'O AU NO KEIA

'O AU NO KEIA

Voices From Hawai'i's Mahu and

Transgender Communities

Andrew Matzner

To order additional copies of this book, contact:
Xlibris Corporation
1-888-7-XLIBRIS
www.Xlibris.com
Orders@Xlibris.com

ACKNOWLEDGEMENTS

My deepest thanks go to:

Ashli, for taking the time to talk with me back in the
beginning before I had the idea for this book, and for
mentioning the Wizard Stones at that first meeting.
Carol Odo, for being an initial contact at Ke Ola Mamo.
Kaui, for being the first.
Hina, for the title that just rolled off her tongue.
Kayla Rosenfeld at Hawai'i Public Radio, for doing the
Wahiawa story and providing a transcript.
Alison Colby at the Farrington Teen Center, for putting
me in touch with Phoebe and Jennifer.
Patty Lei Belcher at the Bishop Museum library, for
helping me research the Wizard Stones.
Adoon Kitimoon, for the cover painting.
Paul Berkowitz, for the maps.
Kathryn Besio and Paul Berkowitz, for the computers.
Julie Walsh, for shipping logistics.
Nicole Mercurio, Matt Stein, and the rest of the staff at
Xlibris, for their help in making 'O Au No Keia a reality.
This company is a blessing for
independent-minded authors.
LeeRay Matzner Costa, for being there every step of the
way. I couldn't have have completed this book without
her support.
The contributors, for their willingness to participate in
this project. Each one, with great trust and openness,
took the time to share with me the intimacies of her life.
For this I will be forever grateful.

DEDICATION

This book is dedicated to the contributors.
It is also dedicated to Bruce and Nancy
Matzner and to LeeRay Matzner Costa.

The Hawaiian Islands.

Ni'ihau

Kaua'i

O'ahu

Moloka'i

Lāna'i

Maui

Kaho'olawe

Hawai'i

100 kilometers

N

CONTENTS

Note on the Hawaiian language: In the Hawaiian language a vowel can be either short or long. When writing Hawaiian, one indicates a long vowel by placing a macron over it. This mark is highly significant because words which are otherwise spelled in the same way have different meanings depending on the lengths of their vowels. For example, it is important for the reader to know that the word "mahu" which appears in this book contains two long vowels, and should be pronounced as such. In writing the original manuscript of this book, I made every effort to correctly spell the Hawaiian words used by contributors. However, due to font limitations, the publisher was not able to reproduce the long marks which should have appeared in this text. I apologize for this important omission, and hope to have it corrected in a future edition.

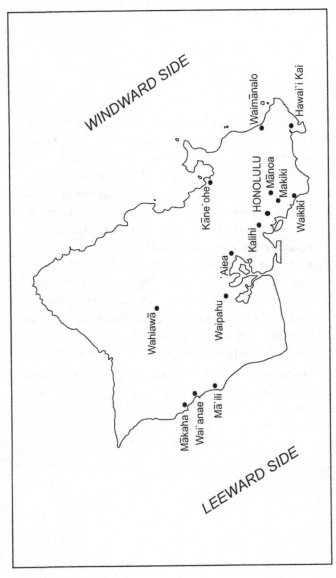

Island of Oʻahu.

WINDWARD SIDE

LEEWARD SIDE

Waimānalo

Hawaiʻi Kai

HONOLULU

Mānoa

Makiki

Kāneʻohe

Kalihi

Waikīkī

ʻAiea

Waipahu

Wahiawā

Mākaha

Waiʻanae

Māʻili

The title of this book, *'O Au No Keia*, was chosen by Hina Wong, one of its contributors. It means "This is me" in Hawaiian and is an apt description of a project which gathers together the voices of transgendered people who live on the island of O'ahu in the state of Hawai'i. In telling their stories, each participant invites the reader to understand what it is like to live in a society which looks down on biological males who cross culturally approved boundaries of sex and gender. These personal statements, which resonate with adversity and courage, despair and redemption, are powerful testaments to the strength of those who follow their own hearts. Likewise, by verbally sharing with us their realities, truths and beliefs, the contributors honor the heritage of Hawaiian oral culture, in which chants are the sources of genealogy, mythology, and history.

We all have stories to tell, but the collection you hold in your hands is significant because so little attention has been paid to the lives and thoughts of people who are transgendered. In my local bookstore I can find scores of books which contain oral histories and personal stories from members of a multitude of different groups, from working-class Americans to adolescent girls, World War II nurses to Vietnam veterans. The list is endless, but incomplete. Missing are the first-person experiences of every-day transgendered people. This invisibility implies that their stories are not worth hearing. In *'O Au No Keia* I attempt to address this situation by providing a forum in which members of Hawai'i's transgender community may act as historians. That is, each contributor has been given the power to construct her own past, as well as present and future, in a format which validates her experiences. This power is vital in a society which valorizes the written word because it exposes to a wider audience the realities of those who are either disinclined toward writing or too busy to set their thoughts down on paper. It is my desire that the effects of this exposure lead not only to a greater understanding of what it means to be transgendered, but also to empowerment for transgendered readers and a change of attitudes among those who are not. By increasing the visibility of transgenderism and giving transgendered people the opportunity to speak for themselves, this anthology challenges stereotypical conceptions of transgendered people as anonymous prostitutes or sexual deviants. As the narratives demonstrate, the transgender population of Oʻahu is extensive and rich with diversity.

The stories in this book are also special because they reflect the cultural uniqueness of Hawaiʻi. For being transgendered on Oʻahu means being immersed in a sea of multi-culturalism. After all, its name literally means "The gathering place." Beginning with the original Polynesians who first settled Hawaiʻi well over a thousand years ago, this island has been well washed with the waves of immigrants. Today, Oʻahuʻs ethnic mix makes it a mini-United Nations. People as diverse as Hawaiians, Chinese, Filipinos, Japanese, Portuguese, Laotians, mainland *haoles* and African-Americans, as well as those from various Polynesian nations such as Tahiti, Tonga, and Samoa, live side by side on this tiny island. This diversity is one reason why the composition of Oʻahuʻs transgendered population is so unique.

One's experiences growing up and living life as a transgendered person on Oʻahu are also influenced by the fact that transgenderism once had an accepted place in pre-European contact Hawaiian society, in the role of the *mahu*. Little has come down to us about this aspect of Hawaiian culture due to the zeal of Christian missionaries who squelched what they believed were "sexually deviant" customs. According to the information we do have, neither effeminate males nor masculine females were ostracized in Hawaiian society. Rather, they were valued members of their families. Male-to-female *mahu* were particularly respected as teachers, usually of *hula* dance and chant, and as the keepers of cultural traditions.

The heritage of the *mahu* role has survived to the present day, in that Hawaiian and part-Hawaiian families are said to be more accepting of transgendered children than those of Western and Asian immigrants. Indeed, the gay marriage bill defeat aside, Hawai'i has gained a reputation on the mainland as a state which is quite tolerant of transgendered people, as well as gays and lesbians. This is a theme which runs through *'O Au No Keia* as the contributors — some of whom were born and raised here, and some of whom came to O'ahu later in life — reflect on tolerant native Hawaiian values and condemning Western ones, and how the intersections of these differing cultural attitudes have affected their lives. The contributors make clear that, contrary to what many outsiders believe, the issue of familial and social acceptance of alternative genders and sexualities in Hawai'i is a complex one, with many shades of gray.

The word "*mahu*" itself is currently undergoing transformation. In old Hawai'i this term meant "hermaphrodite" and was also used to refer to both feminine men and masculine women. In present-day Hawai'i locals use "*mahu*" to refer to male-to-female transgendered people, as well as effeminate and gender-normative gay men. Over the years this word has taken on negative connotations, and today is often used as a slur. For this reason many transgendered people on O'ahu generally neither identify as *mahu* nor prefer to be referred to as such. However, the integrity of this word is slowly being revived by transgendered people of Hawaiian descent who, due to renewed interest in its cultural meaning, view the *mahu* of traditional Hawaiian society as role models. This groundswell can perhaps be traced back to the beginnings of the Hawaiian cultural renaissance, which gained momentum during the civil rights era of the 1970s. That was when, after a lengthy period of repression by state officials and educators, Hawaiians started to revive their cultural heritage on many levels, including language learning, *hula*, traditional craft-making and navigation. Many people also became interested in exploring Hawaiian ancient history and spiritual traditions. However, it wasn't until the late 1990s that *mahu* themselves began to organize for their rights within the larger context of the Hawaiian cultural reawakening.

Spearheading today's small but significant movement to redefine the meaning of *mahu* are the members of Lei Anuenue, the HIV prevention program branch of Ke Ola Mamo, the Native Hawaiian health care system for Oʻahu. As one of the writers for Lei Anuenue's newsletter asked in an editorial, "Can local *mahu* of today reclaim this word [i.e. "*mahu*"] and change it from something ugly and judgmental back to a neutral way of referring to someone? Can a word that once hurt us be used to bring us together and heal us?" Some of the narratives in this book examine these questions in depth and reveal the process through which the term *mahu* is currently being transformed.

Believing that knowledge is power, the members of Lei Anuenue are diligently working to make connections with the general public, specifically targeting Oʻahu's transgendered communities, high school and university students, and health care professionals. One of the goals of Lei Anuenue is to provide education about the all-too-often hidden cultural history of transgenderism in Hawaiian society. Its members hope this will foster greater understanding and respect for *mahu* within the community at large, as well as generate higher self-esteem and pride among those who are themselves transgendered.

***

The genesis of *ʻO Au No Keia* occurred on the morning of December 13, 1999, when I tuned into a news story on Hawaiʻi Public Radio. Community members from Wahiawa, a district located in central Oʻahu, were up in arms about the large numbers of prostitutes doing business in their neighborhoods. Disturbed and disgusted, a group of concerned citizens were working with the police to force the sex-workers, most of whom were transgendered, to leave town. In addition, they were asking church leaders to offer "spiritual assistance" to the prostitutes.

As I listened, I was struck by the attitudes of the Wahiawa residents. For them, the prostitutes were a nuisance, as well as poor unfortunates who needed to be saved. It seemed these community members held little interest in deeper questions relating to the prostitutes themselves: What had led them to sex-work? How did the prostitutes feel about what they were doing? Why were they composed mainly of male-to-female transgendered people? Did they, in other capacities, contribute to the community? And if so, how?

The Wahiawa story showed me that people continue to have a knee-jerk reaction to prostitution without examining, or even caring about, its underlying causes. As April Weiss, an HIV prevention coordinator and outreach worker, explained on the radio broadcast, the community members had never considered that negative social attitudes in Hawai'i towards transgendered youth often result in their getting kicked out of their homes. Faced with widespread job discrimination and no other means to earn money, survival for these young people often depends upon entering sex-work. This naturally leads to their further stigmatization as well as the creation of a stereotype which links, as a matter of course, transgenderism with prostitution.

But how might the attitudes of Wahiawa community members be affected if they knew more about the lives of the people they were chasing out of their neighborhoods? Would community members look at prostitution differently if they understood the factors which force transgendered women into sex work? I imagine that the chances of an anti-prostitute Wahiawa community member and a transgendered prostitute actually sitting down and holding a conversation are not very high, since so many people's minds are filled with negative and one-dimensional images of transgendered people. The question therefore becomes, *How* can one convey information about transgendered people's lives to the larger community?

One way to do this is through books which are easily accessible to the public. For example, the oral histories found in this volume can be used to communicate the idea that *mahu* have feelings, hopes, dreams and *rights* — just like everyone else. If *'O Au No Keia* can be made available in Hawai'i's schools, perhaps the state's next generation will take a different view of those whose gender and sexual orientations fall outside the "norm." In other words, I hope that *'O Au No Keia* will be used as a tool to convey to a wide audience the humanity of a group of people for whom it is so often denied. In doing so it might provide insight, a sense of history, and an appreciation of what it means to be transgendered.

***

The creation of *'O Au No Keia* was a joint project that involved many people in O'ahu's transgender communities. My contacts were facilitated with the help of two organizations. One was Lei Anuenue. I first learned about this group when they sponsored a large conference in late October 1999 which focused on the risks of HIV/AIDS in the Native Hawaiian transgender community. When I approached Carol Odo, its coordinator, with the idea for this book, she was quite enthusiastic about it and spread the word to Lei Anuenue's transgendered members. This led to my initial interviews.

I also received support from Hawai'i Transgendered Outreach (HTGO), a social/support group for transsexuals, transvestites and cross-dressers which holds biweekly meetings in Waikiki. While Lei Anuenue's outreach work targets a population with Hawaiian and part-Hawaiian background, the members of HTGO include not only locals, but also long-term residents originally from the mainland, people passing through O'ahu, and university students.

It is vital to understand that the transgender population on O'ahu is sizable and consists of a large number of communities. Numerous circles of social networks, which often overlap, typically center around factors such as geographical location, age, profession, ethnic background, and/or a charismatic leader [i.e. a queen mother]. Accordingly, due to the size of the transgendered community as a whole, this book can offer only a small sampling of transgendered experiences in O'ahu. However, it still strives for diversity. Participants, whose ages stretch from late teens to early sixties, include health-care workers, performance artists, sought-after *hula* dancers, sex workers, a graduate student, a minister and an ex-military officer. While their accounts provide a glimpse into O'ahu's transgender communities, many more stories are still waiting to be told.

I spoke with contributors during the spring and summer of 2000. These interviews, which were tape-recorded, took place in people's homes, in parks and other public spaces, and lasted between one and two hours each. Some were followed up by subsequent sessions in order to clarify and/or expand on previously discussed issues. Although I began each interview with specific questions regarding people's experiences of being transgendered, the actual process varied widely. Some participants wished to be prompted with questions, while others preferred to speak at length on their own. Likewise, some focused on particular events or issues which were particularly meaningful to them, while others narrated their full life stories. Of course, the oral history of each participant could easily fill an entire book on its own. However, because I wished to present a wide range of transgender experiences in this project, I decided to limit the lengths of individual narratives to under thirty type-written pages. This allowed for a fair number of voices to be included, as well as the opportunity for each contributor to present her thoughts with a generous amount of depth.

My goal with *'O Au No Keia* is first and foremost to present first-person accounts by transgendered people. Nevertheless, I recognize that my own presence implicitly pervades this book. That is, during our semi-structured interviews I asked the contributors specific questions and guided the conversations in directions in which I felt readers would be interested. In addition, editing the interviews into narrative form entailed shifting and deleting portions, as well as correcting grammar. At the same time, the editing process relied on the input of the participants. After transcribing each interview, I removed my questions and rearranged the internal organization of the narratives to read smoothly. Following that, I provided each participant with a written copy of her contribution to proofread and revise. Some discovered that what sounded natural in speech did not appear so on the printed page. This highlights one challenge for readers of this book: the language and narrative threads of oral narratives are different from written accounts. Matters of chronology, vocabulary and speaking style take getting used to. However, the revision process gave contributors the chance to modify grammar and phrases to their satisfaction, as well as to change or remove sentences and anecdotes about which they had second thoughts.

I insisted on this cooperation because historically transgendered people have been unable to control the ways they are represented to the general public. They have been written *about*, most often by psychologists, academics, magazine writers and news reporters who have had little interest in actively involving their subjects in the writing and editing processes. Often, assuming that they will be treated fairly, transgendered people speak with writers and reporters in good faith. Frequently the opposite occurs, as they discover they have been misquoted or portrayed in a negative light. It is no wonder, then, that in the early stages of this project people mistrusted me; previous experiences had made them reluctant to share personal information with someone they did not know. But it was precisely because I wanted to change that dysfunctional relationship between writer and interviewee that I was committed to sharing power with *'O Au No Keia'*s participants.

***

Surely we are privileged that some of O'ahu's *mahu* and transgendered people have agreed to speak and pass their experiences and knowledge on to a wider audience. In doing so they allow insights into the feelings and thoughts of an often misunderstood segment of our society. This in turn creates the possibility for empathy, a seed from which understanding and acceptance may blossom.

I was brought up in Kaua'i in a household where it was OK to be *mahu*, unlike a lot of people I know who were ostracized and kicked out of the house; I was loved within my own household. My mom and dad raised me as a *mahu*. I still did all of the tasks a boy would do, but I also did the tasks the girls would do. I was taught everything. Of course, just because my immediate family accepted me didn't mean that my other relatives were as accepting. My cousins used to make fun of me and call me "Diana." My given name is Dana, which was already *fish*. For some reason my mom had given me a name which could go either way, so it was lovely.

Sometimes the name-calling, which was mostly from my older cousins, was cruel. "Hey Diana!" Diana do this, Diana do that . . . It was a bit degrading because of their tone and the way they used the words. But actually it didn't really bother me, because I never gave a damn anyway.

I was born in 1962. In my immediate family I have four brothers — if you include me, that's five, or four and a half [laughs] — and then three sisters. The sisters all come first, then there's one brother and me, and then three other brothers. So I'm a middle child. I was raised primarily by my mom's mother, my grandmother. But I was really fortunate, because my dad's mom also lived right next door.

We lived in the countryside, in the center of a small plantation town. We ran the theater, which was right in front of our house. On my mother's side, her father was pure Filipino and her mother was pure Hawaiian. My mother's side has ten children; they were primarily farmers and fishermen. My grandfather worked on the sugar cane plantation and while he was doing that, my grandmother and the kids worked on the

23

taro farm. We had a large taro farm which all of the *mo'opuna* took care of, and during my mom's time they also cared for that. But my mom actually went on and attained a college degree at Kaua'i Community College. She was a registered nurse. I believe that she's the only one in her family that attained a college degree. I was proud of my mother. She went to work and went to school, did all of her homework and actually raised all of us. But we were also raised by our grandparents, which is Hawaiian style. So while mom and dad were working, we were taken care of by our grandparents.

My father is Filipino-Spanish-Chinese. My father's side were laborers, too — sugar cane workers. My father was one of twelve brothers and sisters. When they were young, their mother would take them to help the father work in the fields. During my grandparents' days, they got paid a dollar a day.

I would say my parents are very humble, brought up very humble. They weren't particular; they would eat anything. They were raised on canned goods, too and all of that stuff, but they primarily grew a lot of their food, and my father was a fisherman and a hunter, too, so that's how we supplemented all our food. Even today, with me and my kids, I'm thinking, How the hell did our parents feed us with a pound of bacon? You know, you buy a pound of bacon today, I could eat that myself! And we had eight kids, a pound of bacon, eggs, whatever else we ate, and we actually were content. We weren't starving, we were content. We always had enough food in our house. And whatever food we had, we shared. That was the concept we lived by, a sharing and caring kind of thing. If family comes over, share. My parents would constantly *hanai*, or care for, everybody else's kids. They were like that — everybody's kids were always at our house.

My parents were very non-judgmental. They always accepted people as they were. We always had *mahus* at our house. My parents were like foster parents to many other children. When we were growing up, all the un-wanted children ended up at our house. My parents took them in, even though we didn't have any legal rights or foster-home papers. They'd say, "Your mother no like you? Then get all your crap together — you're living here with us." We already had eight kids, but my parents took these other kids in, too. We never asked for money. My parents just gave the kids the love that they needed. I'm sure their parents loved them, but any kid that needed a place to go had a place to go.

My parents didn't harbor any ill feelings — they were loving. Of course, we got lickins when we deserved them, I guess. Oftentimes I got lickins because I was there. Just standing around. Sometimes you're just running around, and if you're associated with kids making trouble, you also end up getting a lickin' because you're in the firing range. "Everybody gonna get a lickin', so you're gonna get a lickin' too."

Our house was located right in the middle of town. Right in front of us was the movie theater. It was very quaint, and old-fashioned style. The theater was destroyed in 1982, after hurricane Eva. The town we lived in had a strong community association. During the holidays they always had programs for the kids, treats at Christmas, Easter Egg hunts, Halloween treats, all that kind of stuff, but the proceeds from the theater went to fund all of those things. We actually ran the films and picked up and dropped off the films, rewound the films, cleaned the theater, and even ran the concession stand sometimes. We did all that. It was community. A lot of the community people would come out and help. When we had the theater cleaning, for instance, they would open up the whole theater during the daytime, and people would come with their water hoses and brooms and mops, and sweep up the whole thing. I think about two hundred people could fit in the theater.

Next to the theater was Kunamoto Stores, something like Arakawa's used to be, a plantation store where you could buy everything — clothes, shoes, fresh meat, bread, everything that you needed to survive. You could charge it on your account. Everybody had a *bango* number. Ours was 2567, and you could go there and charge whatever. Occasionally I would go to the store and charge what I wanted to eat. [laughs] It was real nice.

Across the road in a little lane, on the opposite side of the theater and store, was the only restaurant and bar, called Spotlight Inn. It was run by one of our aunties, Auntie Patsy, and you could get food there and snacks. They had one of those sliding bowling things, they had a jukebox, so after school and after the movies, people would go and gather there. That was our entertainment.

About a block down the road on the other side was the community hall, called the Filipino Hall. It was a huge building, filled with crepe paper decorations all over, and was where all the social dances and community parties were held.

Our town was all dirt roads. The only paved road was the one fronting the theater and store. Also the main road in front of the town, along the beach. Those were the only paved roads at that time, so everything else was all dirt roads. If it rained, there would be all these puddles, and we went and played in the puddles, like kids do.

There was also a huge monkey pod tree growing in the center of the road right where our house was. So cars had to drive around it. About 1970 they cut the tree down and paved the road where my house was, but not the other dirt roads. Today, it's completely torn down and taken away — all the old houses, the mango trees . . . The town was known for mango. The whole island came down there during the summer time. If they came from the other side, from Hanalei, they would always ask for mangos from our side. That was the thing that they wanted from us. So we would always take boxes and bucket loads to our family on the north shore all the time. There was a general store, the Filipino social hall, and a post office down the road. The whole life of the town was in the center. Our house was centrally located. None of these places exist today — they were all bulldozed around 1980. That whole way of life was erased.

***

From a young age, I was my grandmother's *puna hele* — her favorite. She used to call me "Glamour Boy." When relatives came in from off-island, she would introduce me and say, "This is my Glamour Boy." But I don't think I got special treatment because I was *mahu*. I was special, but everybody was special, too. However, I did feel a closer affinity to my grandmother simply because she never gave me lickins. I was raised before all this child abuse stuff — I got lickins! Everybody got lickins in those days. You act up, you act silly, you bad-mouth somebody — you're gonna get lickins. And like I said, oftentimes I was just caught in the cross-fire — guilt by association.

My family knew I was *mahu*. They didn't see anything wrong with it. They didn't make a big issue of it. It was just natural. I had a very natural upbringing. I was loved no matter what. But I was *mahu*. I was *mahu* as *mahu* could be. And the thing is, my grandmother and my mom's brother were the only ones who never spanked me. They recognized how I was and loved me for that. My grandmother would always talk to me each morning, to all of us, whoever was around. She would tell us different things. From her we learned the facts of life, about having sex, who you're having sex with, when you're having sex, when not to have sex. My grandmother taught us about that kind of stuff. Because when we were young, we had sex. I had sex with girls and boys. Because everybody wanted to have sex. And I was just there. [laughs] When you're young you don't really think about it in an intimate way. You just go for the experience.

But as far as being *mahu* and being treated or raised in a special way, I really wasn't. My grandmother would sit me down and tell me stories about this and stories about that, or take me to different places around the island. I thought that everything she told me and the places she showed me, I thought that everybody else knew these things, this family folklore. But it wasn't until her death that I realized that no one else had been told or shown these things. So then I began to think, "Why did she tell *me* these stories? I don't want to be responsible!" Because with the stories comes responsibility.

For example, she gave me the responsibility of caring for the graves of our ancestors. We have many in the mountains which are difficult to find. If you don't know they are there, you won't know. And we have ancestors buried in caves along areas that are populated now, but where the caves are still protected. If people ever want to develop certain areas, I'll have to say, "You cannot, because my ancestors are buried there!" So one of the things I was charged with was to care for our dead, our ancestors' bones. It's an important responsibility. And for some reason or other my grandmother, who had been their caretaker, had entrusted that to me.

27

Throughout my years, starting from childhood, I was also raised by my mom's brother. He was the oldest male child in my mother's family. He was a marine. There were times that my uncle would show up, pick me up and not come back for a few days. My mom would be hysterical — "Where the hell were you?!" And he would say, "I took him up into the mountains." Or, "I took him down to the beach." My mom would be all worried — "He doesn't know anything about the mountains." And my uncle would say, "Well, that's why I'm taking him." Throughout my childhood it was always like that. Even moreso during my high school years. When I had come back to Kaua'i for highschool after going to school here on O'ahu, I was a dropout for a while. During that time, when I wasn't in school, my uncle said, "Hey — if you're not going to be in school, come to my house." So I would hitchhike to the other end of the island, all the way to Hanalei.

My uncle's house was something to behold in itself, because it was a one-room cowboy shack. He had his girlfriend there, and it was in Hanalei Valley; from his backyard you could see the Namolokama Falls. It was beautiful. You could see taro fields in the back and when you walked around there you'd see it was planted with veggies and all the plants that you need — ti-leaves, bananas, mangos, all kinds of leaves that you could eat.

My uncle took care of me and raised me in the mountains. I lived with him in the mountains of the Na Pali Coast, from Hanalei Valley all the way in. He taught me how to run, fish, jump and hunt. Survival skills are what he gave me. He would always brief me before an activity. "We're going to go here and there. These are the things we're going to see. These are things we're going to do. This is what I want you to do. This is what I don't want you to do." Whatever my uncle said, I followed to the T. If he told me to climb that mountain, I would climb the mountain like a goat. If he told me dive into the sea, I would dive into the sea. Whatever he told me to do. Whether it was climb that tree, build a house. Anything I had to do, I did for my uncle, to make him happy. Not just to make him happy. It was also survival.

We would often go and stay in the mountain without any supplies. We were lucky if we had a small zip-lock bag of rice or salt. Or maybe a bag of *poi*. The deal was always that if we don't catch anything then we won't eat anything. We'll just have salt and *poi* to eat. But it never worked out like that; we always had something to eat. The way my uncle worked was, we would go down to the beach and he would throw his net no more than three times, and whatever fish we caught — and we always caught, *always* — I'd clean. On the way home he'd give all the fish away, except for what we needed for the day. I mean, the people we met were so lucky because they got free fish! The first time I saw him do that I said, "Uncle, you're giving away all our fish!" He replied, "Don't worry." Because when we got home we still had our fish for dinner. The next day we went back to the sea and the same thing happened.

By the time I was in my high school years and I had dropped out of school, that was when he was able to show me and tell me more, give me more. Because I was getting to be a young adult already, going through all those changes. Everybody was looking at me, "*Oh, mahu.*" But it didn't bother my uncle one bit.

In fact, the whole time my uncle knew I was *mahu*. People had the nerve to ask him in front of me, "How come you're taking him with you — he's *mahu*." My uncle would turn to them and say, "He's the only one in the family who can handle all of the things that have to be done." That's why my uncle took me with him. I was the only one in the family who was taken with him to those places. No one else. Not any of my brothers, who today are excellent fishermen and hunters. Not any of my other cousins. No one.

My uncle was also one of the family's caretakers of our ancestors. That's why I was taken to learn about that and learn to fend for myself in the wild. He felt that no matter how I was, it was important that I knew how to survive. It was the same thing with my grandmother — how to survive, how to protect myself from any kind of evil that might be following me. Because we believe in the Hawaiian ways, which are very mysterious in a lot of ways. We do certain things to counteract those events we believe are the cause of some kind of illness or whatever. We were raised with all the *kahuna* beliefs, steeped in them.

My uncle was a farmer. He had the most beautiful plants. When we went out to the mountains, we planted in each valley that we visited and stayed in. So we had a garden in Hanakapi'ai, we had our other garden in Hanakoa, then we had gardens in Kalalau. We had gardens all over. And he had stuff stashed in the mountains, like his fishing equipment, nets, spears, all that stuff, he had it hidden in caves, buried here, hanging on trees. He knew all the trees. There were certain places in the mountains where people in earlier times had planted things like Hawaiian oranges. Mostly citrus trees. They're growing throughout the forest, and if one never pointed them out to you, you would never know they were there. I'd be leaning against a tree, and my uncle would ask, "Do you want to eat some oranges?" I'd go, "Yeah, but where are we going to get them?" Then he'd say, "You're leaning on the tree." I'd look up and "boom" — it's full of oranges. Stuff like that.

He intimately knew the mountains, to the point where every tree was known. And that's how I learned. When we went to gather *maile* and *mokihana* and other stuff, we didn't just *happen* upon things — we went exactly to where they were because we knew where the trees were. That's the intimacy we had with the land, and with the ocean as well. My uncle knew where all the fishing holes were, he knew where to find the best *opihis*, the best seaweed, whatever it was we needed to gather. So today I know where they are. And I attribute all that knowledge to my uncle, who was taught by his grandfather, my great-grandfather. That knowledge comes from ancient times. My great-grandfather lived to be a hundred and twenty-seven years old. When you live that long, you get a lot of knowledge. And even though he was that old, he still rode and hunted — and had sex. Not only with his wife . . . he had his girlfriends . . . he came from the era when multiple relationships were OK. As for my great-grandmother, she lived to ninety-nine.

***

My family never made a big issue about me being *mahu*. I just was. There were no ifs, ands or buts about it. I lived like any regular child. The people who surrounded me never gave a damn I was a *mahu*. It was only when I went outside that all the kids were looking at me because I stood out like a sore thumb. I stood out like a sore thumb amongst my own brothers and sisters because I was the biggest. I'm bigger than my father. When I say bigger I mean taller. So I'm taller than both my parents and all my siblings.

All the *mahus* who came to my house were loved and accepted by all of us. The queens would love to come and visit with my family because my family didn't care. You know how it is when you go into a room and people start whispering, "Oh, there's a *mahu* over there." They're pointing or making snide remarks under their breath. We never had that. That only happened when we went beyond the Waimea Bridge, for instance. Or when I came to Honolulu. My whole life I knew how I was and it didn't seem like a problem. It was only when I came out here to Honolulu that it became a big problem. I felt people here made a big problem out of nothing. I remember thinking, "This is nothing — why are you guys acting so stupid? This is nothing."

I was raised as a Christian and I went to Catholic school as a child. I remember reading in Leviticus about all the things you're not allowed to do and thinking, "I'm doing that, so I must be evil." But as I grew older my understanding changed. Because what did Jesus come for? He came to give us one more commandment: to love one another as you love yourself. So as a child, when I read that I said to myself, "That's why Jesus came. So that everybody can know the extra commandment, know how to pray to the Lord and know that we have to love each other the way we love ourselves. The first time he never told us that. He said to honor your mother and father, don't steal, don't covet this, don't covet that. But he forgot to tell us to love one another. That's why Jesus Christ had to come back — to remind us."

People use the word of God for their own good and to blaspheme everybody else. But I believe the word of God is a positive thing that you cannot use or manipulate. Today I don't consider myself a Christian, but I have ideals and beliefs which are the same as Christianity because they stem from a long time ago. Those are the ancient beliefs I have. I just freak out sometimes when I see religious leaders who blaspheme anybody who's gay or this or that. They keep quoting the old testament and don't mention that when God's son was on earth, he said to love everybody.

***

By the time I was around ten years old I knew that I would never fit the norm — I knew that I didn't like sleeping with girls and that I would never get married. I had slept with girls and didn't like it. Actually, by the time I was five years old I completely knew. I was attracted to boys from the time I was small. My neighbors were beautiful boys and were attracted to me for some reason, not the girls. [laughs] What could I do? We were attracted to each other. How I felt inside, though . . . I felt like everybody else. It's just that I had feelings for the same sex. When you're in love or you feel *aloha* for somebody, you just feel that. Maybe people looked at me like I was different, but I didn't feel different inside, and I was never made to feel different. Although I was different I felt like anybody else. I never had to hide anything.

I was already dancing at age three and getting formal training from a dance teacher. My first formal dance training was not in *hula*, but in traditional Filipino dancing. I learned all the provincial dances and mountain dances and the Muslim dances, the barrio dances. So I learned to dance all the dances of the Philippines at a young age. My Filipino grandmother would look at me and say, "Oh, just like *baba e*," which meant I was as graceful as a woman. She was always watching me.

My dance teachers were Jose and Guadalupe Bulatao. Guadalupe was known as the first lady of fashion in Kaua'i, so when we were small they would shape our bodies and make our hands bend like this, and make us do all the movements for the dances. We were just kids — three, four, five years old — learning all of these things. I also had a lot of cousins older than me who were involved in *hula*. Also, I didn't mention this before, but my grand aunts and grand uncles, all of my grandmother's brothers and sisters, also raised me. Because I was with my grandmother all the time, they raised me as well. They just loved me to tears. My grand uncles would take me on their horses into the mountains for three or four days. Of course my mom would just go off — Where the hell were my uncles taking me?! I was only five years old when one of my grand uncles called to me and said, "Come over here. I'm going to teach you how to roll cigarettes." So I learned how to roll cigarettes at five years old. They taught me a lot of things.

Oftentimes, because my mom was involved with community work, she enrolled me in whatever classes there were at the Center. I would go to Red Cross classes, swimming classes, sewing classes — all kinds. Most of the time I would be the only child in the class. And with my grandparents and grand uncles and aunts, I would be the only child around them a lot of times. So you could say that this is where I was possibly singled out and treated differently. I didn't feel different, but in certain circles oftentimes I would be the only child. So if I look back now, maybe you could say that I was taken everywhere while everybody else had to stay home.

Whenever my grandmother was sick, I was called in. Because even as a child I was taught to do healing. I learned to do healing with herbal medicines and massage. The benefit of being around all these people was learning about my culture. That's how I learned my language, my mother tongue [Hawaiian]. See, at the time it didn't seem like I had special treatment, but I guess if you analyze it you could say, Oh yeah, you did have special treatment. But for me it didn't seem that way. I felt normal. I never felt strange. The only time I felt strange was when I came to Honolulu for boarding school. When I came here there was a definite difference. I lived in a boy's dormitory. There were rules and regulations to follow, which I did to the T. But even in there, boys were all attracted to me. And I was attracted to them, too. Needless to say, the dorms were wonderful! It was beautiful. Even now, I'm still in love with people, my friends, from that time in my life.

I think the first time my being *mahu* really became an issue was when I was in intermediate school. I had come to Honolulu for boarding and went to Kamehameha Schools [which are funded specifically for the education of Hawaiian children]. On one occasion when my mother was visiting, some counselors pulled my mother to the side and said, "Oh, we think your son has tendencies . . . He might be gay or *mahu*." My mother turned to them and said, "So what of it?" They were shocked at her answer. They thought she was going to be concerned. In fact, they had wanted to send me for psychiatric treatment in the seventh grade

33

because they felt it was a problem . . . that I was going to be a problem. In my mother's mind there was no problem. Later she told me what the counselors had said. But she didn't care. For her my being *mahu* was totally natural.

Originally I had taken the test to go to boarding school only because of peer pressure. All the Hawaiian children were taking the test to get in, so I took it also. Well, nobody passed or got accepted except for me! When that happened I told my mom that I didn't want to go. But she said, "You're going." She told me that it was going to be a good experience for me in case I went to college because then I'd be used to living away. But I told her that I didn't care and that I wanted to stay home.

My mother didn't listen. She packed my bags, brought me to Honolulu and dropped me on the stairs of the school. "Bye, I'm going back." She left me there to be raised by *haoles*. Our dorm parents were *haoles*. But I never changed the way I was. Of course, I couldn't go around dressed in girls' clothes at school. But I was young. When you're young it doesn't matter what clothes you wear or how you look. Because that wasn't the focus in our up-bringing. We never looked at what people were wearing. We had only *aloha* for them. There was a trail that went past our house. It ran deep into the valley, so if people walked along the trail to go further, they had to pass our house. So we would invite them in. We didn't care what the people looked like. Sometimes the people looked *horrible*. But we were always taught never to judge them — my grandmother would say that they might be angels of God. You never know who might come in disguise. That stems from Hawaiian culture and the way you treat strangers — *lokomaikai*, "come inside," *mai e 'ai* "have a meal to eat with us."

***

Around 1973, '74 the Glades [a well-known nightclub in Honolulu] was still going, and I used to go down there. I was about twelve, thirteen, fourteen then. I would head downtown because everybody was heading there. After living in Honolulu as a boarder, I started to get a little bit braver. I used to run away from school. On the weekends I'd check myself out of the dorms, saying I was going to a relative's, but I wouldn't go. Instead I'd just go around, cruise, meet friends. Oftentimes I would sneak in and out of the dormitory without them knowing.

Later on, after the Glades had shut down, I ended up working for the owner of the Glades. I worked for her and lived with the costume designer of the Glades. After I graduated I worked for her. The Glades was the hottest club in Hawai'i at one time. The best shows were found at the Glades. Today, female impersonation here in O'ahu, at Fusions [nightclub] — everything stems from the Glades. Any drag show in Hawai'i stems from the Glades. You have to compare it with the Glades days. Those days were fabulous, fun days, because downtown was fabulous, so alive and full of color. Unlike today — when you go downtown at night it's just full of drug addicts. During that time it was full of color because of all the queens on the street. Hairdos, clothing . . . As a child, I was very intrigued by what they did. Being already acclimated to show business and performing, I enjoyed glamorous things — after all, "Glamour Boy" was my nickname from my grandmother. So I enjoyed what Honolulu had to offer. I loved the country, too, but I did enjoy Honolulu, seeing all these people on the streets. Of course, other activities were going on which I wasn't oblivious to, like prostitution . . .

It was a rough time, because in Honolulu if people found out you were *mahu*, they would really let you have it. When I came here it was the first time I had ever heard the words "fag" and "faggot" being used to refer to me. I was like, "What?! You're calling me a fag — what the hell is that?" I had never known about that word until I came to Honolulu, and then I found out that fag meant *mahu*. I had never been called that before. But I didn't give a damn. I was raised with the kind of attitude that if somebody is going to come to hurt you, then you know how to take care of yourself. Teasing words — those are nothing. When they come at you and are ready to hurt you, then you know how to protect yourself. So that was my safeguard — I always knew how to protect myself. If anybody was going to come and try to hurt me, I was going to stop them from doing that before they got there. Because I was raised by a marine; I learned how to hunt, fish, kill, jump — so you're not going to do anything to me! I wasn't afraid of people. I was nonconfrontational at the same time. But just because I was nonconfrontational doesn't mean I was afraid. I just didn't waste my time.

There was another culture shock I experienced when I came to Honolulu. On Kaua'i I had been accustomed to greeting each and every person I saw. It's because we were raised with the trail mentality. If you meet someone on the trail, you always say hello. So when I came to Honolulu I was walking down the sidewalk and saying hello to everybody I saw. And people were looking at me like I was crazy. So I had culture shock when I first came to Honolulu. But being called faggot . . . It hurt sometimes. It does. But the thing is, I had been so conditioned to not let words like that bother me, that it really didn't. But I have to admit that sometimes I wanted to just slap people or punch someone in the mouth for being so small-minded.

The time I came to Honolulu to live in the dorms, that was a time when my mother and I kind of had a hard time with each other because she said that I had to live with strangers. I was upset because for my whole life I had been able to do whatever I wanted. But then when I said I didn't want to go to boarding school, she said I had to go. So I had a rift with my mom for all those years. The reason I was in the school was not because I wanted to be there. It was because I wanted to please my parents. If they would be happy then I would be happy. So I was at the school for four years. For four years I pleased my parents. Then I told my mom I wanted to come home on a sabbatical and I never went back.

I was supposed to continue with school on Kaua'i but instead I ended up becoming a high school drop-out. I had straight F's, but only because I never went to school. I felt it was useless for me to go to the school where I was because it didn't have the classes the federal government required. The school wasn't teaching the subjects it was supposed to. So I dropped out. That's when I went to the mountains with my uncle. I learned a lot about the culture and survival skills from my uncle.

As far as graduating goes, I didn't attend high school during half of my tenth grade year and part of my junior year. So I had straight F's during that time. But I was never officially dropped from the lists. I was still on the school roster list, just marked absent every day. What happened to get me back in was, in the fall of my junior year, my parents went to the Philippines to visit my sister. She was living abroad with her husband, who was in the military. So nobody was at home to tell me what to do. Therefore I decided on my own that I would prove to the world that I wasn't stupid. I went back to school on my own and went to the counselor's office and said, "You know what, I want to show you guys what I can do. Can you sign me up for school again?" Boom — He signs me up and gets me back into classes. But that whole junior year I had no rest. No rest for the wicked. I had to take all those English classes, social studies, math — that's all I had. The only class I had for fun was the choral class. Other than that, it was just English, social studies and math. But I did it. I did it because I wanted to catch up. And by the time I got into my senior year, I started attending Kaua'i Community College and high school at the same time. So I graduated with my class, but I also attended college before anyone in my class. Even though I was a high school dropout.

Today I'm a college graduate. A four year graduate from the University of Hawai'i in Hawaiian Studies. Art and music were my concentration. I originally started off in college going for an early education degree, and I'm two credits short of graduating from that. But I changed my major to a Bachelor of Fine Arts. I decided I would do the dance and theater thing. Then I thought, "I don't need a degree in dancing. Let me change again." So I changed to Hawaiian Studies, which was an easy road for me because I had been brought up with all of that stuff. So after twelve years of being in the university system I got my BA in 1992. I was very happy; somebody like me actually made it though a four year college.

Originally I only went to college for intellectual stimulation. I didn't think about economics when I was attending school. I didn't think about what jobs I would have. I just thought that I wanted to do something positive for my spiritual and intellectual enlightenment. I wanted to know what everybody else was learning. Throughout those years I was fortunate to travel around — I continually entertained. I also had a variety of jobs, from working in the sugar cane fields to working in a painting and welding shop. I worked as a Summer-Fun aide, a hiking tour guide, a musician and a dancer. I did the fire-knife dance. For that one dance alone, I usually got fifty or seventy-five dollars.

Hula and dance took me all over the world. Had it not been for another queen I knew, a family member whose name was Tiane Clifford, it wouldn't have happened. I was in a *hula* competition in Las Vegas that year, I think it was 1987, and I hadn't seen her for a long, long time. When I went out for that *hula* competition, she was there also, and she invited me to her room. When I came in I saw it was full of beautiful clothing and beautiful jewelry, and all her implements and prizes and trophies . . . there was all this stuff surrounding her. She was lying in her bed and she said to me, "*Ti*, you see that thing over there hanging? Beautiful, isn't it? You want it? You should do *hula*. All of these things — they're all from *hula*. I go here, there, here, there, and all around the world teaching this and teaching that — *all through hula*."

So she encouraged me. She said, "If you want to travel the world, if you want to have these beautiful things, do the *hula*." That's when it clicked in my mind because I actually had somebody now who was giving me a focus and a direction to go in. That summer, a month later, she came home to Kaua'i, and brought me my first *ipuheke* — my first gourd drum. I composed my first chant on the day she gave it to me. And from that day on, I have only moved forward in the *hula*. I attribute all of my successes to her — she's like my spiritual guide, my *aumakua*, in the *hula*. I feel she is always with me.

She guided me back to my grand-aunt, for instance, who was a *kumu hula*, and I went to live with her. Both Tiane and my grand-aunt were the ones who insured that I would be doing *hula* for the rest of my life. Because they gave me the direction. They said, "You're going this way. Don't turn back for anything. Look ahead and just move forward."

Since then . . . Tiane died in 1992, and my aunt died a little after that. But there have been times when I've been in *hula* competitions with another *kumu* of mine, Auntie Vicki Holt-Takamine, where I've seen their visions on the dance floor, between our dancers. I can hear them calling . . . I don't know, you get these visions, you hear things, you see signs, and you know that it's an indication from afar — from the spirit world, if you want to say that. You have to be able to recognize that kind of stuff. Because I think that's a gift that people lack today. They don't understand signs that they might see, which we call *ho'ailona*. That's one of the things which was instilled in me, even as a child: to be able to read signs in the sky, to understand what the clouds and the stars were saying.

There were people who did that in the olden days, called *nana ao*. Both my grandmother and my grand-aunt who I lived with were very famous for that. People would come to their house and ask, "Auntie, I'm going to have a party on so and so day. Do you think the weather will be kind on that day?" That kind of stuff. She would make her calculations, and if she figured it were going to rain she would tell them not to have it then, and if the weather were going to be good, she'd tell them that it was the perfect time. That's the kind of stuff I was constantly around. People would come and ask these kinds of questions. Both of them were like mystics to me. They did palmistry, numerology . . . they knew those kinds of things. My grandmother didn't even have to have cards to do a reading for you — she read the face. I see that on TV now, people reading the face. But my grandmother did that all the time. She'd often do that to my friends when they came into the house — she'd read them, but wouldn't tell them. She'd tell me to tell them things like, "This one here, tell him to be serious with his girlfriend." All kinds of stuff to my friends, but she wouldn't tell them directly. She'd tell me to tell them.

My grandmother and auntie were the kind of people who always welcomed everyone to their house. They didn't care what the person looked like — they were non-judgmental. That's the one thing I remember when I look back: they never judged people by what their clothing was like, by what their face looked like. They accepted them as they were. That's why, even for me today, I still have that. I don't care how ugly somebody might look. To me, I see something else in them — I see some beauty, some passion, some spirit in them. That's how they were. They were able to have *aloha*. That was one of my grandmother's main rules: *Aloha i ke kahi i ke kahi*. Love one another. It goes back to the New Testament — Love one another as you love yourself. Which to me is really important in this day and age. If you're Christian, that's the most important theme of the whole Bible. To love one another as you love yourself. And also, to help each other. This was the second rule. *Kokua i ke kahi i ke kahi.* Help one another in all that you do. Those were the two rules which we lived by.

When you use the word *kokua*, which means "to help," when you *kokua*, you just do work without being told. You don't have to be told, "Can you come over here and *kokua* us?" The youth today ask questions. They're learning something but instead of using their eyes to observe, listening with their ears, and feeling with the other senses that they have, they don't watch, they don't listen — they just want to ask questions. That's the one thing I have noticed which is different about my upbringing as opposed to my kids now. They don't want to watch, they don't want to listen — they just want to ask all the questions and be told. Even though the answer can be revealed through observation and listening. So the way I learned then is not the way the kids are learning now. It's sad because it makes them dead to the their senses. Even to their sixth sense, they're dead to that, too. That spiritual sense.

When we were brought up, we were not allowed to ask, "Oh, where are we going?" If we were told to get dressed and prepared, that meant for anything. If somebody asked, "Where are we going?" then you weren't going. Or if you asked, "Are we going fishing?" — As soon as you said that then we're not going. Or if they're going to take us to the mountains, they'd tell us we were going down to the beach. You're going to the beach, tell them they're going to the mountains. Because in the olden days there were *kupua* — supernatural beings — and people believed that if these beings knew where you were going, they'd come to *hana'ino* you — make trouble. So that was the reason for all that. It was a cultural safe-guard for us; that's why we did it. Everything that we were was because of our culture. Today, I think the learning is the way it is because we lack culture. To me, American culture is lacking. No more nothing. Hollywood, movies, glamour, magazines, stardom — that's the culture.

At one time I felt like I was falling into that world — "Oh, yes, I want to be this, I want to be that." But then I realized that New York, Hollywood, Paris, all those beautiful places, can be made right where you are. You make yourself whatever you are, wherever you are. If you're bored, it's because you made yourself that way. You can be happy and pleased anywhere. You just have to find the resources in your area, use them, nurture them and preserve them.

***

When I think about *mahus* and think back to my time as a child growing up in Hawaiian culture and learning the *hula*, we were always told that Laka, the goddess of the *hula*, was the god of the *hula*. The god or goddess of the *hula* was in male and female form. We were always told that. They never told us that Laka was *mahu*. They said that Laka had a male and female form in one. We never questioned. All our lives we were taught that Laka was male and female. Then when I got older I realized that must have meant that *Laka was mahu*. That was my introduction to Laka and how something in Hawaiian culture was *mahu*, and that was Laka. A god, goddess of the *hula* is like this.

I also heard stories of chiefs who slept with *aikane*. We were taught about our culture and they said that each of the chiefs had *aikane*. What is *aikane*? "*Ai kane*" means "to eat men" or "to have sexual relations." And each chief had an *aikane* — a man that they ate! I kept wondering what was going on. Later I found out that every chief always had a male lover. We were told that this was because women were believed to be *haumia*, or unclean. A man or a chief who slept with a woman of lower rank than him would lose *mana*. But if he slept with another man he wouldn't be affected. That's why, according to my *kupunas*, the chiefs had these male lovers. They were there to be with the chiefs as a friend and companion. In their time it was an accepted practice and actually bisexuality seemed the norm for most people in old Hawai'i. That's the way I look at it.

The place of *mahu* . . . You can read about *mahu* in certain books. But actually it's kind of unclear about *mahu* in the old days. But in certain stories and books you can read about them . . . Like in this Hula Perspective book, this one anthropologist who went to the area where I live on Kaua'i wrote of seeing a "hermaphrodite" — that's the word she used — teaching the *hula*. That particular hermaphrodite was named Ho'okano and came from where we lived. And according to what the old people tell me, that's what the *mahus* did. They were the keepers of the culture, they did the *hula*, and Laka herself was male/female, which is *mahu*.

In fact, we were told that all people are androgynous. All humans are born androgynous and as they grow up, a person's male or female side becomes stronger. But for *mahu*, both sides are strong. That's why when I think about *mahus*, I think of strong people. I think of soft people. I think of sweet, beautiful people. Stern people. But they're not weaklings. All the *mahus* from my family are strong — they can do everything. They can do everything that a male can do and everything that a female can do.

Oftentimes the line between male and female in ancient Hawai'i was very clear cut. But when you had certain ceremonies that required a male and a female . . . It was like in Elizabethan England in the old days, when males played the parts of the females in the dramas. That's what *mahus* did. They played the female roles in the dramas of ancient times and danced as females in the temples where only males could go. That's what my *kupunas* always told me: the *mahu* danced the parts of Pele and Haumeia and all of these goddesses to induce the goddesses' help and to appease the goddesses. Because the women could not go in certain temples. So *mahus* could play the role of the woman in these places because they were still male. Other people might not agree, but this is what my *kupunas* told me. My source of this information is my *kupunas*, who actually lived through and experienced those things.

If you go into Mo'oku'auhau genealogies, you'll come across people who are *mahu*. But being *mahu* didn't mean that they couldn't have sex with the opposite sex. Because they did. From what I've studied, it seemed that bisexualism was the norm. Hawaiians loved whomever loved them. They didn't have animosity towards any particular sex. If they felt *aloha* for somebody then they loved them. It carries on even today. You'd be surprised — even the most butchiest-looking guys still love queens. I don't know why, but it's a part of the culture which still carries over today. Our role was to satisfy and please the chiefs. And that's how I feel. Even today I feel that's our role.

As far as *mahus* in the culture, I don't associate with being gay. I associate with being *mahu*. For me, the difference between being gay and *mahu* is that there is a place for me in my culture, in my society. There was a role which we once played and still play. So I believe in my culture; I'm an accepted and integral part of my culture. That's why I don't feel anything. Because I know I'm an integral part of my culture. It's necessary for me to be here. Whereas if you're gay, you're not part of society. You're not with the norm. You're an outcast, a "faggot." So I don't like to be labeled "gay." I'd rather be called *mahu* straight to my face. Being called gay is degrading to me. Because I've been called *mahu* my whole life. I don't feel part of the group which is labeled "gay" because culturally that group is not accepted. It's not loved — they are outcasts.

I think some of the *mahus* today still carry on their traditional roles, like in *hula*. A lot of *mahus* today are prominent in *hula*. A lot of them are prominent athletes as well. You'd be surprised. A lot of people don't think *mahus* are strong, but they were strong in the old days and they're still strong today. Some *mahus* that I know are the strongest in their family! They still maintain the strength and ability to do anything. They're working in all kinds of fields today. For instance, they're healers; I know a lot of *mahus* who are doing *lomilomi* massage.

When you talk about today, because we live in Western society, all the norms of that society have been imposed on us. A lot of the old thinking and old ways have gotten shoved under the rug. Because of the new thinking, *mahu* began to alienate themselves and were alienated by the rest of society. That's why you get the gay and the straight today. We never had that in the olden days. We never had gay and straight. Everybody was bisexual, or more open. That's the difference today — because of assimilation into Western culture and Christianity, less *mahus* are willing to or want to show their true colors. They're finding it confusing and difficult to act out their role in society today. So they become drag queens, or go into prostitution — they go into all of those things that are stereotyped for *mahus*. And those are only stereotypes because *mahus* have much more to offer society as a whole. To bring beauty and sunshine and warmth and color and *culture* to the world. It all stems from that Western concept and the Christianity concept. That's the sad part to me, because when you talk about *mahus* and Hawaiian society, they were

43

an integral part of the society. But in today's society they are considered a *detriment.*

Even in *hula* . . . I've held the title of Queen of Hula for a year, which is a contest for *mahus* in *hula*. It's overwhelming for people to accept that a *mahu* can be skillful in dancing. And for women to accept it . . . If a *mahu* walks into a crowd and she looks better than all the ladies there, they hate it. They are upset that a *mahu* can look better than them. Or you go to an area with all these guys, and one *mahu* can lift more than all those guys, a *mahu* can shoot a pig, clean it, cook it and all of that, and they cannot. So although I'm kind of assimilated into Western culture, I will remain a remnant of my culture forever. That's my role. I am *mahu*. I will do all the things that are culturally appropriate for me. And I don't feel any pain.

I choose to live as a woman today. I'm not sure if in ancient times all *mahu* did that. I'm sure they didn't. Because diversity is what made the culture thrive. I give the fullest to my culture when I can be myself by acting out the roles I am supposed to. For example, naming children. Doing all of the different things which traditionally were — and still are — for *mahu* to do. People come to me and ask me to name their children. That's what I'm here for, that's my role. I don't have any other purpose other than to act out my role. And if it's my role to be *mahu*, then it's my role. I accept it graciously. It's not an easy role to play. It's even more difficult because of Westernization and Christianity. It's harder to be in that role and feel comfortable. But I do it. A lot of people don't feel comfortable. They have a lot of fear. They're afraid of things like gay-bashing.

Nowadays it takes a lot of courage for *mahu* to be transgender. Walking down the street, knowing you've got something hanging between your legs. But you look like this. I keep telling people: "I can't change the way that I look. This is only my physical shell; I cannot change that. I have to live with the body that I have." I'm one of those who hasn't had any surgicals done — no implants, no hormones, no nothing.

I have a husband, the man I live with. I don't consider my husband gay. Society might, but I don't. I have three children. They are his natural children. I have raised them for ten years. I'm acting out and living in the role of a woman. I'm not their mother, but I'm their guide. I have guided them all these years. It's been a very difficult role for me to live in today. Not just for me, but for my children because they are subject to the whole gamut of emotions which I go through or I might have felt before be-cause . . . you know how people are in society — we might be out to-gether and people will give looks or snide remarks and the kids will pick it up. Or even now as they're getting older, they know what gay is, they've learned about that kind of stuff, and that it's *bad*. It's made out to be *evil*. It's made out to be such a horrible thing that for my kids — growing up and knowing that I'm like this, and that their father is sleeping with me — it's difficult. But I always have to remind them, "Who's buying your food? Who's loving you? Who's taking care of you? It's us. Those other people on the outside aren't doing anything for you. I'm doing my best for you." I try to assure them because a lot of times they feel bad.

The way I was brought up, when kids had things like events and games, we'd all go and give moral support. Whereas in this situation, I want to give moral support, but sometimes my giving moral support will actually inhibit or hurt my child's performance by making them feel ashamed. So I have to give in and say, "OK, I won't go to that, then." Which is sad. To me it's sad, sad, sad. It breaks my heart not to be able to give one of my children moral support because it might make him feel funny around his friends. It's not an easy situation. I don't know of many queens or *mahus* around today who are in the kind of situation I am in . . . Most of the *mahus* I know are young and single and doing their own thing. But I have a stable family life, I have children to worry about. It's very different for me. I have people I have to worry about twenty-four hours a day. When you're a transgendered person it's something, I tell you!

I have no rights to the children because I have no papers or court documents that say that these are my children. But I know they are because I raised them. That's all I care about. "Just remember who raised you." Every day is a challenge. Every single day. When the kids were younger it wasn't as bad or as much as an emotional kind of thing. Now that they're older they feel more emotions, they're going through bodily changes, so for them it's difficult at times. But I try to guide them like a real mother would. But not to actually be the mother. I constantly remind them that I'm not their mother. That actually I'm in the role of the mother. So it's difficult. Oftentimes they'll yell at me, "You're not my mother!" I'm not. But where is she? She's not around.

This last year I've been going through a lot of turmoil within myself. Depression. But all of that stuff is the result of today's society and the attitudes today, because I was never like that as a child. I look back to how we were originally brought up: care-free. But now, it's no longer "care-free" — you've got to care, you've got to watch, look, listen. You've got to be on your toes, aware of who's looking at you, how you're conducting yourself in society. For me, when I look at younger queens today and try to counsel and guide them, I always steer them back to the culture. I tell them to look at the cultural side, to look at their role in traditional culture, and to try to live and act out that part. If in yourself you feel culturally grounded, then you will always have a place. But if you're grounded in a culture which is not your own, then you're going to feel rejected and unloved. Because that's the way Western culture is.

Actually, I have been more fortunate than a lot of people, beyond my wildest dreams, to have left Hawai'i and traveled. I've gone all over Asia, all over the South Pacific, and all over the United States, including Alaska, as a performer. I've also worked in museums as a conservator of items, of objects. I have training in that kind of specialized work. I'm not working in that field now, but I feel one day it will come into play, because that's another role of *mahus*: to maintain and nurture the culture and art of our people, of the Polynesian people. To *maintain* and to continue the cultural side of our people because if *mahus* don't do that . . . I guess we've got a lot of other people doing that as well, but the role of *mahus* is, to me, to maintain the art and culture connection in Hawai'i, so people from elsewhere can learn and be nurtured by that and be able to grow from our experience here in our homeland. Because when you look at Hawai'i as a whole and Hawai'i as a place, we Hawaiians don't own Hawai'i. We are just a part of this land that you see which is so beautiful. We are the ones that make the land come to life. We give it life . . . the flowers blossom and grow because of us. If we don't continue to practice our culture, as fragmented as it might be, then we will not have a culture to look back on.

I believe the reason we have this wonderful culture today is because of *mahus*. *Mahus* have been the ones in the forefront, standing up when nobody else was standing up, leading and fighting. I'm an activist [for Hawaiian sovereignty], too, so I've been on countless marches and demonstrations, both big and small. I've been at demonstrations where there were only five of us. But I'm yelling like five hundred. I'm not afraid. I don't care what anybody says. If I feel there's injustice, then there's injustice. I can play the games they want me to. I can do it the American way — I can go down to the legislature, I can do all of that crap, I can lobby, I can do all that stuff. But I choose to live in my culture. I choose to do culturally related activities.

I worked as a *hula* dancer in the tourist industry for years and years and years. I worked as a performer, a singer, dancer — I did it all. I was a fire-knife dancer, you name it. All the experiences I've had . . . I've stood on the Great Wall of China. I've been everywhere. So I always ask the queens today, "Why don't you come to *hula*? Because *hula* will fill your mind, fill your soul, your spirit. And if travel is in your blood, that's what it's going to do — it's going to take you around the world, like it's taken me. It's going to take you to places that you never imagined existed. To the places in your dreams." That's how I try to encourage my students. Be in *hula*, and you're going to travel. You're going to learn. The gay community, the *mahu* community in Hawai'i is so small. And I am known for being in *hula*, I'm known for cultural things. I'm known not just in the *mahu* community, but also in the community at large, in the *hula* community. They know I'm *mahu*; I *want* them to know I'm *mahu*. I am *mahu*, and I am proud. What are you going to do? I cannot help how I look. I'm only enhancing what the Lord has given me. What the gods have given me, I just work with.

***

I think about passing on the cultural information I have all the time. I will freely give it out to whoever comes my way and asks for this information, if they in return have that free openness. I don't care about their race, I don't care about their religion. All I care about is perpetuation. That's the most important thing for me. My motivating factor for doing cultural stuff such as *hula* is for perpetuation's sake first. It's not for money, glitz or glamour, fame — it's for perpetuation first. Because the culture lives through perpetuation. There's no other way but to transfer the knowledge from person to person, as they did in olden times. Even though we have tape recorders and we can write books, for the culture to live it has to come through a living entity and be received by a living entity. To me, that's the only way. Of course, books, tapes and CDs are useful. Whatever you have — they're all useful tools. But through a living entity is really the only way.

The way I see it, even for me, you cannot choose to learn these things. You're either chosen or you're not. The word in Hawaiian is *koho'ia* — chosen. You're *koho'ia* for whatever it is that you're responsible, your *kuleana*, to be. *You* will know that. *You* will be put in a place to receive that information. You will be guided to a source, or a *kumu*, you will be guided to that if it's meant for you. Because a lot of information that even I myself have, I was told, "This is only for you." And I feel that it's really for me for the time being to be the care-taker, and I'm sure one day somebody else will come around and be the next care-taker of these things, or be the care-taker of the graves that are in the mountains. That's why I try to give out as much as I can. I myself have a lot of nieces and nephews, cousins, friends who are very dear to me, who I entrust many of the things which were taught to me.

And at this point in my life . . . I'm starting my own school of *hula*. Thankfully, I just recently went through an *uniki* under my *kumu*, Kimo Keaulana Alama, and for me that is just so special, I feel so special. With all that knowledge comes so much responsibility. That's the one thing a lot of people don't realize: you have a strong responsibility to keep it intact as it was given to you, because it's *not* yours. *It's not yours.* It's a legacy from the past that belongs to the future, and it's not mine to hold on to, or possess or covet. The dances are not mine, the songs are not mine, these are what were left behind for me to care for until the next person is ready. And that's how it's going to be for all of the next generations to come. It feels and it seems as though things are hopeless . . . The way the world is going, it seems that people are not optimistic about what's going on. But I feel that there's always a hope that it will be a brighter day, there will be something better up ahead, around the next turn.

I was born and raised on Oʻahu in the downtown area. It wasn't so tough growing up . . . I didn't come from a broken family, but my mother died at a very young age. So I was basically raised by my dad for a few years, and then taken in by family members — older brothers, older sisters . . . I lived here, lived there — the whole bit.

I think my cross-dressing came out in my younger years. I was about thirteen years old when I first started, and living with my brother and his family. I used to see all the big drag queens down on the streets, so I started doing it here and there. I was going out in drag . . . We had thrift stores, that's where I got my clothes. I had to go over to a friend's house to get ready to go out because of course it was a big secret.

I left my dresses at my friend's house, who was already a full drag queen. The only things I would bring home were my personals, like my panties and bras and things like that . . . my little pieces of makeup which I didn't want her to touch. The way I hid them at home was so cute. We had this little table, like a corner table, made out of metal. And the four legs on that table were hollow. You could actually pull the leg off and put something inside it. The legs were really thick, like four by four or five by five, so I would pull the leg out and tuck all my bras and everything in there. One day brother's wife accidentally discovered it. I guess she lifted the table up, the leg fell out and there it went. "What is this bra doing in here?!" It just blew her away. She came from a family that was so prim and proper. She was Chinese — my brother had married into this family that was *conservative*. So she just did not want anything to do with me. She wanted me out of the house, she didn't want me around her kids . . . I was a drag queen — a "bad influence." I was upset because I loved my nephews and nieces; there were only a few years difference between us. I was only twelve back then, and they were around ten, eleven years old.

I moved on to very, very close family friends who took me in as their son, so to speak. I lived there, very happy, very content. The only difference was that I was away from my own family. But I learned to adapt. It made me a stronger person.

I was going out in drag at this time. Back then in the 1960s, because it was like family, the queens were very protective. If you were a young queen and under-age, you had no business being out on the street. The older queens were like policemen — they would watch you. They'd say, "If you're going to stay out, you stay out until eight o'clock and then you're off this damn street, or we'll beat you up." [laughs] That's how it was — they threatened you. They'd watch the time and if they saw you out there they'd be on your ass for that. I remember my friends and I always went hiding. After eight o'clock we'd say, "Let's get out of here and go hide." So we'd still stay out, but just away from them. It was fun.

There were a lot of queens who took care of the younger ones and helped them along, taught them the tricks of the trade. I had a couple of people who did that for me. One queen was in the Glade's [nightclub] show before I ever went on it. Her name was Cookie — Wanda Chapman — and she was one of the dancers on the show. Cookie wasn't a full-time, twenty-four hour drag queen. She was queen by night, butch by day. Although I guess I wouldn't really consider that butch by day, because she had her long hair, but in a pony tail, and no makeup on, being herself, with a tank-top and some shorts — stuff like that. I learned a lot from Cookie. If I were to call anybody my "mother" it would have been her. She taught me a lot about life on the streets, what to beware of. In the later part of her life she wanted to go straight again. She got married to a woman but it just didn't work out for either of them and they got divorced. She never came back in drag. She just continued being butch, as a gay guy. She died of AIDS about four years ago.

I continued going to school. I went to school very sissy. Everybody knew what I was all about. That year, my seventh grade year, I knew exactly where I was going and where I was coming from. When that summer came, before going on to the eighth grade, I did my drag all summer long. I went down and did drag — I got in the bars by putting a lot of makeup on and looking older. I had a good time.

I had another girlfriend who was a queen as well. We started out at the same time and hung out together. When I went back to school the next year in the eighth grade for some reason I told myself, "If I continue with this drag thing, I'm going to drop out of school." And for some reason I just made up my mind — "I'm going to set this drag aside because I want to finish school." So when I went back to school, my other sister, so to speak, saw a new me. I guess I was kind of unfair to her. She said to me, "Everybody still knows you're gay." I replied, "I'm just not going to play the part that much anymore." And I didn't — I just laid low. But she went on to being really loud in school. And the sad part about it is that she did exactly what I didn't want to do — the drag got to her where I saw less and less of her in school until she wasn't there anymore. Next I heard that she was doing big-time drag down on the streets.

I laid low for the next few years and went on to high school and did the same thing. I didn't have a hard time; everybody knew what I was about, but I didn't push it, either. There were a few kids who would harass me, but it wasn't an everyday thing because I think I wasn't as loud as some of the others — the other queens in school were the ones getting it. They were loud, and were doing drag on weeknights. But not me. Actually, a lot of harassment came from the queens towards me because even though I mingled with them I wasn't interested in being part of their group.

After that, I graduated to a community college and took up cooking. I went into the hotel and restaurant business, but that didn't last more than a year because drag was beckoning me. I don't think it ever left me. Then a whole group of us started a little drag show. It wasn't affiliated with the big timers, we just had our little group. We did private shows, private parties, things like that. It escalated from there because we got discovered — the Glade heard about us and wanted to see our show. We did a special show down at their place and they started picking and pulling out of my group. Before you knew it our group had broken up, and that's how I got my start at the Glade.

The Glade was big time — it was a beautiful club and I was thrilled to be a part of it. Even before I got there, everybody knew about the Glade because it exposed drag to the public. I think before I was ever out there they were doing it at the Glade, but it wasn't as much publicized as when it became a show club specifically for drag queens. What was so nice about the Glade was that it was a *home* for the queens. The queens don't have that today, which is so unfortunate for them. They don't have a place they can call their own. Like at this club today [Fusion], we have a drag show, but it's basically for the gay guys.

But the Glade was a home for the queens. And if guys were interested in queens, they knew just where to find them. It was lovely. And today . . . it's so sad that . . . this is only what queens know. What they see on stage, or, for a lot of them, on the streets. I don't know what goes on on the streets today, but I'm pretty sure there are a lot of queens who are out there and that's all that they know. It's so sad. There is so much more that they could have experienced by having their own place.

It was more of a family in the Glade era. The queens were more of an *ohana*; they really stuck together. I think the reason for that was because at that point it was more of a struggle. That life wasn't fully accepted at that time; it was going through that stage of where we were going to stand. So the queens were very tight together — they were always there for one another in case any kind of violent situation came up.

The queens stood together strongly on a lot of things which were related to our lifestyles. Like living together — there were a lot of communes back then. You would have a household of queens; maybe up to eight, nine, ten queens living in one household, which was lovely because it was like a family. We even had names for them, like different "houses" — the Olo Street girls, the Kapi'olani Girls . . .

Back then what also played a major part was that a lot of queens hustled. Moreso than today, I think. But at that time the money was just so easy. I'm not ashamed to say it. It's not like today; we didn't have the AIDS epidemic going on, so sex was more free. You wouldn't even consider it a hustle because it just came to you; wherever you went, the money was always there. But that was just a small part of my life.

Actually, life centered around the club, the persons, the show . . . But if the price was right, I wasn't about to turn it down. "Here's a couple of hundred dollars for you." "OK, sure." [laughs] Ten minutes of your time — all right.

***

Glamour was also *such* an important aspect. No queen would go out of her house without a hairdo. You couldn't come out with that *au'natural* look — if you weren't looking together from high heels to hairdo you'd be harassed forever. I think that was the great difference between then and now. More than anything else, it was the glamour aspect. That played such an important role for queens. You'd go out every night and see them talking about makeup. "I bought this new brand, look at my eyes, I'm painting them different tonight." And it was just such an important thing among the group, the glamour.

You had to be glamorous every day of the week. There was no such thing as looking plain — every day of the week was a beauty pageant. It really was something else. I remember cars being lined up around that block to see the parade of queens. They'd be in amazement over hairdos that were up to the sky, and skirts that were up to the sky too.

***

The show which I run here at Fusion follows almost the same format as the show from the Glade, as far having production numbers and then the featured solos. But back then it was a little different because the featured solos were really featured solos. Like in this show now you have a production number, and then a girl comes out and pantomimes. But back then every featured solo was a talent in themselves. Like Prince Hanalei and his exotic muscle control and dancing. Then we had Brandy Lee, an unbelievable singer. People could not believe she was a guy sounding like a woman, with such a beautiful voice. And of course Tammy Kaye, the female stripper. She was the one people made a lot of complaints about. They said that we were pulling their legs because Tammy came out and looked just like a woman, from beginning to end. She'd take her top off — she'd had hormones — and she was just so feminine and petite. Every little step was just so dainty. There was nothing masculine about Tammy at all, from the face to everything. But they had a whole write-up in the papers on her, that the Glade was pulling a fast one over everybody's eyes, that she was really a woman who the club was trying to pass off as a guy. She was that unbelievable.

So I think the most memorable times I had at the Glade were working with really top-notch artists. Some, like Brandy Lee, are still around today. I work with her at the office. But even before I was at the Glade, I was amazed with Brandy. She is just loaded with talent.

And Prince Hanalei — he was one of a kind. It's so sad that he never passed his talent on to someone else. It died with him. There will never be another Hanalei. Hana wasn't really a cross-dresser. He was right in-between. He was a handsome man with a beautiful man's body. Yet at the same time that body looked so soft and feminine.

The appearance of Hana when he was on stage . . . He came out looking like a man — masculine. But his face was painted like a woman. He had lashes out to the door. He put four or five lashes on each eye and made those lashes really super big. He had a hairdo that was all slicked back but it was high in the air; he teased it and slicked it all back. It was like a beehive. He was just gorgeous in the face. To look at him, being dressed like a man — it was like looking at Satan in a sense, with these evil eyes, especially back then because they painted their faces with the long tails on the eyes, high eyebrows and stuff like that.

When Hana started his act the room was all hushed. He'd come out and look so masculine and proud like a peacock and would strut to music that was so majestic . . . And he'd come out in these costumes which were unbelievable. It was like an in-between as well, something a woman would wear, yet a man could wear, too. Fitted pants that were just so tight, with a bolero jacket — he was famous for his bolero jackets. They'd be matching with these big flairy capes that would just flow when he walked. Hana was such a proud person. And his pants were fitted with Velcro — he would rip his pants off. He'd take off his top and start going into his act, which was all muscle control. It was unbelievable; he was one of a kind. As soft and feminine as he was, at the same time he mixed it up with masculinity. It's hard to explain. He looked masculine but then every step he took was just so soft . . . and proud.

Hana did this rolling of the stomach . . . He had a tape that was coordinated to where if there were drum rolls on the tape, his stomach would start going really fast, really deep. And he had muscle control on his butt — one cheek at a time, or he'd do both cheeks — to the rhythm of the music, of course. Then he put tassels on his butt, a bikini with tassels on each cheek. And he would spin those tassels. First he'd spin one, spin the other one, spin them together. Then he would light the tassels with fire. Spin one, spin the other, spin together. Next, he'd reverse and spin the other way. Hana was just unbelievable. He would get on a chair and stand on his head holding the hair like this, with his legs straight up in the air, split his legs and swing his legs around and he would spin the whole chair around. Then he would do his stomach again. And then shake his cheeks and the fire while upside down on the chair. That was his act. But the fire thing was the highlight. He was one of a kind.

Hana would not stand for any harassment. I've seen him put down people . . . No macho guy can come along and call him a queer because he would put that macho guy right down on the floor. I've seen him take three guys at once and lay them flat on the floor. If he's doing his act and somebody is laughing in the audience — Hana would stop the music, turn on the light, have the spotlight pointed on that person and say in a very cruel way, "Get out." If they wouldn't move, he would get right off the table, grab them and push them right out the front door. Then he'd get back on stage, say, "Continue," and go on with his act. Hana was really something else.

I worked my way up at the Glade. I used to do guest spots in the show, but basically I ran the lights. I learned a lot of material just by sitting in back of those lights and watching that show every night. The show used to be five nights a week at that time. I learned a lot of my stand-up comedy from a fantastic MC, Butch Ellis. She's still in the business today, still going. I learned a lot of my stuff from her and from some of the people in the show. Eventually I got on the show, and as the years went by, I reached the point where I had become one of the directors of the show.

I started off on the show itself as a comedian. It was fun and I enjoyed it. I worked with Stacey Lane, who was *the* comedian of the show. I learned so much from her. Some of the stuff I learned from her I still do today once in a while. God bless her soul. So those were basically the main acts, the stars of the show, the ones people came to see every night. As well as the chorus line numbers. Even the chorus line numbers back then weren't put together for the choreography but rather for the glamour and beauty. That's what all these girls did, just kind of prance on the stage and pooch and look gorgeous with the numbers — one little step kick here, one little step kick there, a hand raised here, a hand raised there. That's all it was. It was the beauty they were selling. And they did a good job of it. As far as femininity, they were just the cream of the crop. I remember lines of people outside, just waiting to get in. There were three shows a night, and for every show there was a line which went halfway up the block. It was like the theater.

The Glade itself was such a classy club. The set up, the two tier stage, was so gorgeous; the lighting system, the sound system, the pit for the band to play in . . . everything was just perfect. There was such a lush atmosphere — red carpeting, red booths on the sides and seating in the center, velvet oil paintings that were painted in black light, black-out paint that were just so gorgeous. The paintings, which depicted stories of Hawai'i, were about ten feet tall, and there were twelve of them, just like columns lining along side the wall. The ceiling itself was really high — it was like a three story building, because the stage was almost two stories, being two tiers. It was beautiful. There were also dressing rooms for the performers both upstairs and downstairs because of the stages. And the entrance way to the club was beautiful, with a waterfall. The Glade was just gorgeous and very grand.

***

The management of the Glade was very liberal. Basically, it was run by a family who had a lot of money in back of them. Their club started off as a ratty little place, a rinky-dinky little place on Hotel Street. It was a broken-down little bar with a tiny stage and that was it. But right across the street was where they built the new Glade, the glamorous club, around 1959, 1960. I remember when I was just a kid, I witnessed the first Glade. I was only about thirteen years old, but I remember seeing that club. I never went in it, but I always stood outside the door looking in and seeing all the drag queens in there. The queens would perform on that little stage, but more as a guest artist kind of thing. The only person who was hired to perform regularly on that little stage was Prince Hanalei. He was the draw, the one who had people coming to that bar.

When I finally got to the Glade, I was already twenty-one, twenty-two. The new Glade was built around 1959. I came out to the Glade about 1969. The show I was on ended in 1977. It survived two or three years after that and finally closed around 1978, '79. They ended up having rinky-dinky little shows. The club brought in some drag queens and Macy Williams was involved in that but it wouldn't go. What kind of killed it, too, was that the disco age came in around that time, so the club had a show first, and then a disco afterwards. I think that's what killed it because it kept all the tourists away — they weren't interested in going to a place like that.

The way our show ended was kind of drastic. Every year we would have big functions at the club. It was Halloween-time. And usually every Halloween I'd run it, but then this one queen who was new around the block wanted to run it that year. So I talked it over with my boss, and he was like, "Yeah, sure." So I told the queen, "OK, it's in your hands, you can run the whole function." I figured it would be a nice night because I could go out elsewhere for a change after doing the show for so many years. So we went out to a bar just about a block up from the club.

But everything just fell apart that Halloween night down at the Glade. The things the queen had planned for the audience — contests, costume things — were very disorganized. This was bad because the Glade was known for having big functions which were so wonderful. My boss became so infuriated that he went to get me and walked me back to the club. He asked, "What's happening here?" I replied, "You told me I could let her run it." He was so pissed. So he said, "OK — you're fired." He fired the whole show that night because none of us had gotten involved with it that night — it had all been left up to that one queen. So as each girl walked into the club he told her, "You're fired. You're fired. You're fired." So the whole show was fired. Of course everybody was pissed. When he reconsidered and invited everybody back, we were all just too upset about the whole thing — nobody wanted to come back. So that's kind of how it died.

The majority of the show didn't go back. Only two or three people did. Macy Williams was one of them. She was trying to pick up the show by putting on other girls. She tried for a year. I was in Oregon when I heard that they closed it. Apparently the city was renovating Hotel Street and the Glade was one of the parts which was not in the new plan, so they had to break it down. I was sad. It was such a nice place. I wish I had a brick or something from it as a souvenir.

***

There was a lot of stuff that went on at the Glade that was unbelievable, that I don't think can be topped here even today. The whole show was just so professionally run. They had two seamstresses who worked on all the costuming and did immaculate work. And when they first started the Glade, there was no pantomime — everything was live, with a full band. They had live music and live singing, so the girls danced to a live band.

The Glade was the first to have a Las Vegas look. The glitter, the feathers, the whole bit. Nobody else was doing it. Hawai'i only had the *hula*, and that was what all the shows in Waikiki were about. They wanted to just stick on the traditional *hula* bit. Nobody had that Vegas or showgirl look. But the Glade broke it open because you had celebrities coming down and picking up on what was going on there and then bringing it back to Waikiki. That's when all the glamour stuff started breaking out in Waikiki.

As far as drag goes, call me old-fashioned, but I feel that instead of advancing we've gone back and reversed ourselves. It was so liberal back then — the queens were so fitting to hold the title "Queen." They would be dressed to the hilt every night, looking gorgeous. Hairdos, makeup . . . everything was so essential to look beautiful and perfect. You couldn't go out just looking simple. If you did you'd be cut down to filth. You had to be glamorous with a ten-foot hairdo on top of your head, wearing the shortest mini-dress you could find, and looking like a million bucks.

But today it's reversed itself. A lot of these queens today don't know anything. A lot of them don't even know how to make a hairdo anymore. I would say that at least ninety percent of them don't know how to make a hairdo. I don't know what happened. I think the Glade played an important part in this because it was where everybody went, so everybody learned from everybody. It was like a commune — the queens lived together as well. It was a thing where everybody was family, and people passed knowledge on from one queen to another and everybody learned. So they lived and so they learned. But when the Glade died, there was no reason to be glamorous anymore. So when the next generation came out, there was nothing for them. They didn't know how to be anything but a real girl — no hairdo, no makeup. It happened so quickly — all of this was lost in a matter of ten years. Today half of these queens don't know how to show the glamorous side of themselves. Only in pageants — when there's a pageant then they'll come along. But even then, it's nothing that they do themselves. It's someone else. "Make me a hairdo." Or, "Paint my face." That's how it has become. Nobody does their own thing anymore. Very few, anyway.

***

I used to hear stories from the older queens about what it was like before the Glade. Before that if you were going to be gay, or if you were going to be a queen, you could be a sissy boy. It was not about putting on the drag. But if you did put on the drag, it was all about being deceiving. Because it wasn't really accepted . . . the drag queen aspect wasn't really accepted. Being gay and being sissy — so-called "*mahu*" — was all right. But to put on a dress was another story. They had a hard time. I remember this one queen, Lulu, who always used to tell me things like that. How the queens had to sneak . . . I remember her telling me about how they used to deceive the military men who'd come along, and have fun just deceiving them. They wouldn't go any farther than that. They'd go out and have drinks with them and party with them, but when it came

RAQUEL G. GREGORY

time to go home with them, that's where the whole party ended. These guys would be left never ever knowing that they had been with a female impersonator.

It was fun to hear those stories. I guess things progressed because I remember Lulu saying that they had come such a long way. She is still around today, I think close to her eighties. She's given up the drag but works for a tour company now, I think. Lulu used to say, "If it weren't for us, you guys wouldn't have it this good." Which is kind of true because they had to fight their way. I remember her telling me that they had to put up with a lot of shit.

But I think everybody, at one time or another, runs across discrimination. There were times when I was insecure about it, but I've come to the stage in my life where it doesn't bother me anymore. When I was younger and it was a new thing to me, there were times where it bothered me when you had people *looking*. But it's all part of the game. It's the lifestyle you chose to live — you've got to be strong in it. Because people *are* going to look and you can't blame them for looking. You're something different. And something different always catches someone's eye.

For a long time I was very self-conscious about what people might be saying about me. I remember when I was younger [laughs] and I'd be walking in the supermarket and I'd see somebody chit-chatting, I'd walk right up to their faces and say, "You've got something to say? Say it now." If I see it now, it doesn't bother me. I think about it this way to make myself feel better: "Well, they could be saying that I look like a tall, beautiful woman. Or they could be saying that I look like a tall, beautiful man. Or could just be in disbelief that I'm a man. It couldn't be something ugly." That makes me feel a little better.

***

Back then there weren't too many problems. The only problems were with the guys who came around interested in queens. They would love to go with queens. But at that time there was a law called the Sodomy Law, so if you were caught having an "unnatural sex" affair with someone, you'd get in trouble. A lot of times, if a man was caught with a queen — even though he knew she was a queen — he would turn around and say, "I didn't know that was a guy!" So he would be set free while she went to jail for deceiving him. And there was no way she could prove he had known.

So one of the owners of the Glade, a lady who was very protective of the queens, took it into her own hands and went down to see a judge friend of hers. After all, it's who you know. This judge told her, "If these 'girls' can do something to let the public know what they're all about, then they won't get into this trouble anymore." So she invented a thing called the "I'm a boy" button, which protected the queens. It was like she killed two birds with one stone because she had an advertisement on the buttons — "Glade, 152 North Hotel Street" in addition to the "I'm a boy" phrase. The queens would wear that . . . it was like an ID for them. Some of them would make their own buttons which said, "I'm a pretty boy," or "I'm a gorgeous boy." [laughs] That kept them out of trouble.

But then it reached a point where you *had* to have a button on. If the police saw you walking down the street and you didn't have one on, you'd get arrested for intent to deceive. Of course, a lot of times the girls weren't really deceiving because it was obvious what they were — you don't see women walking down the street with ten-foot hairdos. But if they didn't have a button it could be charged that they were impersonating a woman, and so men could use that against them by saying, "I didn't know that was a guy." This went on for a while. But as time passed the buttons went away and things became a little more liberal. People weren't really bothering that much with what your gender was.

I think drag is kind of accepted today. Even back then it was accepted, but as more of a novelty. Today it isn't anymore. So what if they see you walking down the street — there are ten thousand other ones. People don't have to come see a show anymore because they can see it on the street. Back then it was a taboo thing. There were lines in front of the Glade of people wanting to come in and see the shows. There were three shows a night and each show was just packed.

***

The thing about drag, it was having all the glamour and the attention. I think that played an important part. I just wanted to be beautiful.

I wanted people to look at me. To look at me in whatever way they wanted to look at me — whether I was gay or a drag queen or because I was beautiful; I just wanted that attention. I felt comfortable in that life, and I enjoyed it.

When I was young drag was like a play thing for me. I took it more professionally when I got into the business aspect of it. I think that was the whole thing — I loved the glamour of it. Maybe part of it was that I was getting attention from men. They were loving *me*. They were attracted to *me*. Maybe it's because in my childhood I didn't have as much love or attention . . . But I was happy with it. Because when you're young and you're so flirtatious . . . I think I had boyfriends up the geeky who were coming to the club to see me. I was getting into so many situations. [laughs] "OK, there's Joe there. And oh, there's John over there. I think I'll just stay in the dressing room." Because I always had three or four of them out there and I'd say, "Oh no. I don't want to make any waves with them, so I'll just stay in the dressing room and play cards." [laughs] But I loved all that attention.

Actually, I think the highlights of my life involved finding someone who was really, really special, and living life with that one particular person. I think I got scarred a lot when I was young — you meet someone and you're just in heaven, on cloud nine, everything is just wonderful, you're living together, there's nobody in the world, except for you two people, existing. It's lovely. But all good things come to an end. Maybe it's not right or something happens or somebody else makes it ugly. And I've had a few of those.

But there were some in my life who were just immaculate. Lovers who were very supportive of me. Like anybody else, you want to have one special person, and you'd like to live your life with that one special person. You'd like to be supportive of that person and have that person be supportive of you.

Rght now I have all these flashbacks going through my mind . . . there were a few who played such an important part in my life. Without them, I couldn't have been the person I was at the Glade. Having them made life so wonderful for me, and even moreso at the club. Today I look at it and feel like I had one wonderful husband with a thousand different personalities. [laughs] The boyfriends I had weren't just pick-ups or one-night stands. These were guys who I was with for years. The older queens can tell you — I always had a rep for that. "Raquel always has a boyfriend, is always shacking up with someone. She was never alone; her whole life she's never been alone, until today. She's always had someone with her." If I break up with a relationship, maybe I'm single for a year, then "boom" I'm right back into another relationship, playing husband and wife. That goes on for maybe six, seven years, and then "boom," it breaks up and I go on to another one [laughs]. But that's how my life has been.

So if I were to say what was lovely about my life, it would be my relationships with all these special guys who weren't there just for the fetish part of it, but for *me*. That made my life. Because that's all I think I wanted in life — to have someone special, to set up house and to share moments together with another person. I have good memories and no regrets. I put them all together in my head now and they appear as just one good boyfriend.

***

There have been so many times I've wanted to see a return to the days of the Glade, but I think times have changed here in Hawai'i. I think high drag is still going on stateside although you do have your simple girls here and there. But here in Hawai'i, no. I don't know why. I don't know if it's because everybody wants to be fishy. I don't think it's that they want to play fishy, I just don't think they have the experience behind them to know what it's all about. The queens come out and say, "OK, everybody else is looking like a simple little girl, so I guess I have to be like a simple little real-looking girl, too." Nobody is really interested in doing the high drag thing anymore. Even on my show, costuming-wise we can give them all the glamour and everything, but I can't force my girls to look like drag queens. I still want them to portray glamour. And I'm proud of them because they do a really good job with that. I've seen other shows that have tried to bring back that era, but it doesn't last because the girls are uncomfortable with it . . .

***

I think back when I was younger it was all about becoming a woman. It was like, "OK, I'm going to go through this — first I'm going to get my breasts and later I'm going to have the operation and then live happily ever after." I think I went through that as well. I said, "I want to do this, I want to do that. I want to have my pussy put in, and then I'm going to find a man and we'll be happy for the rest of our lives." Now I feel, *No*. It doesn't work that way. I've found through my thirty years of being around queens that a very small percentage has that kind of a thing going for them, where they find a husband, move away, adopt kids, and live the straight life. A very small percentage. It's so sad. But I think I faced reality. I told myself, "I just want to be what I am. I don't want to cut what I have off. I enjoy it. I don't think I have any problems with the guys who come around me. I'm just going to be the way I am." And anyway, as time went by it became accepted. You don't have to get it cut off to be part of society anymore. But I think a lot of these queens did it. They said, "I want to fit in, so I want to become a woman. Then I'll be happy." No. I said to myself, "I just want to be what I am — transgendered. I'm happy the way I am." So I think not as many queens are getting it cut off as before. I think now a lot of them are happy just the way they are.

But I've known a lot of queens who play a make-believe game and tell themselves, "I'm happy. Yes, I get satisfied when somebody has sex with me, I reach a climax." No. I've met queens who have said, "Raquel, don't let them ever tell you that. It's not true." Even today, I really don't think they've come to the point where they can make a vagina for a guy that's going to be satisfying. They can feel good and everything, but a natural climax like a woman? Not now, anyway. Maybe they will someday.

***

Back in the Glade days drag queens with other drag queens was taboo. If you were a queen, the only kind of person you went to bed with or made love with was a guy. I think the first breakthrough back then was when a queen went with a lesbian or a girl that was wanting to be a boy. Oh, God — that was such a big thing. But as time went by, it got more accepted. It was happening here and there. It was your thing, so go right ahead. [laughs] And now I hear about cross-dressers who go with one another. But that's Stateside, which is a little bit more liberal than here. They're always one step ahead of us, anyway. I listen to the local girls talking, "Oh no, I'd never do that — she's my sister." [laughs] They have a local term, "'ki-ki boogie." That's where a queen would go to bed with another queen. That will happen here, one day or another. Right now there are queens who once were queens and went back to being a guy and then ended up going with a queen. That's pretty close, so it's getting there. [laughs]

I've seen some older queens who have gone back butch. I'll be honest with you, I've often thought about that myself. Not actually considering it, but I've thought to myself, "What am I going to be? Am I going to be an old drag queen? Or am I going to, maybe at a certain point in my life, resort back to being a guy?" That is, still being gay, but not doing drag. And I said, "No — I think I'll be an old drag queen." I just love the life. I'm going to die a drag queen. I'm going to live it to the very end. If a woman can get old and be an old woman, I can get old and be an old drag queen. I don't have to be picking up on the guys anymore, but I'm still going to be me. And if there's a glamorous event I can attend, I will, to the best of my ability. Even if I have to fill up the wrinkles with putty . . . [laughs]

***

Now, at an older age, what I am trying to do is make everything I've learned rub off on the younger queens. There are just a few of us left. Some of the girls in my show were right on the brink of all of the highlights of the Glade. They really didn't catch the big drag shows, but they were *there*. Some of them are left. And I think some of that is rubbing off on the younger queens. Whatever I know I want to pass on to the younger queens. When we put on a new show we sit down and do arts and crafts. Some of these girls bitch at me, "Oh Raquel, I don't want to do this, I don't want to do that." But I tell them, "You're going to benefit by it someday. If you love show business, then you're going to learn. Later you're going to be teaching this to somebody else." Because I went through the same thing, learning how to do things like sewing beads onto the costumes. All these costumes you see here in this room, the girls in my show made themselves. All the headdresses — every girl made her own — but I was there to direct them on that. These are the things they've got to learn to pass down to the next queens.

So for me, I love the glamour. But I think I've worked enough . . . Now it's my turn to stand up there and do the MCing and show off my wares — and my girls are my wares. When they come out with what I've taught them — the glamour and everything — that's special for me. I love to be in the audience and watch them perform and to hear what people say about the show. This is my reward, this is my high now. I know I'm not a glamorous queen anymore. I'm getting older. But I want the girls to show off my wares. They might bitch and curse at me, but when they come out for everyone to see . . .

It's something I enjoy and I just want to pass this on, so at least there's something . . . Like Hanalei — I love Hana so dearly, but the only disappointing part about him is that he never taught his act to someone else to carry on. He was just one of a kind. It's just so sad that it didn't get passed on. A little bit of me is going to be in every girl that I work with. There's my arts and crafts which I've taught them, how to do with drags. One way or another these girls are leaning the trade and how to be a little bit more professional. Because I'm very strict with the show. Sometimes I think people hate me [laughs], but I don't care. I always tell the girls that my number one concern is the show. You're second. I have to take that attitude, but then they respect me for it.

I have a lot of fines. They pay fines up the gazoo. Anything that goes wrong on the show — if they're not wearing a necklace or something, there's a fine of five bucks right there. Pay the banker. If they don't show up for rehearsal and don't call, then they have to come to work that weekend and don't get paid; they work for free. Before I'd say, "OK, if you don't come to rehearsal, then don't come to the show this weekend." But they didn't mind — it was like a night off for them. It's more effective if you have to come to work and don't get paid. If you get angry about it and don't want to work, then I'll find somebody else to replace you. This system works better, especially with the new girls.

Towards the end of the Glade I took charge of directing the show there. And now I'm using what I learned from people back then, like from Lee Jay Taylor, who was the show's director. I learned so much from her. When she put on a show she paid attention to the littlest details, which for her played such an important part in the show. I find myself doing those same things today with the girls. Necklaces, earrings, the smallest things, make everything look so *classe*. With the choreography, I don't completely take it in hand. I work on it, but I let the girls put what they want in there, too. So we're all one happy family; everybody feels like they have a part in it. I don't step on their feet as far as what they want to do for their featured spots. But if I feel it's a weak number then I'll be very straightforward with them and say, "That number sucks." Sometimes the truth hurts, but sometimes it helps, too.

I'd love to make ten years with the show. We've been the longest running show so far. This is eight years, now — I hope we make ten years. If it does, then I'd feel that I had more time here than at the Glade. Although it feels like I was there years longer, I think I was at the Glade for just about eight years. Eight *good* years. It was just thoroughly show business, not like here. That was just a show club, basically built around the show. But I'm proud of this show. These girls work hard and I'm proud of them. Sometimes they make me angry. Some of the stuff they do . . . they just go stagnant; they don't know they can do so much more. They get caught in certain kinds of numbers and if nobody tells them then they'll just stay there on that level instead of doing other stuff . . . But all in all I think this show has been a highlight of my life.

Also my job — I think I've accomplished a lot in the office I work for. I've been there for thirteen years and have gotten their respect. So I'm really content with my life now. I'm not here to please anybody anymore. I feel like I've paid my dues, one way or the other. Those are the two most important things in my life: this show and my job. My job is my bread and butter, while this show has become more of a pleasure thing for me.

I would like our show to be more than what it is now. But I don't think the gay community is that strong in supporting a drag show. That's the sad part about it. Stateside, the gay communities are very supportive of drag shows. They respect them, too. But not here in Hawai'i. I think

RAQUEL G. GREGORY

it's because it's not a unique thing here — it's an everyday thing with a lifestyle. People aren't amazed to see a drag queen anymore; it's just become part of the lifestyle here in Hawai'i. So I don't think there's that support to help a show along, to give the show an opportunity to really get somewhere.

***

Because I started so young, maybe I didn't have a chance to really sit back and ask, "What's happening with me?" Or, "Should I go straight?" I think that because I started so young, I never had the problem of not knowing where I was going and what I wanted to be. Maybe I didn't give myself a chance to think about all of this. I just went right ahead with it and said, "I'm happy here. I'm going to stay here." Because I met queens later in their lives who were so afraid of themselves, where they had such a late start and then came to the point where they asked themselves, "Am I doing the right thing? Do I want to be a woman? Or should I continue being a guy? How is society going to accept me?" I've seen so many late-comers like that with their heads mixed up. For myself, I think that from day one I never really gave it a second thought and just went gung-ho straight ahead. And I enjoyed my life. Being what I am, I have no regrets.

At one time I used to label myself. But now I just see myself as a person enjoying what I'm doing. And if I should find love along the way, it will be as long as the person who comes along accepts me and loves me for the way I am, and doesn't put a label on me, like saying, "Well, I love you as a drag queen." If it's a person who just loves *me*, then I'm happy.

I think in my younger years I labeled myself. But getting older, I've had time to think about what's happening to me and what I'm all about. In my younger years I labeled myself with things like, "I am a female impersonator." Or, "I am a drag queen." But today I know which gender I portray. I enjoy being a woman. At the same time, in the same breath, I can say, "I know I'm not a woman. But I enjoy being one. Or living as one, in a sense." I mean, the clothes in my closet are all women's. I don't think I have one piece of men's underwear or anything in my closet. [laughs] I live my life as a woman.

I don't know how to label myself. I know I'm transgender. We have different species, don't we? [laughs] Everyone who is transgender has a different way of believing in themselves. Some want to become women. Some just like to dress up as women at certain times and enjoy themselves. Some just want to do it as a profession, as drag queens on stage, and then the next day look like a guy. There are all different types. But people don't know that. They think we're all in one group. Then you have the type who likes to dress up as a woman and would like to be with another drag queen as well. And you have the one who likes being a woman, but doesn't want to go to bed with another drag queen, who respects her just as her sister. So there are many different types of us. But I don't put anyone down. I would just like the next guy to respect me as much as I would him for his beliefs.

I was adopted. I was born illegitimately. I didn't find out until about four years ago that there were some questions about my birth. Well . . . I knew all along there was a problem with who I was and who I was supposed to be. My mother was planning on adopting and she evidently knew that I was born and they told her that she was getting a little girl. But before she came and got me they asked her if she'd be happy with a boy. So there are some questions there. She also told me that when I was circumcised the doctor had said he didn't know how this child was going to turn out. I'm learning this when I'm in my 50s . . . It was hidden all these years. Plus, I had genitalia in which . . . one testes was never fully developed. So there were a lot of things which were coming on physically which were making me wonder.

But my home life when I was child, up until fifteen, wasn't too bad. We had a fairly standard family. My mother and dad split on my fourteenth birthday. From my fourteenth birthday until I got married everything was hectic — I was here, there and everywhere . . . at one time I was at three high schools in two weeks, in two different states. As a result I never did get a good education. I dropped out of high school. I was living with my dad at the time, and he told me just before my seventeenth birthday that I had a choice: "You can either go back to high school or you can join the navy." So I elected to join the Navy.

Joining the Navy was when I really started to find out how I was diferent because as I was going through a physical period at boot camp, the corpsman is walking down the line and checking everybody for hernias, making them cough, and when he comes up to me he starts laughing. Because he had seen that there was only one testes there. But I

73

let that go. Later on in bootcamp there were some guys who said, "You know, you walk just like a girl." So, I'm having these feelings, "God, I want to be a girl; how come I'm a boy?" And all of these things are coming up.

My very first memory is of being dressed as a little girl. My mother denies it, though. The second memory, which I can remember vividly, is being dressed as a little girl in the front yard with a permanent in my hair. I can remember that so vividly because of the rolls and the odor of the permanent.

I've been wanting to be a girl all my life. Like so many other people who were in this situation, there was more than one night that I'd go to bed praying, "God, please let me be a girl in the morning." You know — "I want to wake up a girl. I do not *belong* in this situation." I had these feelings all the time I was in the Navy, and I would cross-dress when I could get the chance. I lived off-base the last year I was in the Navy and I cross-dressed quite a bit. At that time, back in '64, I didn't know the difference between a cross-dresser or a transvestite or a gay person. To me, I guess I felt I was gay. I tried to put this need to dress aside.

I was engaged at the time, and it came out in conversation one night; I told her I used to be gay (the truth was, at the time I really didn't know that there was a difference), because I thought I had put the cross-dressing away. But this revelation ended the relationship just like that. I never really understood that I wasn't gay; it's that I didn't know what else to say. I was just trying to be honest with her.

When I did finally get out of the Navy and found the lady whom I wanted to marry, I didn't tell her right at first. I told her a week or two after we got married, and gave her the option of . . . If she wanted to part, she could do it. Evidently she thought she could change me, so we stayed together. We are still legally married, thirty-four years in July, even though we haven't been together now for three years . . .

My actual transitioning began after we had been been together for thirty years. During our married life, I wanted to dress . . . I used to dress quite frequently. I would send off the kids and wife, and they would go visit her mother, and I'd get dressed. She always wanted me to put it aside. And you try . . . you *try* . . . but it cannot happen. After we were

married, I was trying to figure out how to get out of the marriage because I wanted to live as a woman. But when I found out I was going to be
a father, that side of me really did get put in the closet. Because I took the
responsibility of being a father and husband very seriously. And I over-
excelled in everything I did in order to prove that the female side of me
is not real; that this side of me is a lie. So everything I did, I over-
achieved in. When I finally came out and told one of my friends here, he
looked at me and said, "You've gotta be joking. I have never met anybody
who has more skills, more talents, more savvy, mechanical . . . Anything
you want to talk about, you can go do it. *You have to be joking.* You make
Tim the Toolman Taylor look like a wimp." And in reality I did. I still
do.But the reason for it was, I felt like Cheryl was a lie, so I over-achieved
and I learned everything I could to prove that I *could* do it. All this time
I was living my life for everybody else but me. But I was still finding
these thoughts, these urges — "Oh, gee, wouldn't it be nice to be a
woman for the rest of my life . . . " I don't think there was ever really a
time when I never didn't think about that. I wish I had known more about
this situation, being transgendered, when I was younger. Because if I
had, I probably would have never turned out the way I did — I would
have been living as a woman from the first opportunity.

You have to remember that when I was younger, Christine Jorgensen
was just making headlines. They were really putting her down, so this
was not something you just went out and did. Although today in retrospect looking at it, I'm glad that I did wait and learned what I had to
learn, because it's let me be self-sufficient. When I was coming out and
talking with a transgendered friend for the first time, I asked her, "So
how do I deal with this? I love to do all of these things. I'm a mechanic,
I'm a pilot, you name it I can do it. But does this mean that I have to give
them all up?" She gave me an article about a cross-dresser in Texas who
is very tough, very strong. In the article she told how she used to have a
junk yard, a wrecking yard, and one time she had gone out and had her
nails done with her wife, who was supportive in all of this. On their way
home from the salon, the truck broke down. And she was sitting there
thinking, "What am I going to do? What am I going to do?" But her wife
said, "You're just going to put gloves on your hands and go out and do

it." So that was an encouragement to me — just because I'm living as a woman doesn't mean I can't do the things that I do. I think if my wife were to come back here today, she would say that nothing has really changed, aside from my appearance. I still do everything I used to . . . but now I have more fun than I did.

I think there's a realization that the lie I always thought Cheryl to be, was itself really the truth. That is, *Harold* was always a lie. *That whole fifty years was a lie* because it was for everybody else. It was not for me. When I came to that realization — that it was a lie for everyone else and not for me and that I can be happy — my whole life and attitude changed. I miss my family tremendously because I won't go back to where I was for them. They have to accept me.

There were a lot of things which triggered this change. I was really unhappy in 1994 and '95. We were having problems . . . Carol had left in 1985. She came back, but the kids never did come home. She wanted me to do what I was doing when we first met, which was being a minister. I had been preaching and we were going to bible college. She wanted me to be in church, and I wanted to be in church, but you just can't justify with the church telling you what you're doing is a sin, so how do you keep justifying . . . ?

When we came over here to Hawai'i, we had left our ranch in California which we still own, and I was having problems with it, trying to evict renters. Both of my kids owed me money big time, so they didn't want to talk with me. And Carol had gone back to Louisiana to visit her mother, in Jimmy Swaggart's church back there. While she was there I was on the Mainland trying to evict some renters. And everything came apart — I lost it over there. The judge wasn't doing what he was supposed to do in order to get the renters out . . . I had to get back here . . . And I lost it — physically, emotionally and everything. I went and got a can of gasoline and was going to go and burn my ranch down, and my son, on the cell phone, talked me out of it. He said to come on back, to stop this. So I went back to my daughter's house. I had to take a flight the next day to come back here. I think emotionally I was just really shot. When I got home I had a message on my answering machine from my step-father, saying that my mother was in the hospital and wasn't expected to live through the night. So now I've got this plus the ranch on my mind, I've got my work that I'm very unhappy with on my mind, which is dragging me down . . . I didn't know when Carol was coming home, so I called her up and asked, "When are you coming home?" She replied that *her* mom was in the hospital and wasn't expected to live through the night. And in addition to that, *she was not coming home.* So, all of this was coming up on me . . . Her reasoning was because she didn't want Cheryl to be around.

One thing led to another, and I made a suicide attempt New Year's Eve, 1995 to '96. I should not have woken up the next morning, but I did. I decided that I couldn't continue going on through life like this. My wife doesn't want to be with me. I don't want to really die. So I guess I'd better accept who I am. I made the decision that I'm going to accept who I am. And my life started to change from there.

As things kept on going, Carol eventually did come back for about nine months, but left again. My son came over and visited me, and stayed with me for four days, but then he said he never wanted to see me again, because he didn't want to deal with this in his life. At that time I was already transitioning, my hair was in ponytails . . . I was hurt, so much so that it started to make me look at my life and say, "I have given everything I have for everybody." I grant you, in their minds, I did everything for me, too. And I did, because I had all the toys that I wanted, but I bought stuff in order to make life easier for all of us. And in return it made life fun for me. But I was never able to do what I wanted to do. So when Carol came back in 1996, I said, "That's it, I'm just going to end up being who I am." Her leaving the second time caused us some real bad financial problems. That's when I made the next suicide attempt and I ended up in a mental hospital. When I came out, I found that I was not alone as a transsexual out here. Until I joined the Hawai'i Transgendered Outreach group, I didn't know anybody else. I had no idea that there was anybody else in the world like me, outside of what you would find in pornography magazines. And I would look at those and think, "Oh wow! That's gotta be all a joke . . . It's gotta be a put-on. Men with boobs!?" I just couldn't believe it.

But then my whole life changed, and I realized that it *is* true. And right now I believe that there are more of us out there than anybody has any idea about. Because this is something that you are born with. It doesn't go away. How severe it gets in your life depends! From my own experiences and what I'm seeing with friends and everything, if they come to terms with it in their younger life, they'll live as women, and by society's standards they would be considered gay because the only people they're interested in are men, so society would brand them as gay. But if you look at them . . . I can introduce you to some people who you'd never know . . . there's no way you would know. Society says they're gay, I say they're hetero.

Then there are people like myself, who have come out later in life. Certain circumstances have happened so that the opportunity was there and we took it. The majority of us start coming out anywhere between thirty-five to fifty years old; this is when you'll start to see the largest push to free yourself. Usually if we've been married and had a family, you'll find that we're basically heterosexual. That is, when we come out we're only interested in women. So, in a way, nurture does have a little bit to do with it, but not nearly as much as nature does. Usually in our late forties, if we've been this way, the decision is, "I've got to do this. I have to be who I am." I really have a lot of envy for the people who do it younger, who can enjoy it. I wish I could have. I didn't, I don't regret what I did. Looking at this, in a way it's sort of a male menopause, because it happens the majority of the time in the late forties, early fifties, when you sit down and start talking about it, and you'll find out that it's this realization in life that if I don't do this, I'm *never* gonna do it. It's a change in life. It was *my* menopause, I went through it. My life changed totally. It is no longer like it was.

So my life hadn't been a whole lot of fun up until I came out, but ever since I came out and accepted who I am, my life has just been a ball. I've enjoyed myself . . . I'm more involved now than I ever have been, and I'm even better off spiritually now than I ever was before, because this forced me to come to terms with my spirituality and the Bible. The most difficult place to transition, regardless of where you are, is in the church. And the sad, sad truth of it is, is that the majority of us do have strong religious convictions, and feelings, and backgrounds, and we sit there with this damned if I do and damned if I don't thing. I want to go to church, but if I go to church I'm going to be damned, while if I *don't* go to church I'm going to be damned. One of my ultimate goals is to bring that kind of discrimination down. I'd like to take this message that I have to the mainstream churches, and let them see that we are not freaks, and that God doesn't despise us.

Before, when Carol was with me, we helped start a church here in Hawai'i Kai with another pastor, an attorney friend of ours. Eventually Carol went to work for the attorney. And when this was all coming out — my transitioning — he came down on me big time. He said, "You know, this is a sin." He threw First Corinthian 6:9[1] at me, and I said, "OK, yeah, that's what it says . . ." And I'm sitting there and I don't know what to do with this, so I started reading and studying it. And just by happenstance I picked up a different version of the bible, and when I read the same thing, I found out the word "effeminate" wasn't there. So I went on-line and logged onto Gateway Bible, and they have six or seven different versions that you can compare it with, and the word "effeminate" wasn't in half of them. It had been switched to "homosexual" or whatever, but some of them didn't even have "homosexual," it just said "perverted." So I went to the Greek. I put out a feeler and said, "I would like to know if anybody knows what Paul wrote in the original Greek." I got a reply back that in the original Greek the word Paul used is *molokaios*, which means "soft." How it got transposed into "effeminate" or "gay" is really beyond me. As a result I came to some realizations . . .

At the same time I'm reading this and these realizations are coming to me, I'm sitting here with Carol and we're talking divorce, and I'm looking up scriptures for that. In First Corinthians 7, I think it's 7, Paul's talking about divorce. I already was thinking that Paul's word "*molokaios*" got misinterpreted . . . It was like somebody took these words and put them up in neon on a great big neon sign, because the next thing I remember reading is Paul saying, **These words I speak, not of commandment of the Lord.** In other words, these are *my* thoughts that I'm giving you. So Paul is openly saying to the churches that these are his thoughts, it's not something that's of God. I mean, it's what God wants, but it's still Paul putting things into his perspective. That just really confirmed it, that what all Paul was saying had been misinterpreted and misread. It gave me the peace and contentment that I needed to take care of it.

Then I ended up talking with one of Swaggert's telephone ministers about Carol. The first thing he threw at me was, "Back in Deuteronomy, it says, 'Thou shalt not wear . . .'"[2] It hurt, so I started checking into that. I already felt like, hey, this didn't apply to me anyway, because that's the Old Testament covenant, and I'm living under grace. I guess I had already found this out before I talked with him, because I recall asking him, "If you want me to live by that, can I ask you a question? Do you have children?" He said he did. "Have those children ever been disrespectful to you?" He said, "Yes." So I replied, "And you still have children? Because the Bible is very explicit in Deuteronomy, right before where you're talking about: if the family has children who bring disgrace on the family, you're supposed to take them out to the edge of the city and stone them to death. Do you really want me to live by these laws? Are you going to live by them, too?" So God really opened up my eyes.

For the first two or three years after I came out, I still stayed away from church. I had wanted to go to church so bad, but every time you go, you're going to be ridiculed, you're going to be rejected. If I could pass really good, I could go to any church and just sit there, but I don't pass that well . . . Just by happenstance I happened to meet a young lady (who's one of my adopted daughters), and she told me about Our Family Christian Church, which she had just been going to about a month or so before. So I went. All of a sudden I was in a church like I had preached in before — the spirit of God was there, and nobody was saying anything about me being dressed, because everybody was either gay or lesbian or t but the spirit of God was just really strong. The pastors later found out that I had a minister's background. I told them about myself because I was just thrilled to be there. And they said, "We've got to have you back preaching." I replied, "OK, uh-uh, yeah . . . sure — give me six months to a year. Let me be back in church for a while, and then I'll get back preaching."

Lo and behold, about six or eight weeks later I find out I'm going to pastor a church here in Wai'anae. So I was ordained as a minister within the church, and I co-pastor the church out here in Wai'anae with another

t. This is a story in itself, too. This particular person, Jaime, used to be the assistant pastor of Paradise Chapel Assembly of God here, where my wife used to go to church. This person's wife's name is Carol, which is my wife's name. Jaime has been like me ever since she can remember, but had always put it aside. Nobody knew about it but Jaime's Carol. And the two of them are best friends — they go everywhere together, they talk about things together.

When I finally decided to come out, I told Carol she could tell whoever she wanted to, so she tells Jaime's Carol. Jaime's Carol doesn't tell my Carol about Jaime, though. So, you know, later on we find out that we have everything in life that is just running parallel — same names, same number of children, everything. One boy, one girl, almost same ages. The girl is older than the boy. So all of this is just running parallel. And I'm sitting down here thinking how unbelievable it is, how two people in that church can have so much in common. So now she co-pastors the church with me out here. We started off with about six people, and now we're down to about three. Hopefully we'll get the church to where we'll have more of us.

***

When our kids ran away from home, my son was sixteen, my daughter was seventeen, going on eighteen. There was nothing I could do about my daughter. But my son, we kept trying to get him to come home and settle down, but he was really rebellious and we ended up getting involved in Tough Love. This was in California, the Sacramento area. We were having so many problems with him one night, and we were at a Tough Love meeting, and one of the couples said, "If you guys just need a vacation to get away from this all, why don't you take a vacation. Anyplace you wanted to go?" Carol had wanted to come to Hawai'i since we had gotten married. I had wanted to come but I knew that if I came to Hawai'i I'd never want to leave, because I had spent three years in Key West, Florida in the Navy.

So we ended up coming over here and falling in love with it, and went back for two more trips trying to figure out a way to come over. On one trip, I had job applications, and she had her applications, and we were seeing if we could transfer to here. We went out to the public works center, and as we're talking with everybody, they're saying, "Your applications and everything look good, and we want to do it, BUT we don't hire anybody that doesn't live on the islands." They had the jobs, but they didn't hire anybody that doesn't live on the islands. We hit about three or four places like that. We finally ended up at the shipyard and got the same story: we have jobs, but we don't hire anybody off the island. But the clerk sat there and looked at Carol's application and said, "If you can wait twenty minutes, I'll get you a job interview." Even though they had just been saying they weren't going to hire anybody off the islands. So twenty minutes go by, she goes on the interview, the guy calls back to the clerk, "Can you see if they can find a local address — I want to hire her." So we made a couple of calls around, to the church, and one of their people said that we could use their address. We did. So we're not supposed to be in Hawai'i, and yet . . . they're going to hire us. All this took place in a period of an hour and a half. We came over here, but there were a few little problems before we came — Carol got cold feet. But finally we ended up coming over here.

We rented a house to live in for a while on the beach, but we wanted a house of our own. One day I was out here in Wai'anae, driving back into town from out here, and I got right in front of the pink store, and I just got this overwhleming feeling that I'm going to live right here. I had no idea — I didn't even know this house was here or anything else. It was just like, "This is where you're going to live — Wai'anae." And about six weeks later we bought this house.

For me to be in Wai'anae . . . It should never have been, but it's just that God kept putting in everything, and letting everything fall in place. He said, "This is my plan, this is what I want you to do." All of this has a very big tie-in for me spiritually, because I put all of this together, and it's why I am as happy as I am today. Because I can see where God in my life has taken me from this step, and just keeps putting me where he wants me to be.

I don't understand it . . . Right now as I sit here I praise God that I don't have Carol with me . . . I wish I had her with me, but I am thankful to God because if she had not done what she did, I would *still* be living that lie. I would *still* be away from church. By her leaving, it forced me to come to terms with my life. God put us right here in Wai'anae, with people saying, "You *really* want to live in Wai'anae and do what you're doing?!" Yet it's the best place for me to be now. I feel that God said, "This is where I want you. You're going to live here. You don't know where the house is going to be yet, but this is where you're going to live. You're going to live in Hawai'i, but you have no idea how you're going to live there." But God says it, and "Ding." "Ding." "Ding." So — Why Wai'anae? Because God put us here.

∗∗∗

As a *haole*, when you come to Hawai'i, and you're new . . . First of all you're going to get treated as an outsider or foreigner. You're going to learn that there are cultures around here that don't cater to *haoles* too well. There are communities where *haoles* are not welcome. And probably the worst community for a *haole* to live in is Wai'anae, because Wai'anae is basically made up of people who were born and raised here. They're still local, and a lot of them have prejudice against the *haole*; they're angry with the *haole*. So when you, as a *haole*, come to Wai'anae, you know that you're fighting an uphill battle. And that's what we were doing. Then, to be a *haole*, and not know that many locals and turn around and say, "I have to be who I am." To start to transition — What, are you crazy?!

For the first six months, after I had decided to transition, I would go to work during the day as Harold, come home and get dressed as Cheryl . . . live as Cheryl. All the windows and curtains were shut, the doors were shut . . . I wouldn't even go out into the car port, unless it was night. I was really starting to find out who *I* was. Because that's how scared I was — I'm *haole*, and now I'm doing this God-awful thing, you know. I had this fear people would say, "You're a freak! We're gonna beat the livin' — out of you just for the fun of it because we want to." My friends who did know about me said, "You'd better not go out, you'll get hurt. You'd better quit this if you want to survive." But that's the way it is, and I can't change it.

A *haole* wanting to be a woman, living in Wai'anae — It's the last

rz

place in the world I would tell you to do it. And yet . . . In retrospect, after everything that happened, after the suicide attempt, after coming out of the hospital — the lady who brought me home said she knew a lady I needed to meet, and that was Kim — *I find out that I am in the safest place in the world, because there are so many of us out here.* Just like Kim. You know, it's mainstream here in Wai'anae. It is not a foreign culture here. It is like going into a big city, where you've got the Jewish community, the Spanish community . . . This is who we are. It's accepted. This is the safest place in the world for me to be. It's also the place that everybody who knows me says, "You live WHERE?!" They don't believe it. But it's accepted here, so it's the best place in the world for me to be. I'll never leave here until God just says, "It's time for you to leave." This will always be my home. My dream is to be able to take my house and jack it up, and make another floor underneath it, and start up a school for the t's who are coming out and start teaching them some skills, so they don't have to go work on the streets. Because the t community is rejected, neglected, overlooked . . .

As far as acceptance here in Wai'anae, among my friends, if you were to go back with someone like Kim's family, her family was very rejecting of her. They did not like it. I have another friend, Nohea. Her family was supportive of her. I have a young girl who calls me "Grandma," because I won't let her call me "Momma," and I don't want her to call me "Auntie." Right now she's only eighteen, and in her family there are three siblings: one girl, and two *mahu* (girls who were born boys). In that family, it's been hard for the father to accept, so there have been a lot of problems there. Yet the mother is very accepting of them, and the father tries to be. So it's not that everybody is 100% accepting, and not that everybody is 100% rejecting.

I think in Wai'anae, for the most part, because transgenderism is so mainstream, people have learned to come to terms with it and accept that we are people just like they are. I mean, I've experienced discrimination, but not as Cheryl. I've experienced prejudice, but not as Cheryl. I experienced it in the workplace as Harold, because I'm a *haole*.

But people do make fun of you. One time, I had just come out of my first trip to a beauty shop, and I thought I was looking good. This was at the Daiei store in 'Aiea. There were kids selling candy or something. When I went in I had seen these three kids, and they looked at me. When I came back out, there were some older kids, and there was one kid about ten, who they made come up to me and he said, "Sir, would you like to buy some candy?" I took about five steps, turned around and asked, "*Excuse me?!*" I made a big scene. People just start looking, and I was just putting the kids back down, who had put him up to it. But everybody was really supportive of *me*, not of the kids.

For the kids who are transgendered, it's probably easier here . . . except for their peer groups. I mean, the peer group kids are going to be mean and vicious, and the majority of the time, the ones who are the worst are the ones who are sitting there fighting those same feelings inside and just don't know what to do with it. I think that's true everywhere. The people who fight us the most have these feelings inside, and they're so angry at us because we're living it out and they can't, so the only thing they know how to do is fight. Whether we are transgendered, whether we're gay, or whatever. And I know it. I used to have the same kind of problems. The people who you would *least* expect are hiding these same feelings and needs.

***

The transgender population on O'ahu is larger than anybody knows. I don't know all the avenues, but I'm familiar with Hawai'i Transgendered Outreach. That community is in town, and is made up primarily of older cross-dressers. Some of us are transitioning or transsexuals, but the majority of it is made up of an older group of people who are coming out later in life and are still married. They need a place to get dressed, so they come to the group. It's a very loving community, and I owe a lot to it. But I have a whole different family here in Wai'anae. I'm accepted as "Auntie" out here. My friends out here at first did not understand why I was not interested in men, because I am a woman and I want to live my life as a woman. Because this community has been based on people who live all their life as women, and who are only interested in men. So it's a different kind of a culture. I mean, It's just as different as between the gay

TZ

world and the straight world. They have the same things in common, but they're different. So this culture is different as well.

If you go down into Waikiki, you'll find still another different culture. The culture down in Waikiki is going to be younger queens who are working the streets. I don't believe that the majority of them are doing it because it's what they *choose* to do, but it's because society puts them in that situation. I would love to see that change. Within Life Foundation, there's still another community of t's who are primarily t's with AIDS. So, there are different little pockets, and this is even all the more reason why I want to see the PLU work, because I want to see this get all of us together. We all have the same things in common, but we're just split apart.

PLU means "People Like Us," and it originally came about with Ken Miller. He was one of the heads of Marriage Project Hawai'i, which is a gay organization working to get the marriage legislation pushed through. He started to feel like the gay community was giving the transgender community a bad rap, and he wanted to learn more, because for the most part, the gay community doesn't understand the t community, the t's don't understand the gays, who don't understand the lesbians — It's all just a lack of understanding. So Ken talked to me because I was the president of Hawai'i Transgendered Outreach, and he asked to come to our meetings. I said sure, by all means. So we sat down and talked and he said, "You know, I'd really like to see if there's some way we could get together." I said, "So do I. I really want this." We had hatched this idea that we were going to try to do something to bring us all together, and it was going to be some kind of coalition.

The name PLU came up from one of the first church services I went to with Pastor Billy, who was preaching, and he used this term. To this day he doesn't even remember using it. Well that phrase stuck in my head, and when Ken and I held one of our first meetings, I brought up this term and said, "I think PLU really describes us: we're all people and it's an opportunity to drop labels off of ourselves. I'm just a people like you. It doesn't matter what my orientation is. If we want to get together, we have to learn to drop these labels." So with PLU the whole goal is to get us together to drop labels and to start working together for common goals. When we first founded it and started it out, I said, "You know, we have a lot of goals that we want to do, but for me personally, I will consider it a success if we do *nothing more* than just have one great big picnic or bash or whatever, where all of the different communities are there, and we're working together and playing together. It's more important for me that we are friends first, and care about each other - *ohana* - and then we'll start tackling some of the other issues. Legislation, the laws, the hate crimes, and everything. But before we do that, let's learn to be one big *ohana*."

God has blessed me, because I have been able to be with the Hawai'i Transgendered Outreach group. I also have a family here in Wai'anae, which, for the most part, doesn't want anything to do with the HTGO group, although they are coming around. The two of them are coming together. Because of the Wai'anae family and because I go to Dr. Rodwell [for hormone treatments], I have met a lot of the girls in town. Most all of the girls in town call me "Auntie Cheryl." So I've been accepted into that culture. I could go to town anytime I wanted to and find a place to spend the night and not even worry about it.

Another culture that I've gotten into is the gay community, with the Imperial Court System of Hawai'i. Because of some of my friends out here who are in the Court system, I got involved in it. So now I've got HTGO, I've got Wai'anae, I've got Waikiki, I've got the Imperial Court System . . . That's four families I'm sitting here with. Now I have the church, and the church is a whole different world. It's new people, who are gay, trans, who are all together. God has let me have inroads and respect in all five of these different areas.

Plus, even one more, and that's the mentally challenged community. I'm a member of the Club House. The Club House system is where there are club houses, and these are places where people with mental problems or who are in recovery go and spend their days, and they try to work their way back into society. That's where Kim works. I was a client in the beginning because I needed help. They took me in and accepted me for who I was. So there are six *ohanas* that I have sitting there which are all different. Yet God is letting me have parts in all of them, and hopefully bring all of them together. Because I have got people involved in HTGO from the Court System, I've got people from Wai'anae involved in HTGO . . . Gradually we're getting together. I had a Thanksgiving dinner out here, and there were people here from every group. There were twenty some-odd people, and a lot of them didn't know each other, but people ended up finding out that they had so much in common, new friendships were created and built up. There are a lot of different communities, but I hope we can get them all together.

***

To me, you could take everything that anybody has ever called me. Whether it's "Sir," whether it's "Ma'am," whether it's "Reverend," — you could even put "Dr." on it — anything that anyone's ever labeled me — and all of them pale next to the fact that they call me "Auntie." Because in the Hawaiian culture the aunties and the uncles are revered. They are very special people who, regardless of whether they're your real auntie or not, are called that out of respect. And when they started calling me that . . . I think originally it was because I was the oldest one — out of all of my friends here basically I'm the oldest person. But I think it went way, way past being the oldest person. It's love. And I don't think anybody could call me anything more precious than that. Even when this one little girl calls me grandma, I love that, but I don't think it has as much meaning to me as being called "Auntie." It's a special thing, and it has nothing to do with being *mahu* or anything — It's just Hawaiian culture. You couldn't call me anything to make me happier. I'll be walking downtown, I'll be in Waikiki and someone will call out, "Hi Auntie Cheryl!" I don't know who you are — sometimes I don't know these people. I have my "niece," Nohea, and wherever we go she knows somebody, and so we'll talk, and she'll just talk and talk and talk. She's very good at meeting people. So now it's at the point that wherever we go, there's somebody coming up saying, "Hi Auntie Cheryl." It's just uncanny . . . To have felt like a cork sitting in the middle of the Pacific three years ago, and now everybody on the island knows who you are, and even on the other islands . . .

It's really not all that hard to get in. You have to give of yourself, without expecting anything in return. I guess that's why God has blessed me with all of my skills, because I love to and enjoy giving of myself all the time. If their cars are broke down, I'll go fix the cars, whatever, and I never charge anybody for any of it, because I feel like these loved ones have been taken advantage of all along, and it comes back to me . . . I'll find a little extra money here or there, and then I'll try to give it back to them if I can. If you come in with the attitude that it's gonna be all take, it won't work.

Notes

1. First Corinthians 6:9-10: "Know ye not that the unrighteous shall not inherit the kingdom of God? Be not deceived; neither fornicators, nor idolaters, nor adulterers, nor effeminate, nor abusers of themselves with mankind . . . shall inherit the kingdom of God." (King James)

2. Deuteronomy 22:5: "The woman shall not wear that which pertains to a man, neither shall a man put on a woman's garment; for all that do so are an abomination unto the Lord." (King James)

I'm Philip Herman Kaui Faumuina, but I go by Kaui, my Hawaiian name. I want to have a name change to Chalace Kauilaunaole Limoni. I'm Hawaiian-Chinese-Filipino-Samoan, and was born February sixth, 1971.

Growing up, I never felt muffy or anything — I just felt special because that's how my family made me feel. I knew I was a boy, but I wanted the prettier things in life. It was in elementary school that I knew I wanted to be a girl. Around that time I started getting called names like *mahu. Mahu*, sissy, Alice, fag. . . .

All my life I had only known love, and then all of a sudden there was this hate and this rejection, and I couldn't understand it. My father used to make me take the rubbish out in a dress, and he used to beat me down. I was shamed because even though I knew what I wanted to be, I wasn't ready to be put out like that. I wanted to come out my way. But when I started to get used to taking out the rubbish in a dress, and he knew that I wasn't ashamed anymore, then he started beating me down for that. I got beaten for every single thing . . .

When I was in school the teachers never really criticized me; they just didn't bother, not even my counselor. But the students . . . From seventh grade through ninth grade almost every day of the school year I got beaten for being *mahu*. I tried to be respectful and everything, and I even tried out for the football team to prove I wasn't *mahu*. In the tenth grade I got in and was first string left guard. But as soon as I got first string, I quit the team. Actually, I was small until I joined the football team, but then I got husky and big. After that if anybody called me *mahu* I would beat them up. So that's when I started drag, because I could back

91

myself up. I said, "I don't care what everybody thinks — I *am* a woman!" So I went to school in drag . . . I must have looked like a freak, but in my mind's eye I was the most beautiful thing in the world.

There were four of us *mahu* at school, but there was only one that I hung around with. One I admired, and another I used to feel superior to. I was too afraid to talk to the one I admired because she was just the epitome of *woman*. Even though she looked like a man, her mannerisms and the way she displayed herself were just like *a woman*. I mean, *there* was a woman. You would look past her ugliness and see a woman. I used her as a big role model, and she still is a role model in my mind. She was always so positive. She would always tell me, "Yes you can. Yes you can." It was never, "She was better than me." It was, "I can, you can, we *all* can. We *shall*." That's how she was. Her name is Dee, a.k.a. Diva.

The other sister, Kandi, I had battles with — she was just too loud. Although she was more flaming than me, both of us used to get beaten up. But I felt so much better than her because I thought that here was someone else who was lower than me. [laughs] And the *mahu* I hung with was my cousin and my queen mother, Jamie. That's how it was at school —just the four of us.

Sometimes my mother would say, "It's OK," about my gender issue. So I'd start to feel OK about it. Afterwards she would tell me that it wasn't OK, and make me feel bad. So there would be days when things would be good and then there were days when she was telling me to turn back butch.

It was at seventeen that my mother finally acknowledged me as her daughter. She took me to the beauty salon, and we did our hair, nails, everything. She told me, "If you're going to be a woman, be a *woman*. Women don't wear high shirts and pants up the ass, and they don't wear tank-tops so half their breasts are falling out. They look attractive."

***

I was seventeen when I had my first trick, and it was not pleasant. My first date was for a radio. I didn't like sex, but I just wanted to try it — I was curious. So my date and I were there on the beach, doing our thing, and this guy's wife came out! She started snapping at him, 'You're with *this*?!' I was thinking that she was going to lick me, so I just stood up and started running. I ran into a bathroom . . . Inside were these two girls saying that their sister's boyfriend was fooling around with a *mahu* on the beach so they were going to lick him. Of course, *I* was the *mahu*! So I told them, "Oh yeah, they're still over there, they're hiding on the beach," and I got them to run out. I was so scared!

But after that incident I spent more time at the beach meeting guys, trying to get used to the idea of being a product. I still wasn't mentally there; I didn't know what the hell I was doing. I had to learn to tell myself, "Put yourself away and become a robot. Put away the person you are and become this thing that doesn't feel anything."

Jaime was working in Waipahu and told us that we should start there before we go to Wahiawa because Waipahu is slower and we could practice our walk there. But she really didn't tell me what I was supposed to do. Or even what the prices were. I just followed her. When we got out there she immediately pulled a date, so I was left standing by myself. I was so nervous. There were cars going by, and I didn't know if they were families going to the store or if they were dates. I just sat on the wall and waited. Guys would stop but I turned down so many of them because I didn't want to go. I wasn't comfortable. So for the first few nights all I did was hang out. About one week later this one military guy, a local Puerto Rican, approached me. I went to date him for twenty dollars and it was the worst experience I ever had. He made me do all kinds of filthy things with him. I had to suck his cock, lick his balls and jerk him off. Then I had to repeat everything. He took so long to cum, I swear it took about three hours . . . my mouth was so sore. He also wanted to fuck me and I let him because he threatened to lick me if I didn't. And it was all for twenty dollars. I hated it. At the time my thinking was that I needed the money because I had started hormones. Jaime had treated me with one shot, but she told me that I had to keep up the shots. That's why I needed another twenty dollars. So that's all I was thinking about, my hormones.

After that date I went home and cried for a week. I washed myself, I scrubbed myself so hard to get the filth off me. Finally it dawned on me that all this time I'd been preaching to Jaime how degrading it was for her to do what she was doing and that she shouldn't do it — *and now look*

93

at me. The very one preaching was out there doing it. But she had kept challenging me, "You cannot judge me until you've done it." And then I fell into that and did it. I kept it going because I got my hormones, and the hormones were doing me lovely; I'd do anything for my hormones. I was very faithful to my hormones — that's what I hustled for.

Later I met another queen in Waipahu who showed me the ropes. She told me, "Not twenty dollars — sixty dollars. They want a fuck, three hundred dollars. They're going to pay if they want it." She'd say, "Do your hair like this, dress like this, walk like this. You've got to appeal to them." She took me shopping and showed me the ropes. So this other queen named Bonnie pretty much groomed me. I stayed with her in Waipahu . . . We'd go hustling there and we'd make our money fast. It was trippy, because the majority of the money was from blowjobs. A lot of military were there because they lived in that area. When the families would pass by on their way home, the girls would say, "Drop the bitch and the make a switch," because the guys would literally take their girlfriends and wives home and then *come back out.* It was just trippy, the things that were going on. Here I am thinking that there are certain rules for people's lifestyles *and actually there are no rules.* I learned that everything was sex for money.

Then I went to Wahiawa, where it was about being as presentable as you can be. You've got to be as fish as you can be, you've got to look as womanly as you can because the military men up there don't like the fags, don't like the stigma. But if you look real enough they'll take that blowjob. I guess they'll just tell themselves that you're not really a man. If you don't say anything, then that's OK. But if you say something, then they've got to deal with it. So it's all about deceiving. You had to play that role to get your money. And up in Wahiawa you'd make so much money. In fifteen minutes you're making like five hundred dollars. They were like marathons back then. That's when I learned to dress like a slut, a whore, and to take my dress code up a little bit higher. Because when I first started it was jeans, shirt, very nice, like I was going to school. But when I went up there everyone was wearing latex and boots, and body parts were showing. I was very intimidated by my body because the girls' bodies were *done* - their breasts, their hips — their bodies were *done.*

They looked beautiful. And I felt like I had no business being there. But what I learned from being out there hustling was that the guys actually didn't care what you looked like. They were just out there for sex. Another queen, Alexis, a.k.a. Chocolate, taught me that you dress to be comfortable for yourself, not for them. They're not out here to buy what you look like; they're out here to buy what you can do for them. She said, "You don't have to dress up for any of these motherfuckers. You dress comfortable, because sometimes you're out there forever." So I started dressing regular, and found it was true. The guys came out there and they just wanted to get off. If you were available they would pick you up. Of course, if you looked hot, you'd get the young, arrogant guys who were trying to compare their handsomeness to your beauty and would try to get a deal because of it. But there were older gentlemen who would pay more if you were dressed regular. I guess the older men were trained by the queens who were there before me because the majority of the dates were like, "If you don't tell me what you are, I don't care." I learned a lot about sex from my tricks. I didn't like to have sex, but the money was addictive.

The whole time I was hustling I was trying to find myself a husband. I was trying to live that Pretty Woman role where somebody was going to sweep me off my feet and take me away from this life. There were guys who could have come along and done that for me, but I was so caught up with the money that I couldn't love any of them. From Wahiawa I ended up going to downtown Honolulu, and that was even better! The money was amazing — seven minutes for a hundred dollars. One date, five hundred dollars. That's how it was. What made it even more addictive in town was this one date that just blew me away. All I had to do was keep him company for seven hundred dollars, just talking stories for an hour. Usually I was like, "Let's have sex, let's get it over with." But seven hundred dollars for just talking stories — Flawless, yeah! That's all I had to do! That's why it was very, very addictive when I was out there hustling.

When I was in town things were really different. In Wahiawa I was the one who was performing blowjobs on the guys, so it was trippy for me to go to town where the guy would want to perform the blowjob on me. In Wahiawa you have to be the feminine one, you have to be the woman. But in town, they wanted a woman who had a man's tool. So it was trippy.

***

Mahus don't have pimps because it's our money — we're the ones working for it. I think the pimp thing is from the mainland because it's not a Hawai'i thing. The mainland people brought it down here. But the pimps don't go into *mahu* territory, so we don't need protection. We're beautiful and we can fight. A lot of the girls look small, petite, beautiful; people forget that under all that exterior is a man. We don't need pimps because we have sisterhood. The queens all watch each other. Nowadays, though, when I see the girls out there, they don't watch each other — they fight with each other. In our day, we always asked each other, "Are you OK? Are you hungry? Do you need money?" We always watched each other and took care of each other. It's different now.

There came a time when it was just booming in town — The guys sought you out and you'd tell them, "It'll cost you fifty dollars just to talk to me." And they would pay you fifty dollars! I was getting so blinded by money that when a guy would touch me I'd say, "That's a hundred dollars." And he would give me the hundred dollars! Even though I was only playing around and acting stupid, he would pay. That's why I got spoiled, because I would play these tricks with them and they kept giving and giving.

When election time came up in 1991 for the mayor polls, the cops started busting down on everybody — you couldn't even stop and sit in one place for more than two minutes. It got bad; you had to keep walking and they kept chasing us to different sections of Honolulu. It was getting really nails. Election time killed the tricks because the police were arresting the johns, not us. So they scared away all of our johns. It was bad because we had become accustomed to a lifestyle that we couldn't afford anymore. We were out there doing nothing for a long time. And with the new bills and laws getting passed the dates were not coming around because they were afraid. Next, the only thing you could trick up for was drugs. So you'd get a load of drugs for dating somebody, and sell it.

That's how the majority of us girls fell into it. The next trick was for drugs. The next date was to get the next fix. And that's how you catch HIV, because you lose focus. When you're in the heat of the moment and you're high and thinking of your next hit and the guy says, "No condom," you do risky behavior.

So I was getting sick and tired of being on the streets. Not only was there the risk of AIDS and diseases like that, there was also the risk of being arrested and having a record. Plus there were situations where the john would beat me up, take back the money and throw me out of the car. That's how risky it was. That's why I wanted to get off the streets. See, I really got into drugs because I didn't want to have those feelings of being hurt anymore. I wanted to be numb. Being high on drugs is the only thing that kept me surviving out there. But I knew I wasn't born to be a drug addict, a prostitute, a low-life, a nothing. I knew there was something else that I was supposed to be. I wasn't supposed to be like this. It took me a long time to dig out of that hole that I had dug for myself.

My husband was the one who taught me respect. I couldn't respect my family. They made me pay six hundred dollars rent — and said I couldn't eat with them. I had to buy my own food! I couldn't even wash clothes with them — that's how they treated me. So I hated my family. And my husband taught me to love my family again. I used to think, "Fuck them, they're wrong, not me. I'm not wrong, they're wrong." But he told me, "No matter what, they're your parents. You only have one mother, you only have one father. Say you're sorry to them." I used to *fight* with him! I'd have the hardest time just to say I'm sorry. Every time we'd fight, he'd make me go back and apologize. Next thing you know, I started to see my mom and dad changing — they started respecting me and loving me.

So this man gave me back my family; I could talk to them. Before, I couldn't talk to my mom or dad because I was always afraid. But then I learned to communicate with my family and I used to tell my mom, "You know what is wrong with our family? We don't communicate. It would kill you to tell me that you love me. So I'm going to start it now so you can learn." I told her, "I love you." She asked, "Are you OK?" I answered, "I'm OK. Now you have to learn to say it, too. It's medicine for the soul." So this man showed me how to love myself and how to love another person. He gave me back my family.

I knew that something was missing in my life, and that was religion. I thought that I couldn't pray . . . When I was a child I had lived with relatives who took me to church. They preached to me because of what I was . . . They shaved my hair bald, took me to church, and in front of the whole church used me as an example — "We cut his hair to make him look like a boy, but he still walks like a girl. We have to pray for him to change his walk." That's what they did to me. They made me hate the religion. But it was the religion I was missing . . . After my husband left me, which was in 1994, it took me almost four years to learn what it is to pray, how it is to pray, who He is, what He is . . . I didn't understand anything. But praying is what helped me.

The other thing which really helped me was Ke Ola Mamo. I used to catch the bus from Makaha *every day*, from May of 1999, to come to work at Ke Ola Mamo. And I caught the express home. Every single day it was an hour each way; I was so tired. But it was good just to leave my house. Because I lived in a bad environment at home. All my sisters and them did drugs, our neighbors all around us, my mom was hardly ever home. Fighting all the time . . . I'm not home to watch it. I go to work and come home. If there's a problem there I'm not involved.

I was still doing drugs two years ago . . . It seemed like every time something was good for me, I felt like I had to fuck up because it wasn't real. So I had to keep fucking up! [laughs] Even this year I fucked up — I just relapsed in February. And my friend Ashli came to me and said, "It's OK that you relapsed. You relapse for three months, three weeks, whatever. But today — make it three days because, Mary, I'm coming for you! I'm not ripping you; I care for you, Kaui. You came this far. I knew you from Philip and look at you now." And it showed me that they cared, that Ke Ola Mamo cared about me. They really comforted me!

When I moved up to Waikiki in February 1999 I was crying because I had just moved out of my home and didn't tell anyone what I was doing — I just moved to Waikiki and I felt lost. Then Ke Ola Mamo found out what was going on and where I was, and they came to the house and told me, "Kaui, don't get drowned out in your misery, don't get lost. Work. Drown yourself in work." Ashli and Roxanne said, "Carol wants you to come to work, she doesn't want you to get lost." So I said, "I'm coming to work!" [laughs] And I was just working, working, working, working. All the time. And I was like, it feels so good, and I have to tell them thank you and all of that.

***

Earlier this year Ke Ola Mamo had a retreat for *mahu*. There was a *mahu* get-together five years before this one, but it had been for the old-timers. They had made a camp for three weeks, supplied the food and everything. All they said was, "You *mahu*? You know this auntie? You know that auntie? Come down, swim, eat, carry on . . ." Only three of us from Wai'anae went down for that. So when this retreat came up again, I thought, "Finally — another one!" There were only three old timers from that first one who came back. So I think we've got to have this every six months. We cannot wait . . . even a year is too long. People change, people grow . . .

What helped it happen now was because we've got three girls working in Ke Ola Mamo and they have an excuse for a retreat — HIV prevention. Because if a lot of girls get together often there's this competition style and ripping, and that's what keeps them away. But if you have a reason — like HIV prevention — then we're gonna have fun. We're gonna leave all the competition out and just come to find out information.

The retreat was so lovely. We had girls come from Kaua'i, Moloka'i, the Big Island, Ni'ihau. But the girls from Maui couldn't come because they had just started a drag show. Of course there were girls from all over O'ahu . . . The biggest group of girls, the ones from Wai'anae, were all my daughters. I told them that they had to mingle with the others. "You from Wai'anae know how to hang around with each other, so hang around with everybody else. Mingle, mix, match. . . ." It was lovely. They hiked, learned *hula*, the Hawaiian language. They learned to be women there, and they learned the old style — Whatever the older wants, you do. There were some girls who were disrespectful, but we were able to change four of them. Because up until that retreat they were very high and mighty — If you asked them to do something they said, "Ugh, you do it, I don't want to do it." And there was this one who was so into herself, who was so afraid to carry on and talk story. It took us a hard time to break her out of it, but we did.

The girls from the other islands are *intimidated* by the girls from Honolulu. It's just like when we go to the mainland — we're intimidated by the girls there because they have a bigger place to shop, a bigger menu to go for hormones, but we're just an island. On the other islands the girls don't have hormones, so they have to work with what they have. But we look at them and envy them because we're living here in this chaos — all we want is to have peace of mind. [laughs] But they come here and speak Hawaiian . . . They can gather plants and make them into a beautiful *lei*. And I'm thinking, "Oh my God!" Yet when we're getting ready and getting painted, they look at us and say, "Oh, you guys can paint!" So we envy them and they envy us. It's mutual. But I think that sometimes you have power but just don't know it. I told them, "You girls envy us? *Stupid*! Because we envy *you*, honey. You live with where there are no problems going in or out, you have your families, you have your homegirls."

Because on the other islands the family is tight — *It's tight*. You don't find *mahus* on the streets. I mean, you find *mahus* on the streets, but not like over here where you're kicked out to the curb. There's none of that on the other islands. You know, it's so *special* there. And they all dance *hula* — over here we're Hawaiian and we don't know how to dance *hula*! I'm like, "Ai — you envy us, but we envy you!" So it's equal. But I love the girls from the other islands. They have old drag queen style. I mean, with those Moloka'i, Ni'ihau, Kaua'i girls at the retreat there was not one time my cup was empty. "Auntie Kaui, are you hungry?" They were bringing food, serving me, making *leis* and *haku* . . . They talked with me . . . They stick with you and like to know who you are. There was always respect. It's too bad it's not like that over here.

So the retreat was very successful; it was good for all the girls to meet each other. There were a lot of girls who would not normally talk to that kind of person or this person because of prejudice. They think they're better than the Wai'anae girls or better than the Waipahu girls, so they won't mingle. But by the end of the weekend, it was like, "Oh, I don't want it to end!" That's how it was.

There were seventy-eight people there all together. It was supposed to be for only thirty people! But I recruited and recruited and recruited. It was so lovely and I really want another one. I'm working on it, in fact. If Ke Ola Mamo cannot fund it, then everybody can bring pot luck. I can provide the tents, I can provide the warmers, coolers, chairs, tables, and I can provide the entertainment. All we need to do is to find that spot, and it's right there in Makaha waiting for us, and everybody can come down. So I'm planning that . . .

See, *mahu* have always been organized. But it's been here and there. It's like a puzzle and now we're just slamming the pieces together. You know, for years, since I can remember, everybody used to meet at Queen's Surf to play volleyball and we always had meetings there. I knew for a fact — wherever I was on the island, whatever I was doing at that time in my life — that I could always go to Queen's Surf and they would be there waiting for me. Street queens, working queens, butch queens — anybody could come down to Queen's Surf. People might have attitudes towards each other on the street, but on the beach there was none of that — it was family. Sometimes people acted up — butch queens might say to a queen, "Hey prostitute, get an education!" And the queens would tell them, "You just wish you were a woman!" So the regulars would say, "Don't act like that. We are *all mahu*." They'd tell the butch queens, "Be careful what you say, you might turn into one of them." And they'd tell the queens, "Before you ever were a woman, you were like them." So the next time they saw each other on the street they'd be closer to each other and things would be safer. Like if you're getting beaten on the street, I would beat the person who is beating you up . . .

But then they tore down the volleyball court, tore down the bathrooms — they changed everything. So that's what Ke Ola Mamo is doing now — we're trying to fix the problem.

* * *

I call the older generations the "*mo'o* drag queens" — they are the lizard drag queens of the past. Because that's how they looked — they all looked like *drag queens*. They looked like a lizard in drag. They had that exaggerated face [pulls face back], those big eyes, and as black as they are, they all had blond hair. But the way it was back then was, whatever they said you did. "Do this!" — You did it, even if you didn't want to. That's what the training was.

The first *mahu* rule was, *Mahu* look like *mahu*. The second *mahu* rule was, Don't use your penis on a man because you're a woman. Carry yourself like a woman, present yourself as a woman. Those were the rules, and it wasn't told to us — it was beaten into us. That's how the queens were in those days. If they saw how my hair is right now, they would slap my face! That's because you always had to have nice hair when you went out. And the way they spoke to the younger queens wasn't so pleasant. Actually, it was quite vicious. "Eh, Mary, get the ashtray over there right now!" It wasn't like, "Could you please pass the ashtray?" And you did not *dare* say "Huh?" or "What?" You just got the ashtray and brought it because if you didn't there would be cracks. That's how the girls my age were brought up by our queen mothers. The mothers used to compete with each other. "You talk to my daughter, you'll get lickings. You and all your children will get lickings for touching one of my daughters."

Those queens didn't have hormones in their day. Everything was an illusion — Makeup, hip and breast pads. I learned those things from them. You cannot afford sequins? Then you make something into sequins. They taught me how to wrap buttons in saran wrap, blow dry them tight, and that's what we used for large glitter. That's how it was in those days. But in my days coming up, all of us girls had hormones. The hormones gave you skin, hair, body, personality. Every day it was a ritual to use the hormones. So no matter what size you were, every single girl was *beautiful*.

In my day we used to have respect. The next generation after ours was losing respect, but now the girls who came after them have no respect. It's because of the new Child Protective Service laws. If I had known about CPS in my day, I probably wouldn't have had any respect for my parents, either. See, now if their parents beat them, they can get out of their family and go to a foster home or another family. So parents are afraid. When we do outreach and go to the parents' house and talk to them, they ask us "How can I beat my son? Because then it'll be turned over to CPS." But I say, "Beat your son and teach him the Hawaiian way." If it wasn't for the beatings from my family, I probably would be all fucked up. I hated all those beatings, but that taught me to respect my families, and to respect anybody who was older than me. But a lot of these young girls know about CPS because they're taught about it in school. And the school wonders why the kids act up against their parents — you taught them that!

***

The younger queens know about their options now. I was in the dark ages when I was younger; I thought that we had no chance with this community. But there's a new generation, my generation, that took the stand and said, "I'm working. I'm not mental. I know what I want to be. *You're* mental, you're trying to make money off of what I'm supposed to be." It's just that our species, the transsexual, is always being pushed back. They're really afraid of us. In the old days we were the ones who were told, "Watch the kids, clean the house, do this stuff, because I gotta go and live my life." Because we are such passionate, caring people, because all we want to do is be loved and accepted, we are suckers for it. We're not being suckers for it anymore. "Watch the kids." *You* watch the kids! I never make kids! [laughs] "What, you want us stay home and don't go out? *You* stay home and don't go out!" Now that we're standing up for ourselves they're getting threatened and are trying to shut us down again. But it won't work because we're all so fed up . . .

But if the community can help us help ourselves — and just help us a little bit because we helped them a lot — there wouldn't be such negativity. We could eliminate the prostitution and the drugs. A lot of the girls turn to drugs because they're in a situation where they don't know what to do. They're introduced to it because they want to be numb. It's a sickness — and we can cure it.

***

The way I feel about how mothers and daughters become connected and the relationship between them is that the older queen sees

103

herself in the younger queen. They're attracted to you and vise-versa. The younger queens are attracted because they see the knowledge and beauty in you. What happened with me is that I saw my children — Roxanne, Lili, Akamu, Keisha — going through the sufferings I had to go through. I didn't want to see them go through that, so I used the bait and switch thing: I lured them to me with complements and then tried to instill in them my values. I told them how beautiful they could be, and if I had extra money I would take them out to eat or to buy them whatever they needed, their drag necessities, womanly things. I would take them to drag pageants or bring them around to other drag queens to see . . . I wanted to take them off the streets because I knew that working there was suffering. In the beginning it's an adventure. But once it becomes your job, honey . . .

I had my own place over here in Waikiki. I was a full-time prostitute. I was working the streets *for them.* I would take them hormones, teach them how to be the woman, pluck, shave, hair, everything, shopping, everything. I just took them under my wing, and took care of them . . . I told them, "I don't want you on the street, because it's dangerous; you can get killed. There are drugs, there is disease." But they wouldn't listen — I'd catch them on the streets. So I'd tell them, "If you're going to be on the streets, be aware. Always have condoms." And I showed them how to use them.

I also taught them, "Do not fall in love with your dates because they are not there for you — they are there to use you, so you use them. You put on a show and then you leave." I told them to be aware of their surroundings, to know how often the cops went around, to watch how many times this car went around, to see what guy is looking at you — I beat that into them. I gave them the old school style.

See, I had common sense but I never had education, and I had self confidence but it wasn't the kind of confidence you're supposed to have to make it in society. It was that backstreet, streetstyle confidence. And I tried to teach all my daughters so that they could make it in society. I really stressed three things. One — family. You can have a sex-change, pussy, money, husband, everything, but you're never going to be happy until you have your family. That's the first thing — you *don't* forget your relationships. That's what sustains me. Two — education. Do *not* be a fuck-up. Use that education and *go* for it. Because I don't have my education, and it's the simplest thing I could have ever had, but because I never had it I felt low self-esteem. That was my biggest failure.

And three — prayer. I told them prayer because everything I prayed for, I got. I didn't pray for anything for the first three years; I prayed only for forgiveness. Then I asked for spiritual help and spiritual guidance. And I prayed, prayed, prayed. And I got my diploma, I got my driver's license, I got all these things . . .

I'd never really had an older queen mother to guide me and show me this and that, what is right and wrong, until I met a *mahu* who I admired. She did things I didn't agree with, like working the streets, but she was still living her life as a woman, so I was attracted to that. And she had information about hormones and other queens. With my own children, I felt that I didn't want them on the street suffering like I had to be doing, or being rejected by their family, or just having no focus. I was attracted to them because I wanted to save them. That's what I was trying to do, save them. I taught them that they need their family and that they're not going to be anything without their family. And that they need education because in today's world . . . Back then, the streets were OK, but now everything is education; you need that hook to get a job. You use that as a weapon to get a job in today's society.

I really stress prayer. I say to them, "I know you like to hear me talk story about the old times. Now if you really listen to me like you say you do, then you've got to pray — and pray hard. Prayer will open up the doors to everything." Before thinking about their parents, family or school, they've got to pray to God. If you ask for forgiveness, everything will fall into place. So you need God first, then your family, then your education.

That's what I mean by bait and switch. Usually young queens are so attracted to the knowledge that you have that they'll believe and do anything that you tell them. Because when they become stuck to you, you can pretty much mold the girls into whatever you need them to become. So I mold them to save them from what I had to suffer from. I want to mold them into positive role models. And the majority of the girls who I did that to are positive role models and they're all successful.

Now I have a new challenge because I have a new generation of children. It's different from before. Because of CPS they have their families — but they don't have focus. Because they have things easier, they are kind of spoiled. The old generation, like in 1980, had to suffer and go through things to make themselves successful. In the old days, if you were *mahu*, you'd have to get out of the house; your family didn't want anything to do with you. When I was younger I had to focus because nobody else was going to take care of me. Now there's a lot more awareness out there because the older queens already paved the way. I would be honored if I were known as one of the queens who did pave the way. There are a lot of queens who came before me who I had the fortune to meet and know and learn from. I honor them because they paved the way for my generation. So the young girls say I'm hard on them, but I really love them. I only punish them because it's better to be punished by the person who loves you than by a total stranger who could totally wreck you. Because I'm not only going to punish them, I'm also going to nurture and love them and make them strong.

I've always believed that education is important and that's my biggest failure since I was smart in school — I had Bs and Cs and several As. But because of the gender identity crisis I was going through I couldn't focus. I was more focused on why everybody was calling me a fag, why everybody was being mean to me, why I was being rejected by my family. So I couldn't focus on education because of my family. One minute they would be saying, "Oh, you should've been a girl." And I'm thinking they're telling me that it's OK. But the next minute they're saying, "You fucking fag! Why are you like this?!" And they're telling me that it's *not* OK. So I couldn't focus on education; I was too busy worrying about what was going on at home. I was too busy worrying about what was going to happen if I go to school, how to dress, how my hair looked. I had all these issues so I couldn't focus on school. That's why Ke Ola Mamo goes into the schools and teaches about sexual diversity and HIV. And I think sexual diversity is very, very important to teach in the schools, because if they can eliminate that barrier for transgendered people, and eliminate the distractions and try to soften things at home, that person can be just as successful as anybody else. That's the downfall for gay children — they have to grow up early. They have to be defensive way before their time and focus on things that are not really important for them to be successful in the future.

Education is important. I knew that I was smart, but because I didn't graduate with my class, I felt like a failure for a long time. So I'm very happy I got my diploma, which took me twelve years to get. And I'm starting school again in the spring at Honolulu Community College. I'm planning to study cosmetology. That would be good for me because I'm talented at it already.

After that I think I'd like to go into communications. TV, radio . . . One of my children, Leikia, is a DJ for a radio station and she doesn't have a degree, but she's there. She got there with hard work. People have given her a hard time at work, but she's still going. See, I was my children's role model, but now they are my role models also. I was a big hypocrite because I didn't have my education and I really didn't have my family. And because I didn't have my education and family, I tried to instill these things in my children. "These are the things that you need because these are the things I lack."

So I try to make the younger queens who are coming up understand that if they want to be a part of my family — and I have the biggest family on this island, over thirty drag queens — they have to get their diploma. Whether they accept God in their life is their choice, but that's something I stress to them. Because for me the three most important things are God, family and education.

I also try to teach my daughters about how dangerous materialism is. Some queens, as they go through their birth of becoming a woman, become materialistic. Make-up, products, tweezers, hair, body, cars, men . . . Sometimes they sacrifice friendship over these things. And it's OK, because they work so hard to get it. But in the end they need to realize that they need to pray. Because when they die all these things will not be there for them. When they get hurt, are they going to cry to their materialistic things? Are they going to cry to their car that their man hurt them? The girls have to learn to respect their materialistic things enough to let them go. Because that's what I'm going through now. I've seen the desire for material things taint friendships and relationships. It really affected me when my husband left. When he left me I still had all these material things — jewelry, stereos, TVs . . . But I didn't have me or God. So when he left, I felt like I had nothing; the material things didn't mean anything to me anymore. I escaped that pain through drugs. It took me three years to get out of that.

When I was young I had a lot of dreams and aspirations. But because I was stuck in my sexual diversity crisis I couldn't focus on any of those things. So I built this gigantic wall of dreams, and when it came time to start taking those bricks down and doing them one by one, I was so intimidated that I couldn't focus on anything. And I just got depressed and sad and didn't know what to do. I did other things to comfort myself. Because I didn't know how to become a woman and didn't have information, I went into the sex industry. Everything was based on being a woman — beauty, makeup, hair, men . . . Those were my goals in life. When I was young my goals in life were to become either an interior decorator or a cook. I was interested in these things because when I was young I had to clean up the house and cook. But when they became chores I didn't want to do them anymore. So I focused on being a singer. I used to love to sing. But my parents always used to demand that I sing, so they killed that dream. I also loved to draw, but when I started in the sex industry I started drugs, also. I started tweaking while I was drawing, so I killed that dream, too.

When you're young and have all of these sexual diversity issues, you cannot focus on one brick, one dream, at a time. It's really, really hard. You become stuck and stupid. And that's an issue some of my children are dealing with now. Because I have four of them who are stuck and stupid and don't know how to get past it. Just recently they came up to me and asked me about it and it just took me back. I told them, "All I can say is that I wasted eight years of my life before I finally focused. So pray, pray now. I didn't know how to pray back then. When you have goals but you don't know what to do with them, pray. Really pray a lot." I don't want to sound like I'm a Christian or that I'm saved, but I just want to say that the church is there in my heart. And you have to pray a lot if you're stuck and stupid, because it's the hardest thing. I don't know how I got through that time in my life. It took me eight years. My goal from four years ago was to go to school, and finally it's happening now. It was a long struggle. Four years ago I was in a completely different state of mind . . . Actually, the idea of going to school first clicked in me about six years ago when I was dancing in the shows, because I realized that the shows weren't going to pay the bills, the shows weren't going to do shit for me. So it clicked for me that I wasn't going to be a showgirl, so I can stop acting like I was one. When I left the show I was supposed to get my diploma, but it ended up taking me six years.

***

In the future I would like to create a safe-house and a community center for transsexuals. I'd like to have a training center there for the queens, with computers. Because that's the wave of the future and it's also a way to link up to outside information. They would learn typing and computer literacy and be able to look for jobs and places on the internet. It would be lovely to have that community center run by queens and worked by queens to help other queens . . . We have a lot of queens here who need help.

I would also like to have a hotline for transsexuals, where queens can call to express their problems. And we should have a newspaper for the transsexuals, with stories by transsexuals. We need our own trans-sexual psychologists and psychiatrists, too, along with doctors for the girls to go to. Many queens get diabetes and heart disease, but the doctors focus on their transsexual issues instead and forget about their health. Plus, we need a drug treatment center for transsexuals. It would be facilitated by transsexuals because we can relate to each other. We're not going to relapse because we're for each other — when you're in the community you're for each other, through the good and the bad times. You'll want to get that person back on track because you love them. If you fall down we say, "Honey, get your ass back up and walk, or I'm going to kick you!" We're going to hurt you, but we're also going to nurture you back. That's how we are. We're not going to just kick you out if you make mistakes or miss your appointments, which is how some other treatment programs work. With us, if you miss your appointment, we're going to come and get you.

***

In the past, I used to think there were only three things: *mahu*, sex-change, and butchie, men who act like muffies. That's what I thought. But when I got into the community I was like, "Oh my God! What is going on?! There are just no rules for these frickin' faggots!" *Mahus* and women, *mahus* and butches, *mahus* and *mahus*, *mahus* and butch queens, *mahus* and men, *mahus* and sex-change . . . Oh my God — you guys have no morals, no wonder people think about us like that! [laughs]

I know this one person who had lived his life first as a woman . . . He's an old-timer, like fifty-one, fifty-two, but he was beautiful, with long beautiful hair. He speaks all different kinds of languages, he went to the university. He was beautiful coming out, a Samoan queen. But I only met him after he had already turned back . . . I only heard these stories about him later. He works for a law firm now, and is married with kids. There are a lot of people I know who turned back. I think that's what gave me the idea that I could turn back, too. [laughs] But when I look at him I realize I cannot turn back. The idea is just wrong for me. I cannot look like a man and accept it. So I accept myself as a drag queen — colorful, like a chameleon.

I'm happy . . . I feel like a woman, but I would not have anything cut or done to me . . . maybe breasts or something like that. But I wouldn't have a sex-change. I would not take away what God gave to me. I think the only person I need to love right now is Jesus Christ — that's the only man I will ever love. And that's my sanity right now. [laughs]

There are *mahus* who go with girls and have children . . . Another young one, my daughter, turned back from her drag into a boy to go with a drag queen. And the other drag queen *is my daughter!* I'm mad at him — that's incest! [laughs] The bottom line is that there aren't any rules. There are just ideas of how things are supposed to be. But when you really look at it, anybody can turn and snap at any time. People go back and forth . . . The majority of people who are as old as I am, they flip — they're always flipping. We're pancakes, we're always being flipped to see which side is the best side. Because there were times when I wanted to have my own children and find a girl for myself. But if I did that, I would still do it in drag. If there's a girl who could love me to be like this, and would have my children, then lovely! But I'm not going to play the image of a man — I cannot. So what do you call that? I don't know what you would call that. I really don't have a label for that. But they all flip. There's a queen I know who had a son, even though she's a queen. She was going with a girl who dressed like a man, but who left the queen and decided to go with another man. So you can see what kind of flipping goes on!

People ask me a lot, "What do you call the kind of guy who goes for you? I know that gay men go with gay men . . . So what is a man who goes with you? Is he gay?" I tell them, "There's no name for it. The only thing I can tell you is that they're really confused. A man who goes for an illusion of a woman — they're confused, they're infatuated, they're curious. That's what they are. I don't know any name for them." They ask me, "Why do you think they're confused?" And I say, "Well, first of all, we want straight men because we think of ourselves as women. Even though we're men. But when guys meet us, they have the image in their head of a woman . . . they think we're a woman, and we play the role until they love us. If we finally tell them, 'I was really born a man,' there will be those guys who just cut the line and leave. But there will also be guys who will stay with you because they've met and found this person who they love. They can't just leave . . . They're confused. Maybe they'll stay with you for four, five, six years, but the whole time they're with you, they're *confused*. Because they *love you,* but they won't go *there.* They'll fuck you, you can blow them off, but they won't go *there.* But they love *you,* they love the image, they love the action, the femininity . . . They're in love with the idea that a girl can be so girl, girl, girl, girl, yet do the things that any man will do. So all this is really hard to label . . . It's funky." [laughs] When I first got into it and got confused I thought to myself, "No wonder society wants us to disappear — we bring out questions you just cannot answer!" But I think the best answer that any queen can give is, "You cannot label me. I'm just *me.*"

***

In the past the word "*mahu*" was offensive and degrading and de-meaning, but I have accepted that *mahu* is what we are. That is *our* word. I've accepted that word . . . If somebody says *mahu* in a bad way, I look at them and say, "What is the meaning of *mahu*?" The way you say "*mahu*" to me . . . everything is pronunciation. You can say, "You look good." "You look *good*." "You look . . . good." So what is the meaning of that "*mahu*" which you said? Is it, "You faggot"? Is that what *mahu* means? So I say, "God bless you," and walk away. That leaves them stunned.

Today, we have many names for *mahu* — mermaid, smoke, two-spirit person . . . But when I was coming out my queen mother told me that *mahu* means "dessert." I asked her what she meant. She said that somebody told her that *mahu* meant "cream puffs." And for a long time I used to think, "What the fuck does 'cream puffs' mean?" And this is what I finally came up with in my mind: it makes sense because if you go to a place where they sell desserts, they have jelly donuts, long johns, sugar-glazed donuts, chocolate donuts, the pretty-kine donuts. And if you look at the cream puff, it's ugly. You look at it and you think, "Ugh, what *is* that?" So when you go to buy pastries you talk about and buy all the pretty things, but you don't talk about the cream puffs. They're the ugliest things — you're not going to look at them, you're not gonna bother. And that's very *mahu*. Because when you come into society, you look at the all the beautiful people and talk about them. But when you see that *mahu*, because it looks so different and ugly, you wouldn't bother with it. *But* — if you take the time to get to know that person, you find out that it is a lovely treat. Just like if you take the time to go and buy a cream puff. It's ugly on the outside, but if you bite it you find that inside it's creamy and delicious. So that's my theory — we're cream puffs. [laughs]

Another thing I want people to know is that there's a big conspiracy about *mahus*. We're actually angels. We were sent down to earth to soak up all of man's sins. I was sent up to earth to make people laugh and happy, to give them counseling that they need. Because a lot of people run to us with their problems. For some reason, in our mind and from our hearts, we say what we think is right and it *helps* people. If you look in the Bible when they describe the angels, the majority of the angels are men. But they're *beautiful* men, beautiful boys with angelic faces and hair and gold. They're just the most beautiful things you've ever seen. So that's what we are — angels.

I moved here from Wisconsin in 1993 because of a job transfer. At the time I was married, so I moved over everything. I went through my gender shift at a point when I had gotten laid off from my job, my dad had died, and my marriage was struggling. I was aware that I was going through a crisis and needed to decide whether to ignore it or instead pursue some changes for the better.

I was born and raised in Rhode Island. I'm forty-seven years of age. I attended the University of Wisconsin and earned a Masters degree in leisure service management there. I worked for many, many years as a YMCA camp director. Currently I'm working as an office supervisor for a large office in downtown Honolulu. I'm also pursuing a Masters of Education degree at the University of Hawai'i.

I have a great interest in gender equity in education, and I'd eventually like to train teachers and youth leaders who work with children. I want to teach and demonstrate how to carry through gender equity in the school system, the sports system and the recreation system. Because that's where it begins. Kids learn about gender in school and as they play, and it will carry over into their adult lives. I've also had a lot of opportunities to train college students and young adults through my YMCA work as a camp director. I really enjoy doing that.

Gender equity is about dissolving the myth of gender. Which is, that people who are born male are innately superior to people born female. Gender equity says that there should be equal opportunity in all things, including sports and the workplace, whether you're male or female.

There are a lot of things which have been carried over from the past in our society which perpetuate the myth of gender. You can easily see it in sports and in the workplace. Even now after thirty years of laws providing equal pay for women, they still only make eighty-six cents on the dollar. Why? Because the men are still in power, and they're the ones keeping it that way.

Just recently, the women's athletics department got a track program at the University of Hawai'i. A university that size not having women's track for all these years? You really have to wonder why. It's just wrong. People need to stand up against it. I think that once gender ceases to be such a big issue in the workplace and in the social setting, then being transgendered won't be such a big issue.

Women have proven themselves time and time again to be as equal to men, and in some ways superior — they're better swimmers, some can be better runners. Recently, there was a boxing fight between a man and a woman at one hundred and thirteen pounds — and the woman won. I guess the bigger question is not so much whether we're transgendered or not but rather, What difference does gender itself make?

***

I think of childhood as a time of innocence. You don't really know who you are, what you're destined to be — you're just enjoying life and absorbing it all. Then about six or seven I started giving more recognition to who I am and how I relate to people. I think it was about then that I started to feel more of a connection with my mom, and the female form and social appearance. I wasn't a rough and tough child, but neither was I very effeminate. I'd go out and play sports and climb trees. But I think that when I became aware that my destiny was to be a boy, that this is what I am supposed to be, then I tried to fit in more with boys and get into sports. When I sought friendships with girls other people interpreted it as, "Oh, you have a girlfriend." I'd go along with it, although knowing that I really had no interest beyond friendship. It was the friendship that inspired me, not necessarily physical connection or sexual attraction.

I was about eight or nine when my dad set my brother and I down and told us the facts of life. He did these little graphics with his hands. He did a good job, but it made me realize that being a boy was my destiny. Before that my body had been undefined and I just didn't believe I was headed that way. I was hoping greatly that I would somehow magically transform. I used to think about it so much. I thought that if I kept thinking about it, I would actually turn into a girl. But having seen everything in papers like the Enquirer — the sensationalized stories of people who were suicidal and who were drag queens and being beaten up on — I had no desire to go that direction.

So when my dad told us the facts of life, that was emotionally shocking to me. For the next two years I was really stressed out. Sometimes I couldn't even go to school because I had trouble dealing with my emotions. Plus there was the flak I was getting at school, and I was going through puberty and all these self changes. It felt overwhelming. At times I'd fake being sick so I could stay at home.

I remember one time my mom came home and realized that I wasn't really sick and that I had lied. She got angry, which caused me to try to express to her why I did it. So my parents took me to a psychiatrist. They talked with him while I sat in the lobby. When they came out, they looked at me and shook their heads. Then we left. They never told me what they had talked about and decided. That was around 1962 . . . I was about ten or eleven at the time. The approach then was to ignore gender identity disorders because it was thought they would just go away on their own. The generation before got electrical shock treatment. That's what they did in the fifties. Thank God, huh? I just missed that by ten years. They ignored it, so I ignored it. I figured that no one else thought it had serious consequences, so I might as well ignore it also.

But as I got older . . . Well, when I was eight or nine I had started trying on my mom's clothes and putting on make-up. It was all in secret. Then I learned to suppress my feelings because it was too risky to dress. Later, as a teen, I made friends easily with girls, so I had a lot of girl friends. But everybody saw me having a lot of "girlfriends," and that I was just loose with them. So there was this conflict with me just wanting friendship and people thinking I wanted something else. There were times in a relationship when I would fake it, in terms of being attracted in the physical way, just so I could have the friendship. It was very hard not being able to pursue my true feelings.

Understandably, my mom and I have different memories of these and other events in my childhood. Although she knew I was feeling stress and confusion —which caused both my parents great concern — she later told me they thought it was coming from other sources, such as my difficulty at the catholic school. As a child and later as an adult, it was my own fears and my own misunderstandings of inner feelings that kept me from telling either of my parents about my gender identity confusion — that is, my strong desire to live as a girl and feelings of not being male. It wasn't until I was forty-three that I finally had the confidence, inner strength, and self-determination to reveal to my family this life-long conflict: my desire, and later my plan, to live as a woman.

***

I didn't get into any serious conflict until I was a young adult, at which time I started living on my own and found the urge to express myself returning. I was spending time alone just seeing what I looked like dressed up and wearing make-up. But I never went out. I tried to have a successful life, but it seemed to be conflicting. There was this turmoil.

I think the big thing with me when I lived as Bill was I thought that I tried to do gender really well. This is what my destiny was, this is what people expected. I got a masters degree, I had a career with YMCA, I had kids that I was responsible for. There was no way people would allow me to live as I felt — to live in their community — if they knew my real feelings. So it became this huge, huge secret.

Not even my spouse knew. I remember saying to her when we first got engaged, "There are three things I've got to tell you about." And they were all very serious things. To give you an idea, one was that I had supported an abortion. I drove my girlfriend at the time to a clinic and she had an abortion. That has bothered me ever since because of my values in life. And I was able to tell my fiancée that, but not that I had this gender identity conflict. So we went through our whole marriage without her knowing. It wasn't until I felt a divorce might be upon us that I felt my secret was not threatening to our marriage anymore. I was able to tell her after that. That's how much I held it in. Not even my family knew, not even my closest friends.

All my life I've always been a planner. I set goals: daily goals, weekly goals, monthly goals. I took time management courses and I taught time management at the Free University. I had done the same thing with my life. I planned everything out. I planned out my gender, too, as a way to have a good life. I wore the beard and very masculine dress. I was even into the cowboy thing for a while — what's more masculine than that? How much more macho can you get? I was always rambling. I could never sit and talk with people. I could never tell them about deeper things. It was always surface things.

My dad knew something was up, and in his own way he would always try to get it out of me. But I would always resist. I'd go on vacation and visit him, and I'd bring my laptop computer with me so I would have a distraction. It wasn't until my dad died that I realized that somebody I loved very much had passed out of my life without really knowing who I was. Did *I* really know who I was?

At this time, which was about six years ago, my spouse and I were exploring divorce. I was seeing a therapist and had told her what I was experiencing. So with my dad passing away I thought, "God, I've just got to be honest to my family." I didn't know what to say, so I just said to my mother, "I've cross-dressed, but I don't go out. It's not like it's an entertainment thing for me. It's an expression. I'm not sure where it's going to take me." Right away my she said, "So, you're going to get the surgery?" I told her, "Mom, I don't know where I'm headed with this." It was like she expressed her greatest fear right away.

So then I was having to deal with people who can't accept an in-between-ness. I remember expressing to them that I didn't really feel like a man. But I wasn't sure that living as a woman was the answer. I feel differently now — I made the right decision. But it was because I didn't have a set plan to follow; it was like osmosis — it flowed. And this was the direction in which it flowed. People say to me now, "Oh, you're so natural." But this is just me. I'm not real feminine, and I don't put on a skit about it. I'm just a very honest person with my expression.

119

***

Initially I changed my name to Liam because that's the Irish version of William, my birth name. But Liam was less masculine, less defined. I was trying to get definition out of my life, trying to get rid of all this masculine crap that I'd learned. Like anger. I was an angry person. Always. Anger and raising my voice and being demanding. All those things that men are supposed to do, I learned to do. So I was trying to get these things out of my life. My name. How do you change your name? Some people might just pick something that sounds real feminine — like Cathy. But I didn't want to direct my life by another name. I thought that Liam was safe and legally the same. My mom liked it. She even sent me a bracelet right away that said "Liam," so at that point she was accepting.

But then I started going by Li because I was getting more androgynous and even less defined as a man. Then at some point somebody said to me, "Li, you really don't look like Li anymore. Maybe you should go by Li Anne or something." And Li-am, Li Anne — they have similar sounds, almost the same letters. So there's some association with my original name. Then my initials — Waioli is my new middle name, so my initials are L. W. Taft, whereas before it was W. Taft. You know, you do these things subconsciously and then later you realize that the familiarity remains.

For me it was letting everything flow from the heart and trying not to plan. I think that's what made it real healthy for me. I always thought of it as a transition, until my therapist said, "No, no, no. Every day is a transition. You're going through a *transformation*." So it was at that point that I became more respectful of what I was getting swept up into. The way life is for us, you really don't have control. When you try to control things, you create this negative, opposing energy which can pull you apart. But if you go with the flow and find the ebb tides and the swirls and the little pools off to the side . . . That's what I've been doing.

The first year of my transition was the fall of 1994 through the summer of 1995. By April of 1995 I was living full time as Li Anne. April twenty-third is my re-birth date. So in six months, October to April, I went through this massive change. It was like I got caught in the rapids at some point, and I couldn't keep on top of it all. I wasn't working at that time; I was collecting unemployment and living off savings. I was spending a lot of time socializing, going out to concerts and fairs, inter-mixing with people and learning a whole new social contact, new rules . . .

And my voice — I knew that people identify who you are by your voice, especially when they can't see you. Or they can see you, but your voice doesn't match what they see. When I listen to recordings of my old voice now, I guess I had a real masculine voice. But the thing I was interested in doing at that time was releasing the masculine, that which I had learned as I grew up to sound masculine. Because women's and men's voices are only about half an octave apart. So it's not so much range as intonation, with men being monotone and women being more musical. Also, women often talk in a more unsure way, using tag questions for instance. So a man might say, "Nice day," and a woman might say, "Nice day, don't you think?" There's an inclusiveness, too — women want to be inclusive. I thought, "These are all the things I feel inside." So it wasn't as if I was trying to learn how to sound like a woman. Rather, it was figuring out how to release the "man lessons" I had learned.

***

I think every stage of transitioning is challenging in its own way because as you get more and more into your new life, you risk more. But there are a few stories I remember which had a lesson as an outcome. Like being at Kmart. This was early in my transition. At the time I was married, so I was there with my spouse. I wasn't dressed up real femi-nine; we were just out shopping. I think I had on jeans and a sweater. Because I was still going through the transition, I still looked somewhat masculine, I'm sure. We split up and I went looking for a size 38 B bra.

I went to the women's lingerie department and the woman working there seemed to freak out when I spoke to her. So I just backed off and said, "That's OK, I can find the bra on my own." The next thing I knew the manager had come over and was pushing me out the door. He claimed that I had made a "sexual advancement on one of his associates." Now, this was at the time when the new lessons I was learning were already sinking in, so instead of reacting like a man — getting angry and defensive — I calmly said, "Perhaps you have the wrong person. I didn't sexually harass anybody. I've been shopping here. But when I'm done shopping I'm going to go and cash out and leave and probably never come back." And I meant it. The manager grabbed me and tried to push me out the door, so I called out, "Elaine, Elaine — look at this guy, he's assaulting me." So he let go. He was all sweaty by this point. This guy was definitely transgender-phobic. He started pushing me out with his chest and wouldn't let me go back to where Elaine was. So I just went around him . . . The police came and escorted me out. I was told I was trespassing and "banned from the store for a year."

That was a pretty challenging time. But I don't shop at Kmart that much anyhow, so I'm not going to worry about whether they receive me or not. Sure, there's the issue of pride and the worry that if it happens here it's going to happen there. But it's not a battle I want to put a lot of time into.

Or like going down to give blood — The woman said, "Sorry, but we don't take blood from *mahus*." I turned around and viewed the people in the lobby who looked homeless. So I replied, "But you'll take blood from them?" She said, "Yeah — they're not gay." "Excuse me, I've been involved in a heterosexual relationship all my life." She replied, "Why should I believe you?" I thought to myself, "Is this worth a battle? Nah." I was going to fight it, but decided not to.

Another lesson was getting on a bus. This was early in my transition. I was wearing jeans and a denim vest, my hair was medium length, and I probably looked very androgynous. When I got on the bus, the driver, a big local guy, gave me such a look that it just about knocked me back. I thought, "*Man*," and put my dollar in. I sat down and felt so . . . like I had been slapped around. But then I thought, "Wait a minute. I'm a paying customer, I did nothing to deserve that look. He had no right to do that." So I walked back up to the front of the bus — I'm all riled up now — and I waited for the bus to stop so the driver would look at me and I could tell him what I thought. The bus stops and more people get on, so I pause. And I see him look down at those people and give every one of them the same look. I thought, "God, it's *him*! It's not *me*." That was a big lesson. We all have fears, but we shouldn't put our fears on people, because then we're going to be setting ourselves up for failure. I also remember the time I was standing in line. I was working a delivery job for a temp agency which required me to wear a collared t-shirt. I had a cap on and gloves, too. I was picking up and delivering supplies, and had already dropped my stuff off. I was hungry, so I went to L & L Drive Inn and got in line. I didn't notice who was in front of me. But then I saw that there were all guys in front of me. And I've got my baseball cap on, my masculine-looking shirt. . . . I get up to the front and the woman goes, "Yes, Sir?" So I reply, "Excuse me, but I guess I need to work on my gender expression." She takes a closer look and goes, "Oh, I'm sorry Ma'am!" And that was such a good feeling. Because I didn't ask her to make the change, I just made her aware. It was like the first time somebody called me a bitch. I went, "Oh, wow!" — because they recognized my gender. Now it's different; I get mad when somebody calls me that.

***

For a male-to-female transsexual, there's scorn. People feel that you've lowered yourself; you've stepped out of a successful male role into a role that is not destined for success. I remember my mom asking, "Why are you giving this all up?" As if I was going to put myself into a life of misery and under-achievement. Actually, I think I've achieved a lot more in my new life because there's a better balance in my mind, body, and spirit.

I have gained a whole new sense of who I am, and a whole new sense of capacity, of being able to take control of something. I joke that I went through a mid-life crisis. The only thing different from other people's was the outcome. We all struggle with crisis in our lives. But some people say it's a crisis and they go and buy a car and think that deals with it. I had been unhappy and in hiding. I was stressed out, over-anxious, and over-ambitious. I hid behind my achievements. I had created these expectations that I had to live up to, so there was always that pressure. But I turned it inside out . . . Knowing I was able to do that and survive gives me a lot of strength.

I just got a letter from a woman who was in a university class I spoke at. She shared what she had thought before she met me and her feelings afterward. Because she had heard that I was born male, at first she thought, "This person is a man who is wearing women's clothes — this is really going to turn me off." So she really didn't want to go to the class because she thought I would have nothing to say of interest (it was a class on human development). I'm sure doctors and nurses and psychologists can have this kind of attitude as well. They might decide ahead of time what's worthy of their attention and what they shun. This woman went on to say that for whatever reason she stuck with it and came to class. When she heard me talk and realized that I was a real person with real issues, that I was struggling and that I had a lot of strength, she changed her mind. She wrote, "I'm glad I met you. I'm glad I went to that class."

I always keep in mind that people's first reactions are often times gut-level and are often based on experiences they've had that I have not been a part of. They have this phobia and try to dump it on you by saying, "I don't like you, because you represent — " So I try to be patient and realize that I know myself to be a good person. Once they meet me, there's a fresh start and they can either go with it or not. I guess I just always leave it; I don't try to force it, I just let it flow. I think in this way I have the most success in identifying with people who might even be transgender-phobic, or at least neutral on it and have no interest. My approach is that it just doesn't need to be an issue.

People can suspect my sex all they want. They might think, "Oh, she's kind of got big hands, strong hands." Let people think what they will . . . I'm not going to worry about what they're thinking. I'm not going to put my fears on them. I remember one time meeting with an old friend who is a priest. He sat down with me and he said, "I really have trouble thinking of you as a woman. Your hands are too big to be a woman's, your feet are too big to be a woman's." I almost felt like saying, "You know Father, your mind is too closed to be a priest's." When I realized that I could have said it, I was empowered. In my mind I knew where I stood. You don't judge people by their hands and their feet. Sorry.

***

I think one of things which the mainland has a lot more of than here in Hawai'i is the drifters — the people who just drive through, settle briefly, and move on. Oftentimes, because these kinds of people can be so unsettled with their own life, they can be ones that cause the problems, too. I think that the whole transient part of society which is missing here probably makes it a safer place. There's no really place . . . well, I guess they could still hide here. If you cause some harm you can hide, but it's harder to hide here — it's a small rock. [laughs] I think people try to get along better because of that.

I feel safer in Hawai'i. Perhaps coming here and feeling that it's a fresh start was a real positive force in my life. I thought of myself in a different way because I was in an environment in which I had no history. At the same time I felt connected with Hawai'i through some kind of emotional and spiritual sense, that perhaps I had lived here in another life. The ocean and mountains had been so special in my life while I was on the mainland. Because they were in such close proximity here, I felt totally at home. I felt that the greatest adventure of my life could be here.

I haven't been back to the mainland since my change, so it's hard to say whether I could have done my transition there and been as successful as I was here. I guess after I go back I'll see. If there is any reaction to me, it's probably going to be more based on going back to places where people knew me before. But I think that as I travel around, I'll just be a stranger. Then again people might think, "Oh, she's a strong-looking woman, she's assertive, she doesn't take no gruff." [laughs]

If somebody wants to explore a gender change, it's good to go someplace where you can get a fresh start and not have to deal with things coming back in your face from friends and family. Just get a fresh start, identify support groups in that area, whether it be a church or social groups, and just start over again. Then try to reconnect with your past life. I've heard of people who try to stay in the same area they lived in all their lives. When they change their gender they complain about the animosity and hatred and bias. It's really tough on people, especially when they know you. But if you can get a fresh start someplace, I'd recommend it.

I also think that Hawai'i is culturally more accepting of diversity.

Certainly, in terms of gender expression, because there are so many cultures here and each one expresses gender in different ways, there doesn't seem to be the straight line you seem to find in places like the far west or the deep south, where men wear cowboy boots and hats, and women wear the ruffled skirts. Here, we have a woman at work who wears heavy boots and jeans every day and it's fine; we just think of her as a woman that likes to wear heavy boots and jeans. So Hawai'i's cultural diversity helps with gender diversity and gender expression.

A lot of people say, "It's great you live in Hawai'i because of the *mahus*." But it's actually challenging for a transgendered person to be confused as part of the *mahu* culture. The *mahu* in Hawai'i, from my understanding, are mostly recognized as males who like to express themselves in a female way, but don't attempt to go through a change of sex or to be known as the opposite sex that they were born. It's almost like we're talking about *mahu* as being a third sex, in a way.

Whereas in my case, as a transsexual woman, I'm willing to conform to the point of being one gender or the other because this is how I feel — I am a woman. Also, I want some stability in my life. I just want to succeed, and right now the system is set up so that it only recognizes people to be one gender or the other. I don't know how much I can generalize but at some point we all have to give up our own personal independence to be successful in society, and often times I see local transgendered people really struggling with that. Because they're just not willing to go along with it. They want to remain separate and different.

Recently there was a case in downtown Honolulu. A group of local people were hired at an office as men, and at some point they asked if it would be OK if they wore more feminine clothes, or they just started wearing them. But they were fired because they were told, "We hired you as men, and we have a job where we're in the public, and you need to appear as you are." This is different from taking time off, going through the change, and then applying for the job in the gender you want people to accept you as. But that's hard; a lot of people can't afford to do that.

Hawai'i's transgender communities vary greatly. There are some that are made up mostly of local girls who have a different kind of lifestyle, and who went through the gender change early in life. As women they are attracted to men and are with men. You have another group which is based out of Honolulu and made up mostly of TG women, born male, married to women, lived into their adult years as men, and then went through the gender change later in life. So these two groups are like opposites, although they might mix a little bit at some social events like beauty pageants. But now there seems to be a growing overlap between the different transgender communities more than ever before. There are a few key groups that are helping to deal with this. For example, Our Family Church, based at the Gay and Lesbian Community Center, which has branches both in Wai'anae and in town. It's doing a lot to bring the different transgendered communities together.

Because of the church, I think there's more blending going on, more understanding between groups of people. I know I've had some good interactions at some socials that I hadn't had before. I had always thought of local transgendered people as being too different; I couldn't understand them. Because many are at times very effeminate in their ways and flamboyant. And they probably think of me as being too masculine in my ways and not feminine enough. One of the first things they'll say to me is, "Oh, you need to wear more make-up, girl! You would look so nice if you wore make-up."

What broke the ice was going to a girlfriend's house, someone I felt comfortable with, who lives on the Wai'anae side and had friends there who lived in the valley. They were all local girls who went through the change real young in life and a lot of them did the pageants and were really into the very feminine expression. But at this Memorial Day party, everybody was in shorts and wearing little make-up; it was very relaxed. It helped that we were all a little bit more on an equal plane of appearance.

Cheryl, one of the pastors, is a great mixer of people. She brings people together. She did a few social things and icebreakers, and that helped. I met some interesting people. There were people there who I wouldn't think of as being transgendered. From what I understand they weren't interested in making the full change, but they identify with some of the transgender issues, so there was a whole variety of people there. I'm just glad the admirers weren't there — that can be a hassle. [laughs]

I'm often amazed that after all I've been through and how open I profess to be, how easy it is for me to be biased and closed-minded, also. That is probably because I was brought up to put gender in a box — when you look at somebody you say, "That's a man. That's a woman. Part of that gender equity thing is to teach ourselves to look at others in a broader spectrum.

***

My earliest memories of paddling go back to when I first moved into Honolulu in 1994. I'd see the canoes out on the water and think that was where I wanted to be. I've always been a water person. I've sailed and enjoy white-water canoeing, so it was just a matter of time before I found out where the paddling clubs were and how to get hooked up with one. I spent a lot of time at Ala Moana Park. I would hang out by the wall and watch the women paddle. Of course I was shy to some extent because I was still really new in my new identity, but at the same time I was being me. I was willing to put myself out there a little bit, too. As it turned out, after a couple of times sitting there, I got talking with a few women. They asked me about my interest, and I said that I was interested in paddling. They replied that they had paddles and that the next time I should come with my bathing suit and go out with them.

So that was the beginning of about a month of practice with them in the summer of 1996. They were at the end of one season and beginning their long distance season, so it is kind of hard, unless you're really good at that point, to get started. So I went as far as I could with them, and stepped aside. But I came back right away in the off-season and paddled with the girls all off-season. Right away I thought that it was great because it was the first time I had been involved in a cooperative team sporting event. I'd been on baseball and softball teams, and played flag football and recreational volleyball. And there is to some extent a lot of cooperation in all of those sports, but you perform so much first as an individual. Therefore there is a lot of focus on the time that you're bumping the ball, swinging the bat, what have you. But in paddling it's a total mesh, it's a total flow of six people in a canoe, and the key word is blend, *laulima* — "together," "many hands." Right away I connected with that because I'm really into cooperation. In fact, one focus of my masters degree work is learning through cooperation versus competition. So I just took off with it.

Paddling was also a wonderful social arena in which to learn and test out new social skills. I remember the first woman I met there. We really hit it off, and went out for a bite to eat after one of the practices. We were talking and something led up to her saying, "I need to tell you something about me." It had been because I had said to her, trying to play in a certain role, that there were a lot of guys at the restaurant. "Maybe you can show me some techniques for dealing with these guys." Because they were eyeing us. She didn't respond right away. Later she said, "I need to tell you something. I don't like men. I'm a gay woman. I live with my partner." I replied, "Well, that's interesting . . . Now that you've been honest, I need to be honest, too." So I was open with her. "I also identify as a gay woman. I'm not interested in men, I was just saying I was because I was trying to find some common ground. But also . . . I'm a transgendered woman." And she goes, "Oh?" It was the beginning of a good conversation that gave me strength and faith that people could accept me.

So the first year in paddling I came in as a novice. Because I'm athletic and strong, people took note. They needed Master-age women, so after a month I was asked if I'd be willing to paddle with the master crew. I agreed, so a group of women worked with me on the off-days. We went out in the single-boats, one person seaters, for a month or so. I just really focused and got my skills up to par. Then I was in the same crew every race, the Junior Master Women in 1997.

In 1998 we had a new coach, there were some changes, but I was in the Junior Master Crew, and that year we did really well. We won the Island Championship. Then we went to States, and we took fourth place. Then we had a really good long-distance season. All these things, when you're doing well with a crew and you're going out and doing four hour races, it's very empowering for all of us. And for me it was very empowering because I pretty much have a new set of muscles and a new body metabolism that I had to work with. I have strength, but not like I used to. I have endurance, but not like I used to. I'm heavier on the bottom. There were all these things I had to work with.

So when I was learning how to get into the boat when the boat was flying by you, because you do crew changes in long distance, I had to learn the way that allowed me to get in with this new body. Men tend to just grab, pull themselves up, and with all their upper-body strength can just pull themselves up into the boat. Whereas I had to do more of a swing-in and at least try to get one leg over and hook in. It's so funny, because there was one race where I couldn't get in. I was so tired, and this happens to a lot of women. To me it felt like an initiation. I was up against the same challenges as all the women there. Or sometimes I'd deal a lot with muscle spasms and muscle cramps, which are more of a female thing than a male — it has to do with hormones. Estrogen does induce more muscle spasms and cramps. So there were a lot of things I noticed about my body. Being involved in a competitive regime and putting demands on my body, I found that it wasn't responding the same way as before. But I was elated, because it represented the fact that I was going further and further into my new life.

And then with the long-distance season in 1998, which was the first long-distance season I did, we had a lot of new women come in, so it was a fresh start for me and the others. People meet you who have never met you before, who don't know anything about you. And people were very accepting. Every year in the paddling club, fifty percent of the women are new. So if for whatever reason you want to get a fresh start, you do.

With the long-distance season in 1998, a lot of new women came in who were physically bigger than me. So that was good. Oftentimes I would hear from the coach, "Li Anne, you're too strong! Blend. Ease back." So then when these other women came in and they put us together, it was more like, "Give it all you've got!"

So 1998 was a great year. 1999 was a struggle year because we got a new coach, new girls, a whole new arena of things. And that was the year they had the new rule in place, of gender verification. Even though it hadn't hit the news, and my civil rights case had not yet become the focus of things, the information had been circulated to all the clubs, all the coaches, and the clubs were trying to figure out ways to adapt to this.

The rule is now that when you register, new paddlers need to show a government ID to verify age and gender. What makes that fair is that everybody is required to do that and that you can provide your choice of ID. And because each agency involved with identifications have different criteria, we all have the choice to present a form of ID which shows us in the best light, for whatever reason. For me, I got my license adjusted in 1996, so I ever since I've been paddling, I've had the appropriate identification. That was never a problem. You register with your local club, who registers you with your local association, who in turn registers you with the State association. And this was always the way it was. That was the tier effect of registration.

It was in late 1998 that they passed the rule that the State Association would now require additional proof, and they chose the birth certificate to be that proof. If you didn't have a birth certificate, then passport. They amended that to say that if a person provided them with something they didn't believe was true, that person would have to go through DNA testing to prove one's birth sex. So what they were after in this case was not necessarily to document people but rather to exclude people. It was because I had a really good season in 1998 and the watchdogs who were monitoring this, who had been watching ever since I had started paddling, rallied and made a case against me. They claimed that I caused the team to win, that I caused an unfair competitive advantage, and that it was because of me that my team did so well. Now everybody knows that paddling is *six* people and that you don't win or lose because of *one* person. But it was the good old boy network. The president of the Association, a lawyer whose father is a judge, rallied the good old boys and they passed the rule in December, 1998. Funny, at the last minute they changed the location of the meeting and my club couldn't find it. So they didn't get a chance to vote on it.

People knew about me because I had been in an article in the Honolulu Weekly newspaper in March of 1996. So when I started paddling in '96 and '97 some people would say to me, "Oh, Li Anne, I saw you in the article." That faded away because there wasn't a follow-up; it wasn't controversial. However, one person took note of it and tried to get my local association to change the rule in 1997, using me as an example of how I go against the grain, how I threaten the whole organization. But they wouldn't go for it. They addressed it and said that there was no problem. They had used driver's licenses for sixty years and they didn't see a need to change the rule. But then this person became president of OCRA [O'ahu Canoe Racing Association], and later president of the State Association. A lot of the officials in OCRA are also members of HCRA [Honolulu Canoe Racing Association], so it was just a matter of time before he had convinced a number of people. I had some inside information about what was happening, but it had never really been discussed openly. It had been put forth as a notice that the rule would be changed to verify age and gender. So they put age first. And when they were first confronted about it, they would always stress the age part. "We have a lot of classifications that put people in different order by their age and gender." They kept trying to take the focus away from gender, but eventually did admit that the primary focus was as a gender verification rule. That's how it was put in the minutes — when you look at the minutes of the meeting, it was put as "gender verification rule." This rule says that a paddler who competes in a state race can be protested. And if protested, she would need to provide a birth certificate to the race rule committee.

When we were in mediation about this issue I pointed out to the officials with HCRA that birth certificates were a poor choice because some states allow changes and others don't. I pointed out that it becomes a political thing — it's a matter of where you're from. You discriminate against people based on where they're from. So if Jane is standing next to me and we have the same background but she comes from Alabama, which won't allow her to change her birth certificate, while I come from Ohio, which is very liberal and I can change this document with very little proof, then what's fair here? Of course, they wouldn't hear it at first. But when the point was made again they acknowledged it and came back with a proposal: they would decide whether birth certificates were original, and if they were not original, DNA testing would be required to prove birth sex. You know what they were trying to do. They knew, too, but they wouldn't admit it.

I remember talking about this with my friend and mentor Dr. Diamond at the University of Hawai'i Medical School. He said, "Well, you know this is not going to be easy. You're not *there* yet, and you probably will never get *there*. In other words, *finished*. Because we're constantly changing and growing. There will always be people who will give you problems and discriminate against you. So you've got to choose your battles. There are a lot of fights out there. You've got to choose your battles and ignore the others." So when it came down to it, I felt this was a battle worth fighting for. When I first filed a complaint, it was a fifteen page document. I had all this extra information, research on the birth certificates. The only problem I saw was that I was the only signature on it. I couldn't find anybody else to file a complaint with me.

In 1999, my civil rights complaint started getting known, and somebody leaked it to all the media at once. So in force they called me and came down to the canoe club. I hadn't listened to my messages in a few days, so I didn't know that the different media were looking to interview me. When I came down to the club I found two TV stations there, and a newspaper reporter. I asked them what they were doing, and when they told me I asked where they got the story from. They said they had heard there was a man in disguise paddling with the women's club. I told them that they had the wrong story and there was a different story here.

Then later they found out the truth, and they found the truth to be interesting also, but instead of reporting it in a truthful way, they still tried to sensationalize it: "Transsexual Paddler Making Waves!" So when they came down again, I thought I could ignore them, which I did, but they still followed me around and used their long-range lenses . . . So I decided to tell them, "Let's go off to the side here, I'll do an interview, and then you guys can get out of here." They agreed, but actually they didn't keep to it — After the interview, when I went out paddling, they stayed on shore filming . . . At one point they came up to me and were filming my hands and feet as I was getting ready. I said, "What is so interesting?!" And the guy puts the camera in my face and I went, "Aargh!" [laughs] So that was the beginning of the end for last year. Because there was a lot of controversy due to the media coverage.

Then a month after the first coverage — it took that long — is when we went from regatta season to long-distance season, which is when you have to bring together a lot of people into different age groups to be one crew, as opposed to before, when you could have small crews of people and people who don't get along could stay apart. But now all the master-age women come together, and they are one small group which always has been and continues to be in control. And they just chase people away. They come into the situation saying, *"You* have to get along with us. You have to do it the way we want it." Not only to me, but to others. There was a lot of inner fighting. Little by little people stopped showing up. One day I came to practice and there weren't too many master women there; it didn't surprise me because the numbers had been falling off. So I get there and it looked like there was a circle of people in the distance. While I was locking up my bike, one of my girlfriends — who I thought was a friend — came over to me and said, "We're having a meeting over here." I asked her what was going on. I figured it was some kind of rally cry because of the decreasing numbers. She goes, "There's a problem." I'm trying to think, What problem? I don't know of any problems.

So we went over and sat down and I was told, "Li Anne, it's not that we have anything against you. It's not the rule, but it's the controversy with the media story. And if you keep coming, we won't have a team. *Everybody is leaving because of you."* I should have said a lot more than I did because when they said that I was thinking, "No — the reason they're not coming is because of *you guys,* because you always bitch." But I didn't say it. I sat there and listened for ten minutes because I figured that there was nothing of value that they were saying. I was waiting for something I could grasp onto and respond to. Finally I said, "I can't believe you guys are saying these things. It was three years ago that you came up to me and recruited me to paddle with you. And now you're telling me that my coming here is causing the team to break up? Well, I'll stop coming because you give me no choice. But I'm not quitting the club, and I'll be back next year."

Two weeks later, those women who had sat down with me left the club and went to another club, where they were turned away. So they had no club. The other club knew better. The moral of the story is, I'm a survivor. I'm still paddling. I understand quite a few of those women are not paddling with any club anymore. Why? Because they have never accepted themselves. The thing with paddling is that it forces you to deal with issues. Mostly it forces you to be accepting. Everybody is a different size, different shape, different style, different attitude. But somehow you've got to blend — *laulima*.

This year I paddle with the women who supported me last year. When the most recent media story came out this year I heard that some had voted me off the crew. So the day after the media story came out, I was told I was paddling with another crew. The following practice, the coaches acted like they didn't know what to do with me. They were putting me in left over seats. They were assigning all the seats, and would put me in whichever one was left over. Later I heard that actually there hadn't been a vote. Instead, it was just a couple of people who made the change. The coach's wife is on the crew that I had been sitting on, which I am no longer sitting on. But you know what, another lesson learned: I'm paddling now with open-class women who are stronger, more vibrant, more alive, more together, friendlier. And I love it. It's a whole new energy. And some of these Masters-class women who are overweight, who don't cross-train — they finished last in a race last week. So I'm just thinking, "I'm really glad to be out of there."

The issues they are trying to make of this in my civil rights case, which remains unresolved, are not really there. It is claimed that my being on a women's team gives my team an unfair advantage. But as the head coach told the media, "Li Anne is strong, but she's not the strongest woman. There are other women who are stronger than her." But most importantly, the implication is that people who are born male are innately superior to people born female. You know who believes that? People born male. It's wrong. It's the myth of gender. And I think something like my case will help break down those myths. Because in sports it doesn't matter whether you're a man or a woman. Probably the biggest things are hormones and body weight. It would be great to have mixed competition divided up by age and weight groups. I think this needs to happen. They don't need to worry about what you looked like when you were born, or who you were twenty years ago. I always said, "If you want to hold me to who I was ten years ago, then we need to do that for everybody here. I mean, we were all once teenagers, so why not classify ourselves as teenage paddlers? We were all once babies, so why not classify ourselves as baby paddlers?"

The bottom line is that a rule was passed which is vague enough to be used in the way people want to use it. Because it was written by a lawyer, he's trying to avoid it sounding discriminatory. Instead of having, "You *need* to provide a birth certificate," it's framed around the idea of a protest. He says, "My hands are clear. *I'm* not protesting her. She's being protested by somebody else who's asking her for her birth certificate. We're not requiring her to give us a birth certificate to paddle. We're not keeping her from paddling." He even said at one point, "We don't want to stop her from paddling, we just want to reclassify her. We can set up racing categories for Li Anne and people like her." So I asked him in mediation, "How many people do think would paddle in that category?" He replied, "I don't know." I said, "How many other people do you know who are like me?" "No one else." So people like that, they've got something going on with them. They must have big identity problems themselves. I think balanced people who've got things going on in their lives don't have any problems with my differences. Usually if somebody's giving you a bad time because you're gay or transgendered it's because they've got their own problems. So if someone is bothering me I'll ask, "*Are you sure there isn't something you want to tell me?*"

My name is Paige Peahi. I was born and raised in Honolulu, Hawai'i and I'm twenty-nine years old. I'm Hawaiian-Portuguese-Chinese. I've been living my life as a transgender for over ten years. I noticed a lot of differences in me at a very young age — in first, second grade. I had a high pitched voice, boys wouldn't want to hang around with me, girls would constantly hang around with me. So I had a lot of girl-friends instead of boy-friends. At first I really didn't identify with having a sexual identity, it was just that I felt different. I didn't know what to call it. I felt I was different from the rest of the boys and girls. But I related more to the girls. The boys . . . some things about the boys I could relate to, but most of it, no. I didn't know what it was . . . I was just completely lost. And so I didn't really put my finger on it, I didn't really dwell on it. I just lived my childhood years. When I got a little older, maybe fourth or fifth grade, *then* I started to get a lot of teasing: "Oh, you're a girl, you're a sissy, you're a faggot." But moreso a "sissy," because I had a high voice, my voice wasn't deep. I faced a lot of torment growing up . . .

My family didn't really react to anything because they were going through their own problems. So they didn't really focus on me. And basically I didn't have . . . I did have supervision, but actually I didn't because I got to do whatever I wanted to do. If I came home late, they wouldn't say anything. I pretty much was growing up myself, my own self. But whenever I had any problems, then I would go to my mom. My father didn't really play a role in my life because he was so busy with work. He was a truck driver, with this company for years. He was trying to survive, keep a roof over our heads, food in our mouths, clothes on our backs . . . Basically my father taught me how to survive. But he really didn't play a role in my life. Also . . . my father was an alcoholic and when he was under the influence I was afraid of him because of his temper. I was scared, basically, of a person who was under the influence, and I didn't really face it. So I would always go to my mom because she was there to support and guide me. My mom was basically my mother and father.

I didn't really face my sexual identity until I was in the seventh, the ninth grades . . . between those years. I was afraid to tell my mom because I didn't want to be rejected. I didn't want to be disowned. I loved my family and I didn't want to lose them. So I really didn't say anything until I graduated from high school. Because the most important thing to me was to graduate from school. And then, when I graduated, I met up with a lot of transgenders who were out already, and they looked good; they looked like females. That's what I wanted to be. And I met Kaui. She became my queen mother. She taught me how to survive on the streets, because that's what they were doing. Basically Kaui just introduced me to a whole different new world that I really didn't know existed. Then when I knew it, *that's* when I made the move to do my transitioning.

Before I could do my transitioning I went to my mother. Well, actually, I didn't go to my mother. I went to my sister. I have two sisters and a brother; I'm the youngest in the family. And my sisters knew already what I was going to become. But I didn't act on it. So I told my one sister who I'm very close with that I wanted to live my life as a woman. She said, "Yeah, I knew that. So what do you want me to do?" I asked her, "Could you go and tell mom, because I'm so afraid to tell her." So she did. She went to my mom and told her, "Oh, your son Kaipo wants to live his life as a woman." My mom was like, "So? I knew that already!" That was such a relief to me when I heard that — "She said OK? Fine, I'm going." So I went to the hormone doctors and took my first hormone shot. It was then I just started to live my life.

***

I went to McKinley High School. There were other *mahu* there. There was only one who was really flamboyant, and her name was Tara. She would wear makeup and dress androgynously. But I didn't want to do it yet because I wanted my friends to hang around with me. Tara didn't have a lot of friends. She would hang around with the girls, but they would usually stay away. She would be by herself. From time to time I would say, "Hi, how are you doing?" She would say, "Fine, girl . . ." We would talk a little while, but then go our own ways.

Growing up, there were other queens who I had met who had the guts to go ahead and dress in female clothing and go to school like that. When I look back now, I wish I had done that. But the reason I didn't want to do it is because I didn't want to upset my family. Because they're gonna get a call from the school, "Hey, you know your son is in women's clothing?" I just didn't want to go through that embarrassment. I didn't want my family to face the embarrassment. So I didn't do it. Because my family was important to me.

I still have my family and they respect me for who I am today. My father passed away about seven years ago from alcohol. I'm kind of upset at my father for going that way because I wanted a family. I wanted my father to be a part of my life, but he had his own issues and his own problems. When he passed away I didn't cry. I just was sad. He did it to himself. And ever since my father died, everything has changed. We don't go to family gatherings anymore. We don't have those things anymore because my father is not alive. His brothers passed away, too. After he died, then a couple of months later his other brother died. So there were no family functions again. Those were the most important and good memories to me, because that was a family thing, because I'm so family-oriented . . . Now we don't usually do those kinds of things anymore. That's what I miss the most — the gatherings; seeing all your cousins, telling them how you're doing . . .

It's a funny and sad thing. When I was just about to transition, that's when my father passed away. So he really didn't get the chance to see me during my transition. But I know that my father, deep down in his heart, knew I was going to be this way. He already knew. Because I have a brother who is *not* gay, who is straight as can be. So he never worried about my brother. But me . . . He picked on me a little . . . Actually, I was kind of like his slave, a little bit. He would always tell me to go to the store and buy him cigarettes. So I would always have to do that. I did it

141

because I loved him, because I would do anything for him. That was a way of him accepting me, for me doing something for him. Which is kind of sad.

My family today, we're very tight. When I told my brother, though, he was the difficult one. He was upset. He was not having it. He wanted to beat me up. Right then and there. We were at a family party and I came in full drag — he didn't really dig that. He was upset. Also he was drinking . . . So he was getting on my case — he wanted to beat me up right then and there. My sisters came to my rescue and told him to shut up, that he had better not do that because it's my life. They said, "He does it. Whatever he wants, he'll do. You can't do anything. You cannot change him. Only he can change himself." My brother was like, "What about the family name? Who's gonna carry the family name?" And I'm like, "Wait a minute! *You're* the one who's going to carry the family name!" He didn't understand that this is what I wanted to be. After that incident I didn't see him for three years, until we had a family reunion. We were all invited so we went. And I looked a little bit more female than I looked before. When he saw me, he didn't recognize me. He was asking my sister, "Who's that?" My sister told him, "That's your *brother*." He was like, "What?!" He was shocked. He said, "Eh . . . *Bra* . . . Oh . . . OK . . . *Bra* . . .You look *good*." He was telling me that I looked good, that I looked real. Then he asked me if I was happy, and I said, "Of course I'm happy." So he goes, "Well, that's the main thing." From that time on, everything was fine. Now they are really accepting. And I'm there, I'm there for my family. Whenever they're in need and they need help, I'm always there. I'll do anything for them.

You know, during elementary school I thought I was by myself, and that there was no one like me. I was going through a struggle. I thought I was the only one. How I discovered myself was . . . When I used to go to my family gatherings, there were these two queens who I respected as aunties. They were my cousins-in-law. I didn't know that they were then, but my mom told me that they were *mahus*, and I said, "*What?*" But then it clicked and I thought, "Oh my gosh!" And I'm there, right next to them, observing everything there is to know about them. They would do shows for my family. Like this one time, my Auntie was impersonating

Patti LaBelle and she looked exactly like her — I was standing in front of the stage, just in awe. "Oh my gosh! Oh wow! Oh my gosh! Look! Look!" I was so excited. I was thinking, "That's what I want to be!" I would stay there . . . They would drink and party with all my aunties there, and I would stay there right next to them and listen to what they would talk about and see how they would act. So I was actually learning how to be a *mahu*. It got me thinking, "Oh my God . . . OK — now I know what to do with my life." Everything was confirmed for me. "I *can* be this way."

At this time I was fifteen, sixteen years old. And I would always ask my auntie about them — "When are they coming back? When are they coming back? When are they gonna come and sing and play *'ukulele*?" She would ask why I wanted to know. So I'd say, "No reason, I just want to see them again." I always looked forward to all of the family gatherings because they would always be there to entertain. So that's how I got exposed. I could say to myself, "You know what, I can be this way, too. I can be *mahu* and an entertainer."

Later, one of them was the person who became the choreographer for our performance group; she helped us. She wasn't surprised about me. She told me, "I *knew* you were gonna be *mahu*. I *knew* you were gonna be *mahu*.' She asked, "Do you want to be a showgirl?" "Yes, auntie, I want to be a showgirl." "OK, then you've got to do it this way, you've got to work it this way . . ." So she started to teach all of us. She told her sister about me. "Remember *da kine*?" "Yeah." "Well, she's *mahu* now!" And when she saw me, she said, "See, when you were young, a young little boy, I *knew* you were going to be *mahu*. You were always standing there watching us, how we were acting." I said, "Yeah, because I wanted to be like you, but I just didn't know how. How do you get yourselves looking so real?" "*Hormones, Mary, hormones.*"

***

It's easier to be transgendered here in Hawai'i. People grow up with *mahus* and know how they are, like in taking care of the family. So they know what they're capable of. That's part of why my family accepts me for what I am. Because I'm there to help the family. If I were in a family that wasn't Hawaiian, I think I would have a harder time with my sexuality. I think I would probably kill myself, or run away, get away, or something . . .

When I came out, when I did my transitioning, I met this one sister of mine — we're best friends today — and actually, we were volunteers for the March of Dimes Haunted House. They used to have a haunted house right on Fort Street Mall, the old Crest Building, and so they turned it into a haunted house. I was with my cousins, who were interested in volunteering, and I went with them. So it was our first day of meeting and discussing things. Then this one particular person came in and . . . I kind of knew . . . He was a little feminine . . . We really didn't go up to each other and introduce ourselves until we were starting to put on our makeup for the haunted house. Then he came on over and asked me if I could put on his makeup. So when I was putting on his makeup . . . During that time I had long nails, and when I was putting his makeup on I scratched the bottom of his eye — Accidentally! I didn't do it purposely. But ever since the time I scratched her eye we clicked and became best friends, right up to today. So we would hang out with each other, and basically we were doing our transitioning together. That's how me and my sister Leikia got together. We're best friends and Kaui is our queen mother. She is the one taught us the ropes.

***

The most difficult thing about transitioning was dealing with society. *Torment*. That was my problem. "How can I deal with this?" So whenever somebody called me names, my feelings got hurt really fast. I was so weak. My heart is so . . . so loving, that I'm *weak*. I get really depressed sometimes when society just really puts me down and tells me that I'm not supposed to be this way. That *you're a man*. And my mentality was driving me crazy. That's why I turned to drugs — to take away the problems. But they don't! I learned that over the years — they don't. But they helped me build myself, to be stronger. It's nothing to me now when people do those kinds of things to me. To this day I still face it, but not as much as before. But I still face people calling me names. And I'm like, "*Whatever*. That's *your* problem. *You* deal with it. I know what I am. I'm secure. I love myself. I accept myself for who I am. And if you don't, then get out of my face — You don't have to be in my face."

When I was doing my transitioning I would have to go to the girls' department . . . I traded in my men's underwear for panties, and things like that. [laughs] Which was kind of a bizarre experience, because I would go to the women's department and the women would be like looking at me and giving me looks, and I would be thinking, "Oh, hurry up! I just want to buy this and get out of here." I just didn't want to face that. So that was kind of a barrier for me. But I broke that barrier because I was starting to be faithful to my hormone intake, and things like that.

***

Me and my best friend Leikia met other girls who were tall, transgender, queens, *mahu*, whatever, and then we saw a show called The Glades. A lot of the older girls would tell us stories about it, and that's why we wanted to become entertainers ourselves. We wanted to be just like those girls who were on stage, with lovely costumes and looking so womanly — *That's* where we wanted to be. So one day we decided to put our own group together. We picked the girls, the ones that we wanted, because we wanted tall girls. We didn't want short girls, because the taller the better. They're more exotic, they're more "Wow!" They're more "Ooh! Ah!" So we just came together, and then met this other older girl who had been in those shows — she had actually been the choreographer. So she came on board and taught us everything there was to know about the show that they had before. Actually, the performers taught us the old production numbers that they had learned, so it's like passing it down from generation to generation.

For the first couple of years it was hard because we were just starting out. We didn't have money for costumes, so we had to work it to where we could look at least a little bit decent . . . We would go to the Goodwill and Salvation Army and look for dresses. We'd put some glitter on it, put some sequins on it, to make it look more showy. It was a struggle for us, but then we started to get a little bit better, we started to be on it, we started to be more professional — a little bit. And then people would hire us to do parties. Especially Leikia. Her family enjoys entertainment from transgenders because they've been to the Glades . . . So the family would hire us to do these shows and we'd get paid. I was like, "Whoa! This is what I want to do!"

We'd been doing it for years and years, until we decided that we wanted to go into a club. And what came about was, Fusion Waikiki was Garbo's before Fusions, and they used to have a show and . . . being young, we would get into the club underage and we would be passable, so we'd get into these clubs and watch these shows. I remember thinking, "Oh my gosh, they are *so* beautiful." The show is so lavish. "*That's what I want to be. That's what I'm gonna do.*" So we'd been going to the club for years, and then all of a sudden we didn't see any drag shows. That was our opportunity to go to the management and introduce ourselves and tell them that we wanted to perform in their club. That's how we got hired to do Fusion. We are called The Gender Bender Lip Gloss Revue. Actually, the first name we had was Vogue International. I don't know why we named it that . . . Then we started to really think about it because we began to get more gigs and were getting more recognized, so we decided on a name. And we've been performing for over five years now.

I like performing because it gives me self-esteem. Being in front in total strangers and just showing them who I am. So it really helped me boost my self-esteem up because it had been kind of low because I didn't know if living this way a good thing for me or a bad thing for me. But it helped me a lot, because we were performing for families that were straight. So that was a comfortable thing for me. I have learned that they do appreciate us for who we are. That's how I got to feeling, "Oh my gosh — this is what I wanted!" So it even made me happier and made me feel that I still wanted to do this. I want to have us do it in a hotel, or something. Find a better club than Fusion to house us, to do just daily shows. That's one of our goals. We're still working on that . . .

As for my personal goals, I want to be a part of an organization that serves transgender people. Because the girls are not getting what they need. And the girls need a lot of help. Our community needs a lot of help. Housing, employment . . . There isn't any information about how you deal with being transgender . . . The only way they know is through older girls who have already lived the life and experienced a lot of b.s.

That's basically how we learn, from the older girls, because they've lived a lot. They've lived through hell for us . . . They were paving the way for us and getting society to at least look at our community. Because there's no organization that knows how to help transgendered people. The only people who know are the transgenders. Because nobody can go to school for it, nobody can get a degree for it. You have to live it in order for you to understand it. So I want to be everything that they need. I want to be there to help them get through thick and thin. I want them to have a good life, too. I don't want them to miss the opportunities that are out there.

***

Things are really changing in Hawai'i. Ever since we had the Ke Ola Mamo conference in Waikiki we've gotten a lot of respect from a lot of people from all different kinds of fields. We got *respect*, and that's what we really liked and wanted. That was a good thing, and I think that was a start for us. We're also the pavers and the movers and the shakers. So I think society is more understanding now. They are recognizing that we exist now. But there's also the understanding of being transgender. There are misconceptions. People say things that really aren't true. Hearsay. That's what they use and that's what they believe in. When they see a particular transgender and say these kinds of things we wonder, "What are you saying?"

More and more people are recognizing us now because we're out there, we're in their faces, we're in their high schools . . . We're teaching them about alternative lifestyles . . . So we're doing good. It's about time that somebody did. It's a funny thing . . . When I first started at work, we only had Ashli. That was the only transgender who was in Ke Ola Mamo. Of course, they also had an MSM; he was local Hawaiian. But he wasn't really making any progress. Then Ashli started to recruit girls. And when she started to recruit girls, she asked me . . . At the time I didn't have a job; I was a prostitute, I was on the streets — That's how I was surviving.

Then Ashli gave me a job. A couple of months later Hina came along. It's a funny thing — we all came together . . . There was a purpose for us to all be together because of the wonderful work that we've been doing for Ke Ola Mamo. We're making a difference. We're reaching out to our community, especially the transgenders. And they're really respecting us because this kind of program has never happened before for transgenders. Even the older girls say, "What happened? Why wasn't there a program for us in those days?" We tell them, "Well, we have it now. And we need your help. We need your *kokua*. We want you to be there for us to help the younger generation to live a better life and not go down the wrong road." So they've been really happy that this has happened. They feel that it's been overdue. But now that we have this program we just hope that it will never finish, that it will still be here for them to come and be a part of. And it's so bizarre! Because when we're together, we say to each other, "You know, we really *do* make a difference in people's perspectives and views." Going to high schools, conferences, explaining to people what a transgender is . . .

Transgender . . . I don't like to identify myself as a transgender because I don't know *what* is that word. I can identify with *mahu* because it's a Hawaiian word for us — transgenders. Growing up, that's the word people used. Reading about Hawaiian history, I've noticed that there were *mahus* in the [Hawaiian] monarchy; they had a place. So I could really identify myself as a *mahu* in a positive way, not a negative way. The boys would yell, "Hey, *mahu*! *Mahu*!" And they would mean it in a derogatory way. But I can identify myself as *mahu*. Actually, *mahu* is either more female or more male, so it's like . . . androgynous.

At one time I thought I was a woman, but I don't think I'm a woman now. I'm just right in the middle of everything. That's how I am now. But before I thought I was a woman because society told me I had to be either a male or a female. So I was like, "OK, I'm gonna identify myself as a female then." But ever since we had this conference and we heard from older women, *kahunas*, who told us that we *mahu* had place, that's when I said, "Oh, you know what — I'm not a woman. I'm a *mahu*." *That's* my word; I can identify with that. But anytime we go to a meeting, we've got to say that we're transgender, and I'm thinking, "Oh God, I don't like that word."

***

Don't judge a book by its cover. You have to look within a person. You have to get to know a person; that's the only way you're going to know. You cannot just look at that person and say that the person is stupid, mental, I don't get it. If you don't get it, ask the person. Be friendly. We're people, we're human, we're people. And another thing, too. If they see a transgender doing bad things, don't think that all transgenders are like that. They're responsible for their own actions, like everybody else is. Because I notice that a lot of people think like this. They've experienced a transgender who was getting really obnoxious, so they think every *mahu* is like that. No. N.O. No. There are a lot of transgenders out there who are nice, and there are the bad ones, too. But you've got to understand — they're at a different level. They're going through their phases, whatever that might be. Problems, whatever. And all transgenders are at all different levels. So you've got to see it and relate to it.

Families trying to deal with a transgender son or daughter need to be really nurturing. They can't be telling them that they cannot do that. Do you remember being in school when you were young and the teacher asked you what you wanted to be when you grew up? The parents should let them do that, let them be what they want to be. Accept them for what they want to be. Whether it's being a police officer, or . . . whatever it may be. Because that's how we're taught — how do you want to be? I always wanted to say, "I want to be a woman," but that wasn't realistic when I was young.

For you men out there, don't think that just because a queen stares at you, it means that they want you sexually. And being that you're straight and that you're not into that, you need to recognize something — we're not always going to be into you. So for those men out there who think, "Ugh," with that kind of reaction towards transgenders, don't think that transgenders are necessarily interested in you. They're just looking at something which is beautiful or handsome. Take it as a compliment, not as a put-down or negative thought. But when men say something like, "Ugh," I know that deep down inside it's a fetish for them.

The ones who are the most negative are the ones who really want to have a sexual relationship with a transgender, one way or another. On the street . . . Oh my gosh — *Yes*! I mean, these were my classmates! The ones that hated me the most wanted to have sexual relationships with me. I just gagged — I was just totally tripped out that this guy had been teasing me for *so long*, and the reason he did it was because he just wanted me to do a sexual thing with him. That was so ridiculous! But it's the pride, the macho-ness, the masculinity. I'm just like, "Get over it!" They need to be mellow, they need to mellow out.

And women — they think that we're taking all the men. No, we're not taking all the men because the men are going back to them anyway. Because they're women, they can have children, they can have a family. I think I know that for a fact, men leave [their *mahu* partners]. Listening to a lot of the older girls, in their relationships, and how long their relationships last, I believe it's true because it's happened to a lot of older girls. I never did hear about even one relationship to where they've lived through their whole lives. Like how a man and woman have a relationship, get married, those kinds of things. I'm not really worried about that because I'm happy being by myself. I had a relationship with a guy who was straight — and I consider him straight — and we have a really good friendship because that's what I told him I wanted most of all — his friendship. Not a sexual relationship. Of course that plays a role in it. But I told him that I wanted his friendship most of all because that lasts a long time.

For me, I don't want the surgery. I'm happy the way I am. And my boyfriend accepts me for what I am. If I really did get the surgery, I don't think it would last long. If he really wanted a woman, he could've gone out there and gotten one. But he chose me. Why? Because I'm different.

BUBBLES

My legal name is Breena Keahiolalo-Cravalho. That's not my birth name, but that's the name I'm giving you. I'm twenty-eight years old, and I come from the windward side of O'ahu — Kane'ohe, born and raised. I'm Hawaiian-Chinese-Portuguese. I identify myself more with the Hawaiian side because I grew up with old Hawaiian values. My grandfather was pure Portuguese and he was from Maui. He married my grandmother who was three-fourths Hawaiian and one-fourth Chinese.

One of the two strongest things I grew up with was *aloha*, which doesn't always necessarily mean love; it can also mean sharing of what you have. You *aloha* somebody . . . just your overall being should be *aloha*. The other word is *pono*. I didn't learn the Hawaiian word for *pono* until later on in life, but I grew up with this concept. *Pono* to me means values and morals; it's the way that you live your life. It goes back to the Golden Rule: do unto others as would have them do unto you. So that is the way I was raised. *Aloha* and *pono* are the two most outstanding words I could come up with for being raised Hawaiian.

Aloha . . . It has to come from within oneself. You cannot buy it; it has to come from within somebody's *na'au*. *Na'au* means your innards, your gut feelings. It's not your brain but your heart. Your heart really dictates to the people around you what they perceive. They can look at you and tell if you're a good or a bad person just by the way you carry yourself. And you carry yourself not from your brain but from your heart. If you're a good person it shows on the outside; if you're a bad person it shows on the outside. You can dress up to make yourself look pretty, but once that mouth opens up and your breath, your *ha* . . . in Hawaiian it's *ha*, your breath . . . once that *ha* comes out you can tell, and

153

your *ha* comes from your *na'au*. Also there's the umbilical cord, the *piko*, which is the Hawaiian lifeline. It's everybody's lifeline, the whole world's lifeline. When you're born you have an umbilical cord, and you're still connected to your mother. When you take your first breath, your first *ha*, then you are your own separate being. But you're never disconnected from your mother, because your *piko* was attached to her. That's where your lineage comes from.

***

I don't know if I felt different as a child. I think I felt normal. But I can distinctly remember being around age five or six and playing in the courtyard of my elementary school, twirling around an umbrella. It was a sunny day and I was singing, "I'm singing in the rain." And dancing around and prancing. My auntie was picking me up and I was supposed to be waiting for her in front of the school. Well, I was playing like normal kids do and not paying attention, and the first words out of her mouth when she saw me were, "Why are you acting *mahu*?!" Of course at five or six years old you really don't understand the term "*mahu*." An adult knows it, but not a young kid. Because to me I was acting normal.

When I first knew that I was quote unquote *mahu*, or gay, I was twelve or thirteen years old. That's when I learned the term, and really knew what it was. I pretty much kept it secret . . . I didn't come out to my family until I was twenty years old. I wasn't really introduced to the transgendered lifestyle until I came out of my closet. Let me talk to you about that. When I came out, for three or four weeks prior my family had been teasing me because I was hanging around all these, as they put it, "fags." They were calling me "fruitfly," like I was a fly hanging around all these fruits. I didn't take a liking to that. Then we had our first big family reunion on our Hawaiian side. In the middle of the food line my sister called me "fruitfly." I dropped my tray right in front of her — there was a big noise — and I said very loudly in an affirmative voice: "You know what, Moose?" (Which is my sister's pet name) "You can just call me 'fruit' and drop the 'fly.'" I walked away and started to cry because such a heavy burden was lifted off of me. I was finally able to get it out in the open.

It was a troubling time because for the three years prior to that I had been going to church . . . I was actually trying to deny to myself what I was, my natural path in life. I was trying to change myself . . . not only because they wanted me to change, but also because I felt, at that time, not so much weird or outcasted, but I just wanted to be like everybody else . . . It's like the opposite of Halloween. Men may dress up as women, maybe that's their fantasy, but they can never come out to it. Well, for those three years that I was going to church faithfully, it was like I was going to Halloween everyday, putting on a mask that wasn't me. I was playing a role. People think now, because I wear makeup, that that's my mask. That's not my mask — that is who I am. It's the opposite of Halloween. On Halloween nowadays I don't even go out with makeup.

It wasn't hard growing up. I had a great childhood. My family is very wonderful! I had a very easy childhood. I am an above average student. I never did anything wrong. I was a mama's boy/girl. I always tried to please them; I never tried to waver from what they wanted . . . My only secret was that I liked boys and not girls. But, lo and behold, I later found out that they already knew from the time I was little what I was. But they really wanted confirmation to get it out on the table. I think that's why they teased me. Maybe it was subliminal; they wanted me to go on with my life, so they could adjust and go on with theirs. I wouldn't say that it's a bad thing or that it's a good thing, but I'm glad that it happened. It was fast, it was sudden, and I did go on with my life.

When I was twenty I decided to move to the mainland, and I moved to Salt Lake City, Utah. There is quite a big transgender population there, and that's where I met and talked with the first transgendered people who I really got close to. I thought, "Oh my God — That's what I am!" Because I really wasn't comfortable with being a *man* liking another man — not that there's anything wrong with it; I think any love in its pure form is beautiful. However . . .

It wasn't that I was a woman trapped in a man's body . . . I was a person trying to live *her* life the best way possible with what I knew. And what I knew when I was twenty was that there were boys and that there were girls. There were boys who liked boys, and girls who liked girls, and boys who liked girls, and girls who liked guys . . . Actually, the word "transgender" really didn't come into play until just a few years ago.

155

Maybe when I was twenty-two, twenty-three, and had already started dressing up and taking female hormones . . . Even when I started to take female hormones, "transgender" was a foreign word to me. The way I felt inside was . . . human!

***

Because I have a great family and a great friend support system, I didn't feel freaky or unloved. I never felt outcasted. I struggled with weight all my life, and it has a big part to do with my transsexualism . . . I have been big all my life, and being a person who is overweight, it's . . . it's easier *and* it's harder to pass. You're more filled out than a skinny girl; especially being on hormones, everything fell into place. However, because of my stature it's hard. I carry myself as a woman, I hope other people see that. I know I'm not one hundred percent passable, but I'm me: you take me or you leave me. And you know what? You take me, that's great. You leave me, that's OK by me. Because I am not for everybody. I am not asking anybody to accept my lifestyle. I have my family and I have my friends, and that is all I need. Period. Everybody else, they don't pay my bills, they don't take me to work in the morning, they don't get me up — they don't do *anything* for me. It is me, my friends, and my family. Period. And God. Those are the only people I have to answer to. That's my support group.

And having the confidence has to come from within. There are a lot of pretty girls out there with no self-esteem. But then there are girls who are not so pretty, who have not been blessed with the perfect face, yet they have all the love and beauty in the world because it comes from *within*. That's where we get back to the Hawaiian values. I think I have great self-esteem, especially about my transsexualism, because I learned, through my being overweight, how to deal with people's indifferences in the world. I learned to deal with it. So being transgendered was *minor* compared to the abuse and humiliation I got all my life because I was overweight. Because people see me as a fat person first. That's the automatic instinct. Then they look at my face and go, "Oh . . . She looks a little *different* . . . Is she or isn't she a boy or a girl?" Sometimes they don't know. Sometimes they know right off the bat, sometimes they don't know, and sometimes they just think I'm a girl. It doesn't matter to me; I live my life how *I* live it. I don't live other people's lives, and I sure don't want them to live mine.

One of my biggest challenges was to get over my weight issue. I had to get over, "Will I look good as a girl? Should I stay a boy?" It's a process. This whole thing. It's like an AA twelve step process. You have to go through the electrolysis, silicone, and the hormones . . . everything. It's not like you wake up one morning and automatically you're . . . *a woman*. You have to go through some sort of androgynous period where you look half and half. Maybe you'll still be wearing boy's underwear, and looking like a girl on the outside. There are different levels. But for me, in transition I didn't have a hard time at all. I had my support group. I used them to my advantage to help me. My friends taught me about hormones, told me where to go . . .

I'm able to keep my self-esteem because my mom always said, "True happiness comes from within. It comes from yourself." I believe that wholeheartedly. *Nobody else in this world can make you happy.* No matter what relationship, no matter who comes into your life, you are the only person who says, "I can choose to be sad or I can choose to be happy." I choose to be happy, because there is so much negativity in the world today. Everybody is getting distant, sitting at their computer and talking to people on the internet instead of interacting. And yes, I'm guilty of that, too. However, I have my social life outside of my computer life, and I use it as a means to get to know other people from all walks of life. I look at their experience in life, and apply it to my own where *I* become stronger. That's how I do it, because happiness comes from within. Period. Bottom line. No man will ever make me as happy as I make myself happy. Physical intimacy, that's the only thing a man can give me. Happiness, I can get from myself. And with happiness there is self-esteem. That's how I'm able to keep myself up, and cheery and happy. They say that the eyes are the windows to a person's soul, but I think a smile is a way to a person's heart. Because a smile says so many beautiful things. It can brighten up a person's day who hasn't had a good day. Or even just the word, "smile" — when you hear it you have to smile.

I always tell myself that I'm lucky. I never went hungry, I really never had to live on the street, I was accepted by my family . . . The acceptance by my family of my transgenderism . . . Well, to back up, being gay was no problem to my family. Being transgendered, I don't think they had a problem per se about me being effeminate, or growing my hair, or even wearing make-up. However, I think that they were afraid for my well-being because we live in the time of STDs, and AIDS, and gay bashings . . . Yes, we've had all these kinds of diseases since the dawn of time. However, now it's more prevalent, and it's on talk shows . . . I grew up during the 1980s when the gay revolution was coming out and everything was out in the open and on the table and it was dinner conversation . . . You never had that before. I mean, you had that after Stonewall, in the late 1960s, and then during the disco era of the 1970s. However, it wasn't until the 1980s when AIDS came into play, that homosexuality was brought forth to the table, nonchalantly during a dinner conversation. So I think with that, and being a school child in the 1980s, growing up being *mahu*, I think they were afraid of me being bashed, or of what other people might say. So I think they tried their hardest to make me feel more comfortable, and if that is what I wanted, they always have stood by me.

My mom has come to the beauty pageants I've run in; even my dad came to one of my pageants. He's a little uncomfortable with it, though. He doesn't want to see his only son being *mahu*. I'm sure he would like it if I were a heterosexual male just like him and got married in a normal way, but I am what I am. He has dealt with it the best way he knows how, as a heterosexual male and as my father. I don't look at my dad and say, "Oh, he's a heterosexual male." That's just a given. I look at my dad and say, "He's my father." And he looks at me, and yes, I'm still his son. Even if I get my change I'll still be "his son." But that is *only* for my father and mother to ever call me, nobody else. It would be great if one day they come around and call me "daughter" or "she." They've come around to where they call me Bubbles; my mom has started to call me Breena, and that's fine and dandy, but . . . I am their child. Period. They love me, and I respect them and love them for that. Because a lot of the parents will kick their children out *for shame*. And I can tell you one thing: there was no shame within my family. There was just hurt because they didn't really want me to be this way. I can understand a parent's point of view with that. But as I said, there was no shame in it; they loved me for who I am. They just want me to better myself. They want me the best that I can be.

I know for a fact that my mom and my dad will do anything for me. I have half-brothers and sisters, I have an adopted sister, and I have numerous foster siblings; we're talking ten of us. My parents' love for all of their children, whether they be foster, adopted, half, whatever, is the same, is equal. They love differently, but the same amount. They love us for different aspects of our lives. Because we are their children.

My mom grew up in very hard times. She was a foster child herself. I guess it's every parent's dream to better their children's lives than their own lives. If my mom seemed distant about my transgenderism, my homosexuality, it was because she was not knowledgeable, or she wasn't educated enough, or she was just *afraid*. We all fear the unknown. Everybody. Through education and through my teaching them how to deal with it, I have to deal with it myself. When I saw two men kissing in a club for the first time I wasn't appalled, I was just taken aback. Because I had never seen that before. So I wouldn't expect my parents to automatically understand about what I was feeling inside, because I didn't know what I was feeling inside to begin with.

As spectators in my life, as people who help me on my journey, I didn't expect them to understand what I was going through. I didn't understand what they were going through; I don't understand what everybody is going through. All I know is who I am. I'm the only person that stays with me twenty-four hours a day through my whole life. So I didn't expect them to come around as fast as I was. I know they needed some time. At times I know I was pushy; it was because I was frustrated. And I had fear about treating the unknown to them, conveying my message, conveying my life to them.

***

I have learned a lot of things on the internet, by researching gender dysphoria and transsexualism. I think that there are a lot of different levels because you can be pre-op, post-op, transvestite, cross-dresser . . . There are so many labels, and I guess it comes under the umbrella of being transgendered. By learning through my friends, through the internet, and even on the street, just like everybody else, you gain knowledge through your actions, through your journey through this life.

The word transgender comes in two parts: "Trans," meaning to go from one place to another; you're transporting, you're transitioning. And "gender" . . . to me, gender is what you feel on the inside . . . I believe . . . my biological sex . . . Yes, I'm a male. But my gender is female. Gender has to come from within. That comes back to your *na'au* and your Hawaiian values. It comes from *within*. If you portray yourself as a woman, you're going to be respected and treated as a woman. Yes, there will be some assholes who call you "Sir" even though you look like a girl. But you have to turn it around; you educate them by saying — you don't be rude about it — but you put them in their place. You have to educate them; you educated yourself and now it is time to educate them. You can't expect everyone to just get it or accept it right off the bat. There are gonna be pricks in the world, and you're just going to have to stumble and fall, and learn to deal with it, learn to cope with it.

I have many, many different labels. But the biggest label I have starts with an "h." It's "human." That's my biggest label. Under human I consider myself a pre-operative transsexual. I am also an entertainer, and I guess you would label me as a drag queen, but that is for entertainment purposes only; that's not who I am twenty-four hours a day. That's who I am two hours a month on stage doing a gig. But I would label myself a human first, pre-operative transsexual, female, as my gender.

How do I feel about the surgery? You know, I've gone through so many different stages on feeling, "Do or don't I want the surgery?" And yes, I've read about it on the internet, and this is my feeling. When I was younger I didn't want it. I was happy with what I was, but only because I was still in-between. As I've gone through my process and gone through my transition . . . I don't think it will make me complete; I think I am complete already. I think it will enhance me because I want to get married in a traditional way. I want to do all the things that a biological heterosexual female would do in her life span.

I've been blessed with both worlds. I've been blessed with growing up a boy, and living life as a woman. So I think I am fortunate, and I think transgendered people are fortunate because they know both worlds. They know how a woman feels, but yet we know what a man wants. I don't know if we have one up over women, but in knowledge I do believe so, especially when it comes to a man. And there are other transgenders who like females. You can run the gamut on that. However, for me, I would label them as human also. The greatest thing we can achieve in life is loving of yourself, loving of your fellow human being, the love of your spirit, and enjoying life. And all that comes from within, comes from your *na'au*, it comes from who you are, and who your parents were, because it's passed down.

Lineage is important . . . I know Hina talked with you about the word "*mahu*," and the people who were "the chosen ones" and stuff like that. I don't know if I'm the "chosen one." I don't know if I would *choose* this lifestyle, but it's the lifestyle I was dealt, and I have to deal with it. I did not ask to be a biological male liking other males; I did not ask for that. But it's who I am. Other people have to deal with their own troubles in the world, I have to deal with mine. It doesn't make who I am. I am . . . I am an artist, I am an entertainer, I am a poet . . . I have such a creative side in me, that whatever is outside is really just a casing for the inside. My heart dictates my happiness. In the world that we live in, I choose to be happy.

As far as my transsexualism, at this point in my life — I'm twenty-eight years old — and my feeling about the surgery is, yes, I would like to have it. However, and there's always going to be a "but" to this kind of thing, it will only happen if I'm, one, healthy enough to have it; two, if I can afford it; and three, if it will make me happy. I need to educate myself more about it. I think a lot of girls in the community go head first into this — no pun intended! — but you really have to educate yourself; it's a lifelong, body-altering experience. You can't go back. I need to be *pono* with myself; I have to know that it is right for me at the time that I do it. Right now, I would not do it because I have not educated myself enough to be at the point where I am *pono* with it. I am maybe eighty percent sure that I want to go through it because I want a family. I would not hide the fact that I am transgendered from my children, if and when I have them. However, I will not go out of my way to tell the public, in fear of my children being ostracized, but that's later on, down the road, when I'm financially able, when I'm spiritually able, when I'm physically able, to raise children.

And of course I would have to have a mate. I do not believe that a child should grow up without a mother or a father. Of course, sometimes you cannot help it; the abusive father or the parent that dies, or whatever have you. But being transgendered, I will need the support . . . I have my family, I have my friends. But when you raise a child, if at all possible, you should have a father figure and a mother figure. And yes, I probably could provide both. [laughs] However, I would rather just stick to the female part. The men will do what they have to do, and the females will do what they have to do, and yes, there's crossing over; we all know that. But we all have roles in society. Being a male-to-female transsexual, my role is to educate the public, and to love myself and hold my head up high to my family and friends, so I don't appear as a freak . . . I just want to blend. Not forgetting my past, and I'd still be within the community; but to me there is heartache involved, and . . . not shame, because I don't think I was ever ashamed of what I was . . . but there's heartache. I wouldn't want my children to go through that; I don't want to go through that.

***

One of the people who I most admire, as far as being famous, is Maya Angelou. She has had to endure so much negativity through her life, yet look where she is now. She has written numerous books of her poetry, of her life, of her struggle, and we all have struggles. Every single human being. Transgenders do not have more of a problem than the next person. We have something that we have to deal with. And yes, it's on the physical, yes, it's on the outside. But who's to say that's worse than anybody else's problem that they might be having on the inside? We all have to go through it, our life's ups and downs. [sings], "That's life . . . That's what all the people say / You may be riding high in April / But you may be shot down in May / But you might be singing one more tune / When you're back on top in June . . . "

We live a roller coaster in life. We have our ups and downs, our happy and our sad, our joyful and excitement, our sad, our pouting . . . We have so many different expressions. But in all of those expressions, there's one thing: love. There's love in sadness, there's love in happiness. There's love in every different aspect of life. So if you can love yourself, and you can love your neighbor and respect them with the dignity that you want to be respected with, that should be every person's goal before everything else. Then everything else will fall into place.

Maya said one thing that really changed my thinking. It was something like, "I do what I do with the knowledge that I have. And when I know better, I do better." So knowledge is power, love is power, being *pono*, having *aloha*, and having it come through your *na'ao*. That's power, that's love. And coming from above, your ancestors, to know where you came from, to have goals and to know where you're going — that's power. Because if you don't have any direction of where you're going, you'll never reach any destination.

***

I want the all-American dream. I think everybody needs to have a goal or purpose for why they're here. We're born, we go to school, we go college, we have boyfriends and girlfriends. . . . It is the journey, not the end result. But what did you do with that journey? What did you accomplish? This isn't about getting into the pearly gates of Heaven, because that will come automatically. If you worry about that, you're worrying for the wrong reasons. I don't believe that I need to say twenty million Hail Marys and Our Fathers just to get into the pearly gates of Heaven. I believe that if I live my life as a decent human being, with good morals and good values, and treat others how I want to be treated, with dignity, with respect, and with pride of who I am, and not put other people down for what they believe in, even people who shun me, we are all children of God. We're all in this *ohana*, this family, which we call the world, together, whether you be Vietnamese, Arabic, Asian, Polynesian, Micronesian, Melanesian, American, European — I don't give a flying fig what you are. You treat me with respect, I will afford you the same feelings. That's what I want for the future. Material things . . . money, whatever — Yeah, that's fine and dandy. But if I have food on my table, a roof over my head, and love in my heart, I'm happy. That's the way I feel.

We need to stop and smell the roses sometimes. To just sit back and observe your life. We're all in this together, in this human race, in this world race. We have to think about other people. But the love has to come from within, first. That's why I want to do this book. Because it will give other people the opportunity to see, "Hey, transsexuals are just like everybody else." When somebody pricks us, we bleed. When it comes down to it, we are all in this together. Yeah, we're gonna have our differences, but . . .

Especially living in Hawai'i, and as I sit here and look up and down this street, you can see so many diverse ethnic cultures melting together in one place. I see Hispanics, Afro-Americans, Africans, Filipino, Hawaiian, Chinese . . . If only the world could be more like the people on this street, living in harmony like this . . . If you really think about it, right here is so beautiful, because there are places in the world where you can't live so free. There is a difference between Hawai'i and the rest of the world. I think we are afforded the opportunity to live in a free environment where, yes, people might look at you strange. However, they respect you because we're all . . . at least fifty, sixty percent of the population is of mixed culture. Like I've said before, I do identify more with my Hawaiian self. However, I have some Portuguese values, I have Chinese values, I have American values, I even have values and I'm not even part of their nationality or race . . . it all carries over. But under the umbrella of human race we all have pretty much the same values. What it comes down to is love, for yourself and for others.

So comparing transsexualism in Hawai'i to other places in the world, the only difference is that they do not have the same avenues available we do here, and are not afforded the same respect as transgendered people living in Hawai'i are. Those people might not have the knowledge, the resources, and the support groups we do because they may be living many, many, many hundreds of miles away from each other.

In Hawai'i we're afforded the luxury of living on an island that is forty-five miles by thirty miles. To get to a person, it will only take you an hour. People on the mainland might have to travel a day to get to the nearest transgendered person. So they do not have the close-knit family that we have. And when I talk about family, we treat each other as family. Yes, we're all friends, but we're all in this together and all the transgendered people, whether they're pre-op, post-op, transvestite, whatever, in Hawai'i we're all in this together, and we're close — a close-knit family.

Most of the transgendered here, because we live in Hawai'i, are part Hawaiian. I think I know of only two or three who are full Hawaiian. But that's only because there are only a few full Hawaiians left. But yes, we are the melting pot of the world. To me, not only are our mothers our umbilical cord, but if you really think about it, Hawai'i is the *piko* of the world. We're in the middle of the Pacific Ocean, we're thousands of miles from any continent, and we're smack dab right in the middle. And where does everybody come to? Where does everybody talk about? Everybody talks about Hawai'i. You go to Bangladesh, people know where Hawai'i is. You go to the North Pole, they know. Everybody knows where Hawai'i is. But then if you ask where Madagascar is, or where Belize is, people aren't going to be able to tell you. But everybody knows where Hawai'i is. We're in the middle of everything. But we're also away from everything.

We have a little more opportunity to be who we want to be, because in Hawai'i we're so laid back, we're comfortable. We live in paradise, for God's sake. And people who say this is not paradise, they should be shot. Because we the best surf in the world, we have great sand, sun, people, food . . .

There *are* cliques . . . the Filipino girls who hang around with each other, there are the Hawaiian girls who hang around with each other . . . However, when we come together, we come together as one. On the mainland, they might come together, but they come together as separate entities, much like . . . how the Olympics are. They come together as a whole, but they don't; they're competing against each other. And here there is no competition. Because, and going back to the word aloha, we have open love and respect for our fellow transgendered person, because we know what they're going through, as well as they know what we're going through. As I said, we're all in this together.

If there's anything at all that I want the next generation to learn, it will be to love yourself, and to not be afraid to share that love with others. Because everything else will fall into place.

***

BUBBLES

I think what Kaui said about us being angels is right. If you look at all the passages in the Bible, or if you look at a lot of the pictures, what do you see? You see an angelic pretty boy. That's all I am and that's all I want to be: somebody's pretty angel. [laughs]

MELY

My name is Mely Silverio. I used to be Rommel Silverio. I was born April fourth, 1962 in Manila, the Philippines, in a district called Sao Paulo. I grew up in Cezon City in the metropolitan Manila area. I am the eldest of three kids.

I came to Hawai'i in 1989 under a scholarship of the East-West Center Population Program to pursue my Ph.D. in sociology at the University of Hawai'i at Manoa. I had already started a Ph.D. program in sociology at the University of the Philippines. I finished my Bachelors in statistics, and my Masters in demography there. When I moved to Hawai'i in 1989 I was still Rommel. That was eleven years ago, August 7, 1989.

I think a major feature of my life has been the fact that I've always been, or at least for the most part of it, overweight. I've also always been effeminate, or feminine, in my actions, and as such I would be the subject of teasing and jeering and name-calling. I had many hurtful experiences, not only from people who didn't know me, but also from people who knew me — friends and even family. Even my own parents would sometimes join in. It's sad, but you have to understand that I grew up in a Catholic culture where machismo, or the macho culture, is predominant. The man is the man of the house, and the woman follows the man. So I grew up in that culture as an openly gay man, which made it hard for me. Somehow I was able to survive it. But what also complicated my life was that I was overweight. And so the jeering and the teasing not only focused on the fact that I was what we call *bakla* in the Philippines, the term for gays back home, but also because I was overweight, and they made fun of that.

When I came here in 1989, life went on for me as Rommel. As before, I had crushes on guys. I've always liked guys. I've always been sexually attracted to guys. I've always been expressive of my attraction to them, to the point of being comical. Some of them took advantage of that; some of them just ignored me. I guess I didn't attract that many gay men themselves, despite the fact that I was also a gay man, because of a lack of physical attraction.

Sometime in 1996, though, I started medical therapy to treat my acne — Acutane. Taking that medication meant that I had to have a liver function test. The results showed that I had fatty deposits in my liver because I was overweight. Therefore, the doctor suggested that I lose weight. Since my weight had been a problem for a long time I asked the doctor to help me, since it's one thing to say, "Lose weight," but it's another to actually be serious about it. I asked him for any medication that would help me achieve that goal, and he put me on Phen-fen. This is a banned medication today, but back then, because I was about sixty pounds overweight, I was a perfect candidate for the medication. In the end, I lost about eighty pounds — which I'll slowly gain back if I don't watch it.

I noticed that as I lost the weight I was looking better than I ever had before. Somewhere along the line, I started to imagine myself being a woman. Actually, I've always seen myself as a woman, but I didn't have the guts to do it before. So when I was about thirty-four, thirty-five years old, I said to myself, "If I'm going to do it, I might as well do it now, while I'm young." Because for me, personally, I don't see the point of going through the changes when I'm in my sixties. I would rather do it while I still have the time to be what I want to be, to establish myself in a career as Mely, to find someone out there, possibly, who would share my life, who would share his life with me, and I with him. Who would stand by me through thick and thin.

Now I'm happy being female and playing the role to the hilt. Because people have always seen me as a woman anyway. Even when I was growing up, they tended to group me with the girls, like whenever it was recess time when I was in kindergarten. All the guys would be playing in the jungle gym and I'd be left behind in the classroom with the other girls, and we'd be sitting there talking to each other. That kind of thing. I think they already saw that I was different. Even when I was still small I felt different. So it didn't shock people when I made the change. Since I've always been feminine, the next step would naturally be to go through the gender transition itself.

I started the hormone therapy in June of 1996. I was so scared that first time I was in the doctor's clinic. I asked him repeatedly whether he used a new syringe to inject me, because, as a student of sexuality — HIV/AIDS is an area of specialization in my Ph.D. work — I've come to know that it's transmitted through contaminated needles. So I kept on asking him, and he kept on assuring me he used new needles. Anyway, it passed. And the rest is history.

My transition was a turning point in my life because people were simply amazed at what was happening. Number one, I lost eighty pounds. That alone would amaze a lot of people. Number two, I was turning into a woman. This, on top of the other, shocks people, to say the least. What used to be a fat, effeminate openly gay individual who sashayed through the corridors of the University of Hawai'i and the East-West Center, where I live, who was pimply faced and didn't have an ounce of self-respect for himself before, and who found solace in the books — suddenly turned into a social butterfly somehow, because . . . he transformed into a she. I was getting shapely, getting curves in the right places . . . My face has become extremely effeminized over time, and men and women have both expressed shock and amazement over what I've done with myself.

Some of the guys who I never thought would even say hello to me before as Rommel would smile and stop and say hello. And, if I'm not mistaken, some would even be hitting on me. This is self-affirming in a deeper sense because you won't hit on someone you don't like, at least in terms of physical attraction. So it was very reinforcing for myself to go through this experience. Except, at the same time that some people are amazed by the changes that I've gone through, others probably envy the spirit and determination that I had and the positive results that came out of it.

So you have a mixture of responses from people: amazement and admiration as well as envy and hate. Not to mention the fact that you're talking about a society which has not yet come to terms with its sexuality. And you are at the forefront. I mix with people who knew me before as Rommel. Yet now they see a different creature unfolding before their very eyes. An entirely new creature, in a different shell, in a different presentation to the outside world. So you expect all kinds of responses.

It's self-affirming sometimes to hear women themselves come up to me and say, "You're looking good," and actually mean it. Or men who actually hit on me or express their liking for me, or would even wink or smile when they see me — It's also affirming in a way which tells me I'm doing something good. Because my logic is that they wouldn't be doing that if they didn't think I looked good.

***

In terms of my professional experience, I did the transition when I was working at the East-West Center as a research assistant for my thesis advisor. It wasn't easy because some people, despite their education, are still burdened by their own prejudices and biases. So I had to deal with their biases and prejudices and learn how to deal with them in the most diplomatic way. Because we're talking about my profession. I think I succeeded quite well, actually, because I've always believed in the goodness of man and that everything will turn out right by themselves. Pettiness will never, ever win.

I remember when I gave notice to the director of the institute that I was going to start to wear a dress to work. She said to me, "Well, it's up to you. It's your life, it's up to you how you want your life." But it's the way how she said it, rather than what she said. I mean, I could say "hello" in different ways, which could be a receptive "hello" or a very caustic or acidic "hello." So in much the same way she was very condescending, to say the least. Perhaps she didn't think that I could actually pass. So the first time I wore a dress I came up to her office and I said, "Hello, Ma'am, I'm here." And you could see the shock on her face. *Because I looked good.* I was down to my lowest weight, I was lean as I could possibly be in all my life. I had that confidence about me in my gait and in the way

I held myself up because for the first time in my life I could look at myself in the mirror and say, "This is me." That's the source of all my happiness. I think that the people around me who cannot adjust to the fact that I am what I am are the ones who have the problem.

***

Every second of my life since I started my transition has been a challenge. Right now I think the biggest realistic challenge in my life is weight management, in terms of the physical part. Because the estrogen makes it difficult for you to really stop eating or gaining weight. The curves are developing, and the curves require fat deposits. So the tendency of the your body is to gain fat, water retention comes in naturally, and here you are — you'd like to keep the weight down to look more curvaceous and appealing, so it makes it difficult. So that's one of the challenges which I face right now. Easier said than done about exercise and dieting because I love to eat. I know how to cook and I love to cook.

The other challenge for me would be the successful integration into the mainstream society. I only started four years ago, so I'm still learning the ropes. I'm still going through what I would see as puberty one more time, but this time from the other side of the fence. It's learning everything, but this time relearning them as a woman, as a girl, not as a man. Although I cannot turn my back on that part of my life, because that's who I am, and that's the foundation for what I would be.

Another challenge is finishing my Ph.D., which is due soon. If I'm not mistaken, I would be the first transsexual to defend a dissertation at the University of Hawai'i, which makes me proud because I think it would pave the way for other transsexuals and transgendered women to follow in my footsteps of higher education. Remember what they say, "Be all you can be."

I've been offered a job at one of the state agencies, the Department of Health, and I'd like to take that job. But also I'm scouting around for some postdoctoral research fellowships that may applicable in my field, which is sexuality and HIV/AIDS, and I would like to focus on the GLBT community, in terms of the social dynamics of HIV/AIDS.

If I could find a teaching job too, I would like that because I think

I'm a natural teacher. I've already been teaching for a while. I usually teach courses in social statistics, survey research, research methods. . . . Lately I've taught sociological theory. Students like me and I like them because I'm more open and less repressed about my feelings. You're talking to someone who's wearing a. . . You're talking about a man wearing women's dresses. Now if that's not liberal or independent or flexible enough, I don't know what is. So I'm not subject to the same repressed feelings and anxieties that other repressed straights might have. So I can deal with students as their . . . older sister. Which makes me discharge my duties as a professor or instructor more efficiently, more smoothly.

I'll never forget the first time I stood in front of a class. It was a social statistics class. You could hear a pin drop when I got inside the classroom. Because it was still early on in my transition, and even up to now people can still tell quite a bit [that I'm transsexual], but back then people could actually tell. But I had to do it. I was quite scared at that time. But I made it. After the initial shock on the part of the students, we got along fine.

I like teaching, and teaching as a woman was something I had only dreamt about before. Teaching I dreamt about. But teaching *as* a woman — that's something which had been a double dream for me, and I was doing it for the first time in my life. So I was quite happy. The situation might not be perfect, but it was the situation that I had always dreamt about, so I was quite happy.

I did experience discrimination in trying to get teaching jobs. I could sense the reluctance on the part of those who were hiring me sometimes. In fact, at one of those jobs I had applied for the person alluded that my sexuality would create problems. I guess I've proven that person wrong because I got very good evaluations.

Being their teacher, I broaden students' horizons because they never thought that someone like me could actually be teaching them. The stereotypes or images they have of people like me are those walking the streets, drug addicts and drug pushers — in general, problematic people. I have problems of my own, but I am just lucky that I've stayed away from those problems. It's a matter of self-presentation, telling them that transgendered women are just like them.

***

In Hawai'i I think what helped me transition is that I'm Filipina; it's a multi-ethnic society here. So in a way that lessens the burden of bias against me. I am in a place where I'm not the minority, in terms of my racial background. If I had done the transition in a predominantly white area, they would have to deal with two features of my personality — my race and my sexuality. So here in Hawai'i, it's just a matter of focusing on the sexuality rather than the race. It was easier for me because I'm Filipino, which is one the biggest ethnic groups in the state. In fact, the governor himself is Filipino.

It's a lot more difficult to transition in the Philippines because I wouldn't have the access to the female hormones as much as I could when I'm here. Also because of the limited income I would have there; the stronger dollar makes it possible for me to access those hormones here. Back in the Philippines I might be able to do that, but at a much later time when I could already establish myself in my profession. Plus the fact that, although Philippine society is receptive towards its homosexual population, it is only to the extent that the gays do not intimidate them. So I think that someone with a Ph.D. would intimidate a lot of those straight men and straight women because they are more used to seeing transgendered, transsexual or gay men or women in fields like theater, arts and beauty parlors. They're not willing to accept the fact that there is a teacher who is a transsexual. So it's a lot more difficult there.

Plus, we do not have the laws which you have here in the United States that protect my rights as an individual, first and foremost, regardless of my sexuality. So in a way that makes it easier for me to live my life here.

Only my sister has been supportive. My brother and father have not been totally supportive. Even my sister is cautious about supporting me because of her loyalty to my brother and father, which is understandable. I think the more important point is that I still love them, despite how they feel towards me; I just pray that in time they will come to love me. Because of me, rather than what they see on the outside.

In the Philippines people have stereotypes of what a transsexual is. They don't see transsexual women in higher education. They refuse to acknowledge the truth that there are some of us who could actually invade the exclusive domain of the straight people, and we could actually debate and argue with them eye to eye, and make them beg for mercy. They can not accept that. And I was in statistics and the field of mathematics — can you imagine that? It's quite difficult for them to fathom that. "How can this gay faggot actually add one and one?" They may not say it directly, but it's not what you say but how you say things. It's the condescending tone and condescending context of what you're saying. So there's this bias and prejudice against transgendered people in general because there are preconceived notions of what we should be.

***

I've always loved wearing dresses. I like looking like a beautiful woman. I've always adored beautiful women, because I wanted to be them. I wanted to look like them. And being what I am now gives me a chance to actually try to become one of them, which I've been successful to some degree. Being pursued by guys, it's a wonderful feeling.

I don't know much about relationships yet as a transsexual woman. My serious relationship before was with a married man, which of course didn't work out. I'm now in a relationship, and I'm still learning the ropes of becoming a wife, a lover, best friend. I've been so used to being independent all my life, that it's difficult to unlearn some of the things I've done before, because I've always stood by myself, and now I share my life and make decisions not for myself alone but for me and my partner. Hopefully I would learn those ways in order for me to share my life with someone because it's not enough that you wear those pretty dresses and put on make-up and everything. It's also wonderful to have someone in your life to share your life with, to share your happiness with as a woman.

For me, a transsexual woman of the twenty-first century has her career, but at the same time is focused on her family, whatever that family may be. It may just be a husband, it may be a husband and an adopted child — because as transgendered women, the technology is not yet there for us to have the children. Who knows? Fifty years from now we may be that advanced. For me a woman is independent, has a career, is loving, is capable of all the feelings of any other genetic woman. And I believe that she is beautiful, both inside and out. That she shares compassion with other transgendered or transsexual women who have less circumstances than her. It's a matter of being gracious, of sharing whatever you have with the rest. Especially your fellow sisters. On the other hand, it means you have those petty jealousies and petty fights and conflicts with others over little things, too minor to even mention. I think a transsexual woman is just like any other human being; her goal is to live the life that she always wants to live. There are no limitations. The only limitations are in your mind.

JONZ

JONZ

My birth name is Jonz, but my stage names are Venetia Pleiades or Venice Alexio Chandelier. I'm twenty-nine years of age. I was born in Oklahoma, but I've lived here almost twenty years now. My father is full-blooded Native American, and my mother is half Hawaiian-Portuguese.

When I was about seven years old I discovered I was different from the other children. Because I liked Wonder Woman, I liked Charlie's Angels, I liked all those unsportslike television shows. And I liked old movies — Bette Davis, Joan Crawford, Lana Turner. I think what attracted me the most to these kinds of women was that they were strong enough to not need a man to save them. Yet they were able to maintain their femininity. That's what I liked about them. And that's what the stars of Hollywood of old had. They could still be vulnerable, but not give everything up for a man.

I had kept my feelings inside until about seventh grade, when I went to intermediate school. My aunt was a campus walker, and she was a dyke lesbian. So I felt safe and secure. I was more relaxed. I guess people just assumed, and they never questioned my sexuality or my interests. I went back into repression from about eighth grade until I was eighteen because I went to a couple of other schools where I wasn't as comfortable. AIDS had just come out too, so it was not a good time to be fully out and comfortable with yourself. There was a lot of ignorance back then.

I always wanted to be an entertainer. Growing up with Boy George, Dead Or Alive, David Bowie, I was thinking to myself — even when I was as young as ten — "That's me. That's going to me up there one day. I don't know how I'm going to do it, but I'm going to do it." I would always fantasize. I would play my music and imagine myself lip-syncing or singing the song, and putting on makeup and going on that stage and doing it. It wasn't until I was about twenty-four that the fantasy came to life.

Actually, after I was twenty-one, because I was experimenting with my life and stuff, I was more open and I got to meet more people who led me to believe that it's OK to be who we are. There was a point when I was going out to clubs; I was in a club-kid stage, not in drag yet, more like colored hair, wild makeup, ugly clothes. I think every person goes through that androgynous stage before they make the transition. But some don't cross over, they just perfect what they do. When I met the other queens I thought, "One day I want to be like that." I wanted to be an entertainment star, but then I also wanted to be like the queens, too. Because they got the attention, they got to do everything they wanted. So I said to myself, "I'll give it time." I was just getting comfortable, wading the waters, and then the transition went into place. I think it started just a few years ago. The makeup started getting better, I was looking more and more feminine, and the androgyny started fading away. I started experimenting with songs, seeing what worked with me, what didn't work. Just having that willingness to go out there and make a fool out of yourself in front of all these strangers. But at the same time building confidence in yourself. It was in '97 that I took it really seriously.

You know, you grow up with all these insecurities and fears, and I think the only way for me to overcome them was to go on that stage. Everybody could see me, flaws and all. And if you can go out there and do your stuff, even if the crowd doesn't like you, just give it all your best, and then you really come to terms with your insecurities. I know I have insecurities and I feel self-conscious about myself, but I'm going out there in front of all these people, do what I do, and then if they like it, they like it, and if they don't, well at least I'm strong enough and secure enough in myself to do that. And that brings me a step higher than I was before.

The first time I went on stage in full drag, it was in 1994 at Hula's [a gay bar] for some party. I had a catsuit on and I did this number and it was so horrible, the makeup was so horrible, but that's when I noticed,

OK, I know how I look, I know how I was, so I know how to improve on that. That's how it started. Then The House of Chandelier started around 1995, so we started having all these appearances. In 1996 we were at our height. Every week we were doing a show someplace. We opened for RuPaul, we did the Gay Pride Parade, we actually did a show in the parade, as it was going from Ala Moana Park to Kapiʻolani Park. We did fund-raisers, we entered pageants. So all that experience kept adding up. We were a new kind of entertainment.

We brought vaudeville back. Vaudeville and burlesque had been popular, but then it got too dated, and there was a lack of interest. So we hadn't had that for many years, so we decided to bring it back, but in our own style, a more colorful style. You know, some of us, when we were starting we were not that pretty, we were not that professional, but we just went out there and did the show, and people liked it. The costumes were colorful and we did props. Like in one show we made a little house and put it on the stage and moved it around . . . Every show we did always had props. Plus we used a lot of slapstick comedy, because somebody — myself — would always have a tendency to take a misstep or forget a piece. But instead of getting all upset about it, we created a comedy bit out of it. We'd end up pulling off each other's wigs, pushing each other down, grabbing people from the audience, pouring drinks on people . . . That's what made us unique. Because no matter what happened, we just went with the flow.

I don't have a structured style of performing. Each performance I do is always different. You can never predict what I'm going to do because I don't know what I'm going to do. If I slip and fall, then I guess I'll do a break dance or something, or strip, or roll around. If the wig falls off I just put it back on and continue. People like that. They like someone who can go up there and not walk off the stage and be embarrassed. Someone who can just have fun with it. That's what we did; that's what we were known for. That's what I still do.

I think I'm just letting myself go with the wind right now, seeing where it takes me, and being open to all my options. Because it's a very competitive business. For me right now it's an enjoyment. I don't want to make it into a career, because once you do that . . . Unless you're really dedicated to the craft, like that's what your set career is, otherwise it will turn into a business, and then you lose the whole interest of performing. Like with Dragon House. I'm doing this show just for experience. And I'm doing it to help me out. To see the different kinds of audiences there are out there. Trying to do the best I can. And if they still don't like me, well, at least I went out there and faced the music. So my future is . . . whatever happens, happens. And if you leave it like that, you might be very surprised at what happens. I mean, I never thought we'd perform for RuPaul or Alexis Arquette or Candis Cayne, or all these different people. Never in a million years.

When I first started performing in drag, what really surprised me was the following and attention. Because when I was growing up and in school, I was pretty much a loner child. I didn't have a lot of friends; I was a very lonely child. Even at home, I never got any attention, ever. So now as an entertainer, I feel more confident about myself and I like who I am; the popularity is amazing. Going someplace and somebody knows my name, even though I don't know who they are. It makes up for childhood. I guess it's like I'm having my second childhood right now.

My style is a cross between Lucille Ball and a B-movie . . . Oh, I know — a cross between Shannon Tweed and Lucille Ball. Campy glamour, that's what it is. So horrible that you've got to love it. And a little bit of Elvira . . . My style is funny, like a B-movie actress, from the 1950s. One of those movies where she's trapped on a planet and there are these creatures coming after her, and she has this space gun, with her corny lines. So that's my style, I'd say, my personality. But each time it's always different. It depends on how I feel.

When I'm on stage, I change. On the stage, even if I'm not feeling well, I still give it one hundred percent. That's really the only time my personality changes. Of course, I play the personality of whatever song comes on. And like I was saying about the actresses and how I had always wanted to be like them, when I'm on stage, it's my chance to be them, to be another person. I can be who I want to be on that stage, with everybody watching. And when I'm done, I turn back into myself again.

***

As long as we don't talk about it, my mom is fine with what I do. Because she still can't accept that whole side of myself. She's very conservative. On my mom's side of the family, my cousins enjoy it! My youngest aunt and my lesbian aunt, they love me regardless. They tell me that they'd rather see me do what I want to do and be happy than waste my life away and have regrets later in life. They really support me. My youngest aunt said, "You want to go out there and do this? Do it! You're young and you have your whole future ahead of you. I'd rather see you pursue it even if it doesn't work out because it's better than being old and saying, 'I should've done this, I should've done that.'"

My father's side is very interesting. I haven't seen my cousins for many years, and it's just now that I'm getting to know them again. They live in Oklahoma and they look at me like I'm a movie star. I talk to them about the shows . . . Living in Hawai'i, sometimes I take the whole scene out here for granted. But my cousins are living in a place where everything is black and white, so they don't have that around them. Anything they see is on E! Network or *Too Wong Foo* or *Priscilla*. So when I tell them that this is how I live, that this is my everyday thing, to them it's like, "Wow!" It's like I became a movie star. They're just in awe. They'll ask what kind of makeup I use, what kind of clothes I buy. They have all these questions. To them, it's like I'm living a fantasy life. For me, it's real, but for them it's different because they're not around it. It's like they're watching TV, with their cousin living that life.

As for my older relatives, I'd rather get to know them first. Then if they ask, I'll tell them. Because they're very conservative. I want them to trust me and get to know me better *and then*, when the timing is right, then I'll mention it. Because I'm not ashamed of it. I mean, if they ask me, I'll tell them.

I think it's much more tolerant here. Because Hawai'i is naturally a very together state. People look out for each other. The spirit of *aloha* is alive here. And moreso with the gay community, the transgender community, the lesbian community. That's what I like about Hawai'i — there's no segregation. When you go to the mainland . . . Let's take queens for example. You have Asian queens in one area, white queens, black queens, Latino queens, and they're all in groups. But when you come here . . . Well, yeah, you do have girls from this side of the island or that side of the island. But they all know each other and help each other out.

For example, if a girl from the Gender Benders show has a fund-raiser, all the girls from the different shows will come and support her. Whether they perform or not. Even if their own girl is also competing. Like for the upcoming Queen of Queens Pageant. We have Jerrine from the Paper Dolls and Maddy from the Gender Benders competing, and the support is just amazing. And they're supporting each other. Like if Maddy has a fund-raiser, naturally she'll invite her fellow contestants to perform. She'll announce that these are the girls who are also running. Fund-raisers on the mainland usually don't do it that way. They only feature themselves and their friends, their cliques. But in Hawai'i the togetherness is there.

I've had four friends of mine in the same pageant. So you cheer for them equally. Contestant number one — clap. Contestant number two — clap. Contestant number three . . . I'm tired already!! But that's what we have here — togetherness and support. There's none of that bitter-ness. None of that, "Why are *you* running?" Like when I run with my friends, it doesn't seem like a competition, but it's like you're having a show and you're all part of the package. A whole package of entertain-ment. And that's the way it should be. Not, "I want the title. I'm going to beat you." It's not like that here. Sometimes the girls on the mainland get *so* into it, *so* serious about it. They spend all this money, they do all this stuff . . . They forget why they do it. And that's sad. We do have it, but on a very small scale. We joke about it. We might say things, but it's all in good fun. But no matter what girl runs in a pageant, there's always equal support. I mean, you might like someone a little bit more, but the sup-port is always there for everybody. It's not like, "I want this person to win, so I'm not going to cheer for you." I'm going to cheer for everybody up there. So that's the difference I see between Hawai'i and the mainland.

I think that's why when a lot of the mainland girls come here, they like it. And that's what I like about Hawai'i — the sharing, the equalness, everybody being themselves.

***

Everyone knows about the Glades Revue. I don't know very much about it, but I know that it was the show of shows; they just went all out, they had the big hair, the loud makeup, what's known as "high drags." And they featured the legendary Prince Hanalei, the fire dancer, and all these other old-timers. I really feel that the Glades Revue set the pace for the drag shows in Hawai'i. That was during the 1960s and 1970s, when it wasn't OK to be like this. It was considered freakish and weird. But these girls went out and did it. They paved the road for us.

I don't remember much about the shows in the 1980s, but in the 1990s there were the Garbo's and Glitter Revue, Serena and Friends, and then the Paper Dolls came out. All those were more of the pretty girls. Everything was all pretty girls. It was good for the time because that was the introduction to the transsexual world. People would come in and they would be "Wow!" Because back then when people thought of a female impersonator, they would think of Uncle Miltie, that stereotypical image. But they would come here and see this person who looked just like a beautiful woman. They didn't know it wasn't a woman. And that was a trend in the early 1990s. Pretty, pretty, skinny girls. The Paper Dolls came out and Raquel G. Gregory, the MC, brought back the old Glades, she brought back the comedy, the loudness. The Gender Benders came out a few years after. And they were discovering themselves. I think they've really excelled. They appeal to the young set, the girls are pretty and very talented. Then we came out around the same time, and we spun off into Dragon House and The Pleiades. And we have our own unique style.

I remember when we performed at Ernest Lab Theater [at University of Hawai'i]. That was interesting. That was my very first theater performance. A nightclub is one thing, a ballroom is another. But a full theater is just . . . It's what the Muppet Show is like! When the curtain rises, all you see are all the faces looking up at you, and the light is really heavy . . . I had nowhere to hide! Because in a club, for me, I don't have stage fright. Sometimes you get a moment where you're just not feeling the crowd . . . Lucky for me, at Fusion, I can always work off somebody in the audience. If my friends are there, I can play off them. Pageantry is different. There's all that lighting, you're under all that pressure and

JONZ

stress, and you can't really work off anybody. Because you see *everybody* there. But theater is different. Theater is different because it's like you're in a box, a glass box, everything is all set. You know that the lighting is going to be here, so you've got to stand right here, or else you're going to look horrible. You've got to remember where all the setting is, and if you mess up on that, you mess up the whole thing. So that's a different kind of pressure from a pageant or club. Not like a club, unless you make your own set and do your own choreography. For me, I just go wherever. Because all I have is that spotlight. I can go here, I can go there. There's that freedom. Pageantry is different because you have to go in a limited area; it's like you're in a maze. You have to walk around and go up here and go up there; it's all structured. Theater is different because everything is all constructed around sets. So you can't play on this side if you're meant to be on the other side.

For me, clubs are easier. The lighting isn't as harsh. And there's that freedom to just go with it. So if you trip and fall, it's not ruined. It's not going to mess up everybody else. You just go with it. Wig falls off? Just put it back on again, and continue the song. Lucky for me, and I knock on wood for this, but I thank God that whenever things happen to me, they always happen at the right time in the song, where I can play it off. The first time I noticed that, it was a political fund-raiser for Tracy Ryan. I think she was running for City Council. And I did Diana Ross for the first time. Big mistake. I ran out, I tripped on the stage and plop! Right in front of the whole City Council! Andy Miratakani, Patsy Nino, Neil Abercrombie . . . I just saw the shock on their faces. And it was just at the point in the song where it says, "I was so right / I could feel the emotions." And I just got up . . . because I *had* to. I didn't want it to look like I fell. So I made it look like I fell and then was rising up. That's when I learned that when you fall, you just go with it. Lucky for me, with the songs I've chosen, when I slip, when I slide, or when I lose my balance, it happens at a time in the song when it suggests something I can play off of. Or I'll slap somebody or take their money or something. And that gets people going! They like that! Because they think I staged it. But it's *not* staged! Because I'm naturally clumsy. So when I'm on that stage in heels and on that slippery floor . . .

I remember for one number I did, I was with two military boys, and they really didn't know what they were doing. At one point I was turning around behind them, and all of a sudden I slipped. So to save face, I dove right between their legs. And they're looking at me like, "Woah — What was that?! Do it again!" I was like, "No, I'm not going to do it again!" And there are times when I'll do these wild turns, but they're just to save my face. I think you can apply this to your everyday life. Because people are all set on how you ought to live life, you have to do things a certain way, and if it doesn't go, you get upset. But I know now that if something falls, you just have to live with it. If something doesn't work out, you just have to go on and continue. I mean, if I can go and fall in front of all these people and still continue the show, any disappointments I have in life, I just have to work with them. This didn't work out, so I'll just have to make the best of it, or try something else.

I think I'm very lucky to live here, in a place where you can be accepted for who you are. I don't know what it's like growing up transgendered on the mainland, but I think because in Hawai'i there's just so much acceptance, it's easier. Even with my co-workers. When I told them I was a showgirl, they were all excited! They asked me, "Do you know this person? Do you know that person?" Because they're either a classmate, or a cousin, or a sister . . . A lot of my co-workers used to go to the Glades shows when they were my age or younger. So they see it as someone carrying on the tradition.

I mean, for the Glades Revue, there were busloads of people, families, honeymoon couples, for anniversaries. I remember once at Fusion there were two things I saw happen which just amazed me. There was a bachelor party at the Gender Bender Lip Gloss Revue. And I was like, "Wow." They were all *haole* guys. And the bachelor guy, he was in this black and white striped outfit, with a ball and chain! I remember another time, there was a group of around twelve men, all sitting in the back just watching the show. They were big Samoan guys. I thought, "Hmm, this is interesting." It showed me how open minded these people were, to come and watch this.

Sometimes people do say negative stuff, but I've learned to deal with it. I'm so used to it. Because in high school it was worse, I was yelled at. I've always been put down. You get used to that, you become immune to it. Because you just tell yourself that you're secure about who you are. At least I can ask, "Can you be true to yourself?" At least I'm doing what I want to do and I'm doing it how I want to do it. Not all of us can. That's why some people become insecure — they feel threatened because this person can be who they are, and they can't. They have these set guidelines for how they're supposed to live, what they're supposed to be like.

I think the younger generation of performers are more free to explore. They don't have the hesitation that we did. "Oh, should we try this out?" People are more accepting now, so they're just free to be. They're very uninhibited, and that's always good. I mean, you already have society telling you, "You can't do this. You can't do that." So you don't need to be doubting yourself, "Can I do this? Can I do that?" The problem, though, is that some of them have the tendency to forget the people before them. And I've always made this point on stage; I've always said, "I'm glad I'm here today because of the generations who came before me." I'll dedicate numbers to them. Like if I'm doing an old disco number and there are old-timers in the audience, I'll say, "This goes to the Glades girls because if it weren't for them, I would not be standing up here today making a fool out of myself. It's because of them that I'm not getting arrested or getting shot at or being ripped at. Thank you."

TRACY AHN RYAN

TRACY AHN RYAN

I'm forty-four years old, and I came to Hawai'i in 1974 from Connecticut. I came out here with the intention of going to school, which I did; I graduated from the University of Hawai'i. I had a lot of issues when I came. I wanted to be far away from my family, and this seemed like a good idea. The first year I was here, I was still trying to deny who I was. I didn't want to be transgendered. I was living a phony life, trying to pretend. And I couldn't live that way. So about a year after I got here I told my college roommate that I wanted to cross-dress. I had been crossdressing secretly while I was growing up, but that started me openly doing it. Then I discovered that there is a community here of a lot of transgendered people. I found some friends who were transgendered, and I hung out with them for several years while I was in college. I wanted to go full-time [as a woman] early on, but I made some bad judgments.

I bought a beauty shop. I thought I could run the beauty shop because then I could have an income and I could be any way I wanted to. But it didn't work out that way. Instead, it ended up costing me a lot of money, and I had to work in a straight job as a man in order to pay all the bills I had. So then I got depressed, and I drank a lot. I was pretty much an alcoholic for years. In 1986 I decided I had enough of that. I woke up. I had a moment where I said, "Wait, I know what I want in life. Why can't I do that?" That's when I started transitioning, and set up what I wanted to do. And since then . . . Well, I've been living full time [as a woman] since . . . 1991, I think.

I went about my transition in a fairly organized way. Before I transitioned, I used to go out on weekends. I would dress up and go out

191

and go shopping or something, go to Ala Moana [shopping mall]. The problem I had as a cross-dresser, before I transitioned, was that I had beard shadow problems. I had to wear a lot of make-up. Plus, I had neighbors. I always wanted to pass, so I had to wear a wig. In the tropics these are big negatives, especially if you go out during the day. And one of the things I wanted to do in transitioning was to go through electrolysis, so that I could go out as myself and not have to be in disguise. I mean, that's the whole point of transitioning. Once I did the electrolysis I felt that I was pretty much ready.

Then I had to go and get my name changed. When I first went to do this, I found that they didn't want to give me an ID with an "f" on it. That was around 1990. I thought that was really irritating, so I got some political help. I went to the legislature and talked about my problem to some people down there who I knew were gay-friendly. I spent about a year fighting with Hawai'i's Attorney General's office on this ID policy before they agreed to change it. Eventually they agreed that I could get a civil identification card and leave off the gender altogether, which meant I'd have a blank card. So that kind of suited me at the time.

Then I was ready. I had changed my name; I'd had electrolysis; my hair was long. When I went out, people were mistaking me for a girl. Even if I went out in men's clothes, I got called "she" a lot. So I figured the time was right.

Then the issue was, How I am going to deal with my career? Because that's always an issue. Are you going to be able to have a job? I knew I was very valuable to the company in which I was working. I work in a small company, tax accounting. I work personally with a lot of important clients with whom I'd built up a rapport, so I knew that investment in my career was there for me. That being the case, it wasn't too difficult because everybody wanted me stay on and just become Tracy. They were cool with that. So I really didn't have a lot of problems.

Now, I can't compare that with how it might have been on the mainland. I think that in Hawai'i the attitudes are a lot better because transgenderism is a lot more open and known about here. It's not necessarily respected, but it's understood better, it's seen more. The visibility makes people more used to dealing with it than in various mainland places. Here's a real simple comparison: where I grew up in Connecticut, the idea of being transgendered in school — in high school — is just . . . like a fantasy for anybody who's like me. But you come out here, and there are lots of transgendered people in the schools, even in the junior high schools, who are braiding their hair, wearing make-up, and being very open about it. Of course, they get some grief, being in a teenage situation — teenagers are like that. But it's a much different mindset. There's the idea that *it can be done*, existing within the person who wants to do it. And that makes a big difference.

A lot of people have various problems with their transition, and there are different things which create problems for you. The three biggest problems are, first, where you transition — and like I said, I think Hawai'i is a better place than maybe some other venues. Second, your attitude about your transition. It's very important what your mindset is. If you view yourself as someone who is going to be discriminated against, who is going to be facing obstacles, who is touchy and unsure about yourself, then that attitude translates into the attitude that people pick up around you, and they react exactly the way you predict. I think you really have to make as positive a thing about this as you can. For instance, if you say you're going to tell your family, then you shouldn't go and tell them, "I have this great *problem* to talk to you about." That's *not* the way to approach it. You have to have a positive attitude about yourself, and you have to feel that if some people are not going to accept you as a transsexual, so be it. Some people wouldn't have accepted you as a straight person. That's just the way life is. You can't run your life worrying about what everybody else is going to think. So you have to have a good attitude about what you're doing.

The third — and most obvious — thing, which I don't think is necessarily the most important, is of course your own ability to pass yourself off in your new gender. If you're very large and very hairy, or bald or if you have a very deep voice, then you're not going to be able to pass. Therefore you're going to have to deal with your transgenderism on a day-to-day basis. In Hawai'i there are a lot of transgendered people who are very what we call "fishy" — they're petite, they've got very Asian features, they have very delicate bone structure, not much body hair.

They transition and people see them as women quick quick quick [snaps fingers], like that, and there's not an issue of them being transgendered, so their transition is easy. With someone who doesn't necessarily pass, it takes a bit more fortitude and a bit more guts.

One of the ironies in our [transgender] community is that we all have a tendency to look up to the people who are prettier. There's very much a pecking order . . . We have our pageants, and we really admire the people who pass. We want to hang around them, we want to be like them . . . But if we think about it, the real heroes in our community are the people who don't pass and can't pass, who go out there every day and live their lives, and just try to get along with people and not develop a real hostile attitude about it. So a problem that many transgendered people face is that the physical aspect of transitioning is enormously expensive and difficult, and it's not helped in any way by an unaccepting culture.

Our community itself has a lot of pathos. There's a lot of pathos out there. There's so much wonder and joy in beauty, and in pageantry, and the affection the girls generate for each other. And there's so much pain in being a pariah in the community, and not having a broader community understanding of how much our little community has to offer the big community of the straight world. We have a lot to offer. For example, a lot to offer in helping men and women understand each other better. A lot to offer in a lot of ways. We've got art, we've got entertainment, we've got all sorts of talents. We need people to understand that.

***

There were people before HTGO [Hawai'i Transgendered Outreach] who had been doing things on and off with support groups. I have to give Bill Woods some credit. He was active in what was called the Sexual Identity Center, and what is now called the Gay and Lesbian Community Center. Over a period of several years he had run support groups, and I went to one in about 1988. It wasn't that good at that point; numbers had come down from what they had been earlier. And with most support groups, you kind of see they are like waves, there's an up and down. Then I met this guy named John, who's a cross-dresser. We talked about the need for a group. Then we had a couple of other people we had met who were cross-dressers. They all came together, and we talked about having a group. So we said, "Let's just do it, and we'll have meetings at John's place."

At that time, the Gay and Lesbian Center had a referral service, and they started referring people to us. We also started getting the word out on it, so pretty soon we had a group that met every two weeks, and it's been meeting pretty consistently every two weeks with a group anywhere from eight to twenty-five people for ten years now. So the support group has been a large success. Over the years, I think over 200 people have come to those meetings.

I think the group filled a very good niche, especially for people who are transitioning. These are people who are living in the male role . . . a lot of them are married, and they need an outlet for their cross-dressing. Or they feel they're transsexual and they need to know where to start. I think a lot of people have come in just as beginners, been with HTGO for several years, and really gone through the whole transition, right through surgery. So I think we fill a very important role in the community.

For a long time we had a newsletter which covered pageants and the community at large, not just the smaller community which was involved in our support group. But since I left the group, nobody's been interested in continuing the newsletter. I guess it's too much work. So it died out. But it's a good thing to do, because obviously we have a very large community in Hawai'i, a very open community. We have hundreds and hundreds of people who go to pageants, who aren't necessarily going to be joining up with a support group, so I've always felt that it was important to tie the entire community together with something. I think the newsletter was useful in doing that.

I think the transgender community here in Hawai'i is similar to those in some places on the US mainland. Generally our community is divided according to aspects of transgenderedism, and also along class lines. There seems to be an orientation towards gay / transsexual / working class on one side, and straight / cross-dresser / middle class on the other side. These are two completely different communities. Now obviously this is a very simplistic way to look at it — there is a lot of overlap between these two groups. But when I look at the community, I see that there are a lot of transgendered people who are very closeted and try to live a very male role. This is what I see as a very middle class pattern. It's a pattern that I went through, it's a pattern that a lot of the people who come to HTGO have gone through, and it's a pattern that most of the people who have come to Hawai'i, who have moved here from the mainland, have gone through. Most of these people who've transitioned here came over from the mainland in their thirties or forties, and used that route to our community.

Then in the local community I see people who have come from poor and working class backgrounds, mostly people of color — Hawaiian people, Filipino people, various Asian and Polynesian people, and some local Portuguese people, and working class, lower class people — who transition in their middle to late teens, rather than in their forties. They never go through the male stage. Rather, they're involved in an entire cultural phenomenon that ties them to the gay community, to prostitution and to street life. They develop an entirely different world view, an attitude about things different from what this other community has.

All the time that I've been here, I've felt that although people have different aspects to themselves and live in different communities, it's important that they understand and try to support each other. There's been more of that in the last ten years, thanks to HTGO and other groups. But there's still a long way to go, and there's a long way to go on the mainland. When I look at the transgendered community on the mainland, I see that, to a very large degree, it's oriented towards a middle class attitude, and towards people who transition late in life. It doesn't reflect a large number of transgendered people within inner cities in the United States, who are Mexican-Americans, Latinos, Blacks, poor people, etc., who are largely engaged in prostitution and may be engaged in drugs, but also who are very much interested in developing themselves in terms of their attractiveness. They're into pageants and beauty and the culture of femininity and a lot of things which the middle class group doesn't have in common with them.

So it's kind of been a division which I think everybody in our community recognizes. I think that it's OK that there's more than one community, as long as people don't have an attitude about it. That's more or less a problem. It's tough to build bridges, and you really have to have a strong political mind, a diplomatic mind, to help bridge those gulfs.

The other thing I see is that the middle class group has a lot of leadership. In fact, a lot of times it seems that we have too much leadership; we have too many self-appointed leaders, too many leaders who don't really have any followers. And of course, if you're really a leader, that means you have followers. It doesn't mean you've decided you're a leader, it means that there are people who actually look to you to make decisions and to represent them.

On the other side, in the working class group and among the people who are more involved in street culture, there seems to be the opposite problem: there is a lack of leadership and it's almost each person for themselves. There's an over-competitiveness. There's a lot of rivalry, a lot of rivalry on the streets. There's camaraderie and support in prostitution among transgendered people, but it also tends to lead to rivalries over various issues that come up on the streets. There is rivalry which is fermented in competition, such as the pageants. Pageants can be fun, but girls can get very competitive and jealous of each other. They can lose sight of the fact that in being transsexual, we're all in the same boat.

We've got to realize that the other girl who may have pulled off a big stunt and beat you in the pageant isn't really your enemy. Rather, it's the guy who is trying to get you arrested for sodomy or prostitution, or keep you from having the straight job that you want. *That's* the person you should be focusing on and trying to bring around, not one of your sisters who you're competing against. And that's a lesson that I don't think has been fully absorbed in that area of our community.

It has gotten better. Now there is a realization of the importance of unity and political working and organization, moreso than there was ten years ago. There's a better understanding of the variety within our own community. For example, I've talked to people who are local, who grew up in Hawai'i, who are familiar with the street aspects of transgenderedism, and to them, the idea that any queen — in Hawai'i we call transgendered people "queens" — would go with a woman . . . ten years ago it was a taboo. If you were going to be a queen, then of course you were interested in men. But now that attitude is largely changing. What we find is that there are more local queens who are and have been involved in street culture, and who have transitioned when they were fourteen and fifteen, been women their whole adult lives, basically not had any experience as men, but have still ended up in relationships with lesbians. Not with heterosexual women, but with masculine women. And that's become something that's accepted among queens; it's no longer viewed in a negative way because it's become more common, and people have said, "OK, well, that's fine."

***

Prostitution has been the royal road of the transsexual for thousands of years. Things are different now. There is an accepted role . . . not completely accepted, but an acceptable role for a lot of people working in straight jobs who are transsexual. This is a great relief to those who have come from the middle class group, because many of them could never deal with what the prostitute deals with. Particularly if they are heterosexually oriented, it wouldn't be appealing at all. But for the younger queens, people starting at fifteen and sixteen, they're males, they have a male hormonal level, they're attracted to men, they're effeminate, they're in a high school situation — which is probably somewhat abusive, and certainly not friendly — but they can get themselves dolled up and go out on the street and have sexual encounters with good-looking straight men and get money for it. It's very appealing to a lot of young people who are oriented this way.

Plus, the streets have been a nurturing environment for our community to a certain extent. Now in saying that, I'm not condoning or defending them. I'm just saying that prostitution has been the only role a lot of girls in our community have been able to survive in. It's given them an income; it's given them a position in the world; it's given them some feeling that they are of use to somebody for something; it's given them the income they've needed to pay for their surgery to transition; it's given them a sense of community . . . It's like going to work and seeing your coworkers.

This is very different from female prostitution on the streets where female prostitutes are mostly isolated from each other, except for the one or two other girls who have the same pimp. Everyone else is a rival, not a friend. With the transsexuals, there are no pimps involved, they're just all your friends. You go out and see the girls you see every night, the people with the same interests as you, the people who are in the same pariah class as you, so you identify with them. There is a tight bond which builds up out there, which is a very nice thing to have.

Of course, you have a lot of negatives, as well. You have violence, the risk of death, AIDS, and you have the potential for very serious drug problems. Drug problems . . . I get different responses when I ask different people from the streets how they look at the current versus past drug problems. One friend of mine who has been down there for fifteen - twenty years says, "Well, most of these hard drugs which are there now have always been there. We had ice fifteen years ago, we had cocaine fifteen years ago." But then you'll talk to other girls who'll say, "Fifteen years ago most everyone stuck to marijuana. And nowadays it's different; ice and crack are endemic."

As a political measure, I like to blame the government's crackdown on marijuana for doing this, and this is the most common view on the streets. But the girls who are using ice and crack will only say nice things about these drugs — while they're using. So you're not going to get a full range of opinions from people who are actively using down there. I think it's unfortunate because some of the these other drugs tend to . . . I think they make people less friendly, less mellow. It breaks down some of the feeling of comraderie and sisterhood that used to go on down there.

I mean, it used to be, that was the route that queens took. You would have a mother queen down there. You would leave home when you were fourteen or fifteen. A lot of them would be thrown out of their houses. So they would go to live with other queens who would teach them how to be prostitutes. I've heard from straight outreach workers who worked with AIDS and stuff, who saw this as a terrible thing — "Here we are, taking our own sisters and turning them into prostitutes." But they didn't really understand the culture of our community — prostitution is not viewed that way by this community; it's part of the culture. It's an economic necessity.

You go when you're fifteen years old to live with a thirty-five year old prostitute, and she cannot support you. So she's going to teach you how to survive, and the way she knows how to do that is through prostitution. It would be fine in our minds if we could get you a law degree, but it's just not going to happen. It's just not realistic. Realistically, even in 2000 Hawai'i, the fact is that for a lot of transsexuals, the route to survival is still going to be in prostitution. And what I see is that we should try, as a community, to make prostitution as safe and as respectable an occupation as we can, if we're going to deal with that reality.

***

There is some discrimination against transgendered people here in Hawai'i. I know of a number of cases, four or five, about one or two a year, where girls are doing perfectly fine in straight jobs . . . Then new management comes in or there's some change, and someone discovers that this person is not a woman. These are usually cases where people are hired on the understanding that they are a woman. Then it's determined that they're not, and they're just fired — "Get out! You can't work here." Or, "You can only work here as a man. Cut your hair and come back in slacks, dear." And this is just not reasonable.

There's been some discussion in the transgendered community about whether we should push for inclusion in anti-discrimination in employment, for it to cover us. In the situations I'm talking about, we should be able to fight under sex discrimination. Because in a situation where you're hired and people see you and understand you to be female, and you're doing a perfectly good job, but later on they discover that you're transgendered and they fire you — that's sex discrimination. The only thing they fired you for is that they found out you had a penis. That's classic sex discrimination. So you should be covered in those cases. And we've made that point. But the problem we've had with most of these cases is that transgendered people won't fight. They just walk. They may try to fight but they get discouraged. They may leave town, they may go back into prostitution, go back into drugs, get depressed . . . We've had a number of negative things go on with these situations. So it's been very rare that we've been able to mount an effort to fight this discrimination.

But a secondary problem is that a lot of these people don't have adequate job skills. If you're looking to spend seven thousand dollars on surgery X and five thousand on surgery Y, and you want electrolysis and hormones, you're not going to do it making six dollars an hour working at Burger King. And believe me, you could get hired. Queens will get hired at fast food places to work counters because in Hawai'i most of the counter workers are foreign and have accents. Employers like to hire people who can speak good English because the customers are more comfortable with that. So queens can get hired to work in entry level jobs, if they're willing to do that. Again, the problem with the entry level job is that if you're going the transsexual route, it's simply not going to pay your bills. So if you get into a nicer job . . . You know, a lot of the people who work in prostitution and are transgendered are fairly intelligent people. It's not any kind of a stereotype. They're intelligent, they have abilities, some have some college background. They're worthwhile people. So it's out there.

The situation in Hawai'i is one where transsexuals were doing much better in the work place when we had a very tight labor market. If we go back to 1989, '90, '91, we had a very tight labor market, with a labor shortage. The de facto minimum wage was about a dollar an hour over the legal minimum wage. Nobody made less than about seven dollars an hour. Even in fast food, where the legal minimum wage was like four fifty because of the labor shortage. And at that point a lot of transgendered people left prostitution and moved into straight jobs.

Now, in the last ten years what's happened is that our Hawaiian economy has suffered terribly. We've been in recession for about ten years. The only thing that has kept massive unemployment from occurring here is that we've lost about one hundred thousand people to the mainland. About a hundred thousand people have left the most beautiful place in the world to move to the mainland for employment. And they are mostly young, productive people. For transgendered people that's actually been a bit of a help. They have stayed here because of their local roots and because they feel more comfortable in Hawai'i. Most of us have stayed here, even though there is discrimination in Hawai'i. I am familiar with the business world, and I believe that most business people are really much more interested in how much money you're going to make for the company. If you make money for the company, they don't give a damn who you are or what you look like. That's the truth. If enough transgendered people understand that, and find the companies which are willing to look at you in terms of productivity — and most companies will — then you'll be OK. Occasionally you will find employers who are pricks. That's going to happen. But if you get into a good local company and stay with it, you should be able to handle it.

***

I ran for the Hawai'i State Senate in 1996 as a member of the Libertarian party. . . I first got involved in politics when I learned that the penalty for prostitution was going to be changed to six months in jail. One of my best friends is a prostitute; I'd seen her go to jail for thirty days. She is a very nice person. It was completely senseless. So I got mad. I went down to the legislature. I took time off from work. I organized people. I banged the drums, I fought the legislature. And the governor vetoed the bill. The Libertarian party is in favor of ending laws against prostitution, so that's why I got involved with it.

I didn't know anything about running for office. No one in the Libertarian party had ever been elected and they didn't know anything about running a campaign; they were giving me advice so bad it was laughable. The national party has some very good brochures, but I didn't have them available when I ran. I had friends in the Democratic party, and I asked them about running campaigns, and they happily told me A, B and C. So at least I knew A, B and C, and I knew that I would need to try to raise twenty-five thousand dollars. I also could copy . . . I saw what my opponent was doing, in terms of literature and what the look was, so I just copied her. I figured she was in office, so she must know something. She sent out a four by six inch card with a picture of herself on it and some of her accomplishments, so I sent out a four by six card with a picture of myself, and some of the reasons to vote for me. I just copied what she was doing.

During the 1996 campaign we had Dragathon. That was our fund-raiser. The queens came out and they performed for me. We sold tickets . . . I think they were twenty dollars each. We had it at the Dole Cannery, which has a nice big ballroom. But it was kind of disappointing because the campaign people hadn't organized the marketing very well, so we ended up having to really hustle tickets. We had it in October, and you should really have that kind of thing in March. So we made a lot of mistakes. But it was good fun. I had a lot of straight people come who were supporting my campaign, and they enjoyed themselves.

It was good to see the community together and understand that there was something we could do as transgendered people other than sit back and take it. It was something we could really do. So it was a very gratifying experience. I made a little twenty minute speech. It was a "bring us together and support each other" type speech. I said that the reason I supported prostitutes and drug addicts was because I don't feel that I'm any better than these people. I may be a college graduate and this that and the other thing, but we're really all in the same boat, and if we don't stick together, the boat is just going to sink.

In the end, we didn't get enough money, just thirteen thousand dollars. Plus, I wasn't a very good candidate. I realized that I was much better at debating and talking about issues than I was going out door to door and meeting people and being a glad-hander. Luckily, the lady I ran against didn't seem to like campaigning any more than I did, and was probably happy she didn't have to do it. She is a very nice, Asian woman, a very nice lady, but kind of like me — very shy about doing all this that goes along with being political.

It was a very interesting experience. I heard later from my Democratic friends that my opponent didn't know what to make of my campaign. I think people were surprised that I did as well as I did. I was kind of disappointed, I thought I should have done better. We got thirty-one percent in a head-to-head race, she got sixty-nine percent. And the Libertarian party was excited, because they're used to getting like ten or fifteen percent, even in head-to-head races. I did better than any

Libertarian candidate in the United States in a state legislative race, in terms of the vote.

I know that a lot of my votes were earned, they weren't just protest votes. People heard my message, liked what I had to say, and voted for me. So we did have an effect. Plus it was a good district for us. This Makiki district is kind of a swing district; there's a good balance of Republicans and Democrats. The Republicans are a fairly moderate group in Makiki; there are not a lot of socially conservative people. The Democrats are fairly moderate. They're socially fairly liberal, but they're not necessarily big spending liberals. So it was a good district for me to run in with my message. And I think that kind of helped.

After the campaign I wrote my post-mortems in the gay press and the Libertarian press, and I was very proud by the selection of people who supported me. I had Republicans supporting me, I had Democrats supporting me, I had liberals, conservatives, business people, welfare people, old people, drug addicts. And I had people who were working in prostitution, who were not just voting for me but who were going out and volunteering and doing work for me and raising money for me. And you don't see prostitutes doing very much of anything beyond the end of their own nose. So I was very, very proud of the people who supported me. I found it a very edifying experience to have done that and to realize that I had given a lot of people in our community something . . . something better, something to hope for. Something to say that, "Yes, we matter."

I've learned a lot in the five years I've been involved in politics. I went in very naively, like most people do, with a lot of principles, and not a lot of sense. So I got kicked around. It takes time to understand the system, and to understand that you don't have many real enemies in politics. What you have is a lot of bad ideas and basically some bad systems, bad systems which chew up good people. There are bad ideas which aren't rebutted publicly, because there isn't any financial interest in rebutting them. That's what you have in politics.

I think the real key is to get people to learn that the art of politics is the art of making friends, not the art of making enemies. Once you learn how to operate in the system, it can be a beautiful thing. But we as a community, the transgendered community, haven't learned that. The gay community has learned it to a certain degree; the transgendered community hasn't learned it at all. And I see transgendered people who want to be political, and they try to copy what gay people have done, without the money and the votes behind them that the gay community has, and they don't understand why they're not succeeding. And they don't understand the role of numbers in politics, how power is manipulated in politics. So they don't succeed. And they also focus very narrowly on transsexual rights, which to me is not the way we will win our rights.

Winning our rights means focusing on other people's issues, working on other people's problems, putting ourselves into the community in a way so that liberals, conservatives, bankers, gravediggers, all sorts of people can come into contact with us and see us as a viable part of the community, not as some pariah group only interested in screaming about their own rights. And when we do that, then we can go into the same mode that the gay community has, and say, "Look, we're everywhere. We're part of you. We're in your lives, we're doing all these things in the community." And then people will say, "Gee. I feel a little bit differently." We have got to demonstrate to people that we're worth having rights, and then we'll have the respect and we won't *need* to fight for our rights because we'll have the respect anyway. So that's got to be the first thing.

I work politically with a lot of conservative groups. I'm not afraid to go and work with them on their issues. And I've been very surprised that when you stop talking about one or two things which are of interest to you and listen to some other people's issues, and can find the common interest, it makes things a lot smoother among people you originally thought were no so friendly. So I've developed very good relations with a lot of very conservative people, with business people, with Republican people. I am not making the point that achieving transsexual rights is a liberal democratic agenda that I am pushing. Had I done that, I would have encountered the same resistance faced by the people who believe this is how we will achieve our rights. Sometimes it's easier to go in the back door than the front door, because the front door is the one which has got all the guards.

Every year there's another anti-prostitution bill to fight. Every two years there's another campaign to organize and get involved in. I may run for another race in 2002. People are always asking me about that; we'll just have to wait and see . . .

I'm Hawaiian-Filipino-Indian-German-Spanish. Give me tequila and I think I'm Pocahontas! I was born here in Honolulu, although my ancestors come from the Big Island . . .

Growing up I had a really tough time. I left home at sixteen — that's when I decided to become transgendered. At the time my mom was living in New York City and I was staying with an aunt and her husband. When I decided to transition I told my aunt and uncle, who were my legal guardians, that I wanted to "come out." Of course they thought something was definitely dysfunctional with me. My poor aunt cried her heart out, while uncle tried his best to help me understand that the decision I was making would end up leading to severe ramifications. But I didn't care what I was headed for — I just wanted to experience a side of me that kept yearning to "come out" and express itself.

Deep down inside I knew my auntie and uncle loved me very much, and that they were just scared and worried about how hard it would be for me to be accepted in the world because of the lifestyle I was choosing. Eventually our discussion ended with the decision that I could not transition until I was old enough to move out on my own.

I totally disagreed with their decision, and felt it was time for me to move on . . . At that moment I headed for my room and began packing up my things in two big plastic trash bags. Then I left — and never went back.

I went to live with a lesbian couple who seemed very supportive of me being gay. But they advised me not to transition because of the health problems that might happen if I underwent hormone therapy. I considered their advice, but thoughts of transitioning still burned inside me like a torch held by night marchers finding their way through the darkness . . .

So there I went again, back on the move. This time I went to live with another auntie. This aunt said I could stay with her and transition if I wanted to. Yes!! I had finally found someone who was willing to support me. So, with written consent from my aunt, I underwent hormone therapy. I was sixteen. Within three months my physical appearance began to change; I was looking more feminine. All my aunt requested from me was that I continue to go to school.

So I stayed enrolled in Farrington High School. There were several other TGs who were in school at the same time, and that made things a little more comfortable for me. Although we had our own little cliques we would see each other at pep-rallies, school plays, and other school events. One of the TGs was named Madonna, and I owe her a lot of credit. She taught me a lot of different things about being transgender. She encouraged me to keep on going even when other people put me down. I remember her always using that line, "Girl, they're just J [jealous]."

There was an incident that happened in school one day . . . I went to the cafeteria to have lunch when a male student stood up from his seat, pointed at me and yelled, "faggot!" Then he threw his open milk at me. So I threw my entire lunch plate at him — he felt humiliated because mash potatoes and gravy were all over his face! He picked up his plate and threw it at me, but I ducked, so it hit some other student, who started to throw *his* food . . . Then everyone in the cafeteria began throwing their food! I stayed ducked down and got out of there fast. Afterwards, the school security campus walker came looking for me and escorted me to the principal's office. Later I was expelled. So I eventually gave up on school and began attending GED classes . . . I received my diploma last year.

***

As time passed I engaged in prostitution. I'm not going to lie — it was fun! I made money — and lots of it — but silly me spent it foolishly. The men made me feel so lovely! They bought me a lot of exciting things — designer bags, pagers, stockings, a cellular phone, dildoes, you name it. [laughs] Out on the streets the other girls were really nice people. It was like one huge support group for transgenders. Regardlesss of what we were doing, everyone knew each other and respected one another. If not, you were taught fast! When I was eighteen my mother came back from New York City. She wanted to see me. This was because she had heard a lot of things from other people about me, and she needed to see for herself. When she did get in contact with me I was doing the hotel-hopping bit with a few other TGs.

I can clearly remember that day when the phone rang and it was her. Oh my gosh — I didn't want to answer it! I didn't know what to expect, but my roommate kept saying, "Just talk to her." I grabbed the phone and answered, "Yes?" She called me by my butch name, and asked me to come and see her now. I told her I couldn't because it was 2am and I didn't have a ride. She asked me to come early in the morning and I agreed. After I hung up I thought to myself that I should run away . . . So many negative thoughts kept going through my mind. Finally I said to myself, "Face it!" And that's exactly what I did the next day.

In the morning I took a taxi to my aunt's house and walked up to the front door. My mother looked straight at me and asked if I was her son. I said, "Yes, mom, it's me." She reached out and hugged me so hard and long that I was nearly out of breath. Then we sat for a long time . . . We discussed how I was doing and what I was doing. I was honest; I told her I was prostituting. But she didn't seem that upset, which puzzled me. Later I found out that my auntie had brought her to the area where I worked as a prostitute, and both of them had seen me working. Right after that both my mom and aunt went straight to the bar and got drunk!

My mother didn't want me prostituting but couldn't really do anything about it, so all she asked was that I take care of myself and be careful at all times while I was out there. She also asked me to keep in touch with her.

Now that my mother knew the truth about what I was doing, I felt free to do what I wanted — I didn't have to answer to anybody anymore! I continued to hustle big time . . . I considered myself a bonafide prostitute! I worked in bars and for escort services, but I also held a

211

straight job to make it look like I was doing good in the eyes of those who credited me for at least holding a "real job." Everything seemed flawless until I got hit on the head with a crowbar . . . I had met a guy in town who wanted to date for sixty dollars for a bj. We drove up to a parking structure where we planned to do the "deed." As I reached into my bag to grab a condom he pulled out a crowbar and cracked it on my head, splitting it open. Luckily, I was drunk on tequila and didn't feel too much pain. We ended up in a struggle . . . I got out of the car with the crowbar in my hand and started hitting him with it. Then he managed to start up the car and began chasing me. He tried to bang me up against the walls of the parking structure. Eventually I got out of there, and he drove off.

I ran all the way back to town where I saw one of my friends. She rushed me off to the emergency room at Castle Hospital. When it was finally my turn to see the doctor, he began asking me questions like, "When was your last period?" I replied, "I never had my period." He said, "Oh? Girls normally start their period during this age. It's strange that you haven't started your period yet." So I turned to him and said, "I'm a male, not a female. I have a penis." And how he blushed! He turned fully red . . . At that moment my mother came running through the door screaming, "Where is my son?!" Instantly the doctor laid me down, numbed up my head, and began stiching me up. He did a messed up job because he was paranoid from my mother's snapping.

So after all that I decided to stay off the streets for a while. And I found a husband. After I met him he taught me how to smoke crack cocaine, roll my own joints, drink alcohol, and take many other mind-altering substances. What an experience! But through it all I grew to love my boyfriend for all the simple and outrageous things we did together.

I remember one time when we drank a whole bottle of tequila and walked into a concert ripped off our asses! While we were walking towards our section of the arena a gorgeous *kane* grabbed my ass. My boyfriend had seen what what happened, and before I knew it began punching him. I started shouting, "Stop it! Stop it!" But they still continued to fight . . . Then, all of a sudden, eight security guards jumped on them, separated them and carried both out. Outside, my boyfriend started yelling at me — He blamed me for what happened! He screaming, "Come here, bitch!" He was ready to pulverize me! I didn't dare go anywhere near him.

I stayed in the concert the whole night. I hoped that by the time it was over, his temper would have simmered down. But when I walked out of the concert, there he was, running towards me like a charging bull! I began running, but he tackled me and began punching me over and over. I started hitting him back and screaming for help at the same time. Luckily, some local boys came to my aid and mobbed him. I ran off and found my way home three days later. But we still stayed together . . . our relationship lasted for six more years . . .

***

When I was born my grandmother gave me the name, "Ano." This could be a name for either a boy or a girl. It refers to a person's behavior; their way or style; who they are, whether they are good or bad. Before she died, my grandmother told my mother that I was going to be *mahu*. My mother didn't want to believe it, but sure enough my grandmother was right! As I think back, my mother told me stories — When I was two or three years old I used to wear her wigs and high heel shoes for fun . . . Later, when I was eight, I was sexually abused by an older man who came to live with us from the Philippines. He would always lure me into his room and shut the door behind us . . . He would make me perform oral sex on him for hours . . .

While growing up my hair was always long because I would run away from home on the days I had to go to the barbershop. Boys used to think I was a girl and would check me out. When they found out I was a boy they teased me and called me "fag." I would go home crying to my uncle because I was hurt by their teasing. So my uncle ended up enrolling me in karate and kick boxing classes. I got pretty good at it, and when boys would make fun of me I'd beat them up!

I remember a time when I was walking to the bus stop to catch the bus to school with a bunch of girls who were my classmates. A group of boys who were already at the bus stop started laughing as we approached them. One of the boys called out my name and began slapping me on the back of the neck, saying, "Wassop *brah!*" I told him to stop it, but he continued to push me around. Finally I stepped back and gave him a roundhouse kick to his head. He fell down — and went into an asthma attack! At that very moment the bus came and everybody quickly rushed on. Before I got on I grabbed his books and threw them under the bus tires. And from that day forward no one bothered me at school.

***

Ohana plays a very important role in being a transgender, a *mahu*, in today's society, especially here in Hawai'i. Having a family strengthens us transgenders to go out into the world and be all that we can be!

My own family really couldn't seem to accept the idea of me being transgendered. So I ended up doing my own thing. I prostituted, drank, did drugs — you name it, I did it. I had absolutely no focus; I did what I wanted, when I wanted. Since my family didn't care for the idea that I was muffy, I turned to the streets. There I met a lot of other queens who were like family to me. We ate together and slept at each other's houses. We literally did things as a family.

Even if my family didn't want me to be muffy, I knew that deep down inside they still cared about me and wanted the best for me. Although sometimes they were bitter at family parties and other gatherings, I was still respected as a family member. This is where the saying, "Blood is thicker than water" truly reflects its meaning.

It's funny — My uncles would make fun of me and stuff like, "Eeaah, look at him! Look how he is dressed!" But my aunties would yell at them and say, "Shut up and leave him alone!" My aunties adapted to the idea of me being transgendered pretty well. Actually, I always helped my aunties with taking care of the kids, cooking and cleaning, so they always backed me up if someone had a gripe against me.

***

I think that once a person decides to become a queen, everything in life becomes a challenge. You have to be secure with who you are. Because if you're not then you're going to become a "confused queen" and you'll be prone to becoming suicidal. See, anybody can put on a dress, but can you handle the ripping and criticism that society has towards homosexuality? Not many of us have the mind to overlook the negative remarks that other people have to say. Some of us really take those negative things to heart and do crazy things that sometimes scar us for life. But if you can be accepted by both family and friends, then the negative remarks from people don't really make an impact anymore.

Today my family accepts me for me, and their children all call me "Auntie." I have proven that, with or without them, I have a purpose here in this world, regardless of the lifestyle in which I choose to live. I went through my drug recovery cold turkey; I prostituted to survive; I drank my life away to ease the pain when my emotions haunted me because of the lifestyle I chose. Having gone through it all, I wouldn't give it back or relive it again. I'll just chalk it all up to *experience*.

We are faced with a lot of challenges because of the lifestyle we lead. It's not an ordinary lifestyle. People don't have to accept it. But if more people can understand the trials and tribulations that we go through just to live our lives, then hopefully things will get easier. Some people do understand, but not all: we have feelings; we cry; when cut, we bleed. We are human! We are not animals or aliens — we are God's creations!

So we deserve the right to be acknowledged as human beings, not labeled as "psychologically disturbed." For the longest time, we were called "psychologically disturbed" because people didn't understand what we were. And we are sick and tired of being labeled that! If you really think about it, who are the ones psychologically disturbed here? *I* didn't disturb anybody. *They* are the ones who are disturbed by my presence.

ATZ

My name is Hina Leimoana Wong. I was born and raised here on
Oʻahu, but I have roots on the Big Island, Maui, and of course I have ties
with Molokaʻi, too. My adopted family — almost like *hanai*, except not
from babytime — are people from Niʻihau who live on Kauaʻi. So I have
roots all over the place. That's my family life. My background is Hawai-
ian-Chinese-Portuguese-English.

I grew up here and went to school . . . I started off in my old neighborhood, Maʻemaʻe, and then went up the hill to Kamehameha, up on
Kapalama Heights. I'm a graduate of the class of 1990. I continued on to
the university, straight out of high school. I spent a little bit longer than
I expected at the University of Hawaiʻi, because I fooled around and
didn't pay attention to school. After six years I graduated with a bachelors in Hawaiian Studies. My focus was on language, partly because I
enjoy traveling, meeting people, especially being around Polynesian
people and at Polynesian functions.

Although Hina Leimoana is not my given birth name, taking this
name had to do with my family. It had to receive approval from my
family, and it had to empower me. Because your name, your *inoa*, is your
mana. *Mana* is your spiritual power, your strength. It's your essence, your
being. It's neither good nor bad; it's how you make it. Everything has it:
mana. So when somebody calls you by a name, they have to be calling out
the good things in you, or things that empower you.

As my given birth name I have a Chinese name — Kwai Kwong.
And Kwai Kwong means precious moon, the precious brilliance of the
light of the moon. For my choices in life, and for me to decide to pursue
this avenue, this perspective, I had to choose an appropriate name. And

Hina, in Hawaiian stories, is the goddess of the moon. She's the mother of Maui and she's the mother of Moloka'i. Maui the one who fished up the islands, Maui the one who lassoed the sun with Hina's hair, Maui who slowed the sun down so that his mother Hina could beat her *tapa* with enough time in the day. There are many, many forms of Hina. She was renowned throughout the South Pacific and was always known to be a beautiful woman coming from a far-off land, or coming from an isolated island. She comes in and she captures the heart — either of the many, or of one in particular, who is usually a chief. Hina just goes through the islands and she touches people. The more I read and the more I hear stories, the more I'm learning about Hina and her many tales. And since assuming that name, those kinds of adventures and those kinds of experiences have come my way. Under Hina, I went to Las Vegas, I won a *hula* contest there in 1996. I won in Tonga the Miss Tonga Galaxy 1998-99 . . . Just the kinds of things I have done, the people I have met, the relationships and affairs that I've had — they're all Hina.

***

I always knew I was different. I never really wanted to act on it. Although I remember many times loving to run around in mother's shoes, seeing which outfit I would look nice in. It wasn't just like I came out, today being a boy and tomorrow being a girl. It was a slow, slow, slow process. *Slow.* It happened over a period of seven or eight years. It starts off with letting the hair grow out, cutting the necks off of t-shirts, plucking your eyebrows . . . And of course being around the Polynesian scene, they wear wrap-arounds — *lavalava, pareu.* . . . Then the look got more androgynous. You can buy clothes that kind of deceive, buy big clothes, wear lip-gloss, have a shoulder bag, wear girls' boots . . .

For me it was different because I didn't have to grow up on the streets. I didn't grow up being punished excessively for being soft. I mean, my parents talked to me on a couple of occasions. My mother said that I was effeminate, that I was too soft. "Don't walk like that. Stand up straight. Don't make your hand a certain way." Now that I look back on it, she was really, I suppose, afraid. Afraid for me, afraid of what would happen to me if I were seen as being too soft. One, she didn't like the idea. Two, every mother is worried for their child, and she knows what the world is like. So it was kind of difficult, but my parents handled it in their own way. My mother and I weren't seeing eye to eye for a while. Not drastically, but you could tell that there was uneasiness. We didn't know how to relate to one another. Sometimes we were abrasive when we were in each other's company. But she is still my mother . . . I love my parents, both of them. Although I was raised more by my grandparents on both sides than my parents, I still have a lot of contact with them. My father, whom I live with — I love my father. I don't know what I would do without my father. He is very supportive, just not verbally. Meaning, he didn't kick me out because I was like this. And no matter what, even to this day, if he says, "Oh, this is my son," I just stand up and smile. And I feel no pain because at least my father said, "This is my son," and did not disown me. He doesn't have to acknowledge me if he doesn't want to because he's my senior. But he does.

My father did say to my sisters one day that it was really hard. He said, "You folks don't know what it's like because this is my son. I'm seeing my son look more like a woman every day, dressing in women's clothes, and having a boyfriend." My boyfriends were big. They were men. Polynesian men. They were nowhere near the typical gay man. But that's not to say that I didn't have encounters with women. Because before I allowed my life to take this route, coming up in school I always tried to deny to the majority of my school mates that I was like that. "Oh, no — I'm not like that!" So in high school I wasn't out about myself. My closest friends knew, without saying or without me actually acknowledging, "Yes. I am *mahu*." In fact, I hated the word *mahu*. There's just a lot of stigma attached to the word *mahu*. That was the *last* thing that I would want to be called. I hate to be called fag, queer, faggot, homo, gay, sissy, bend-over buddy . . . You know, the typical stuff. And they fly it at you when you're not expecting it. But actually I would rather be called *mahu* than any of those other names.

I did my very best to cover that up. Not only did I paddle canoe for six years, I was also the football manager. I tried out for football my freshman year. The first day we suited up with the pads and I went out there on the field . . . I didn't know what I was doing and got knocked silly all over the field. I was sore and tired and I was like, "I can't handle this." I think if I had known how to play the game it would have been better because I didn't know how to play it. Most men assume you know the basics, but I didn't know squat! Not a thing. I didn't know which way you're supposed to run with the ball, I just ran with it because that's what I thought all of the boys are supposed to do. But I made some friends, and they said, "Stick around, hang with it." But I said, "No, I'll just be the manager." So I used to run with them and warm up with them. Sometimes go into the weight room with them and train with them after practice, and be right there in with them and the coaches, reading the plays, and picking up the guys after they had gotten hit and fallen down. They would come to me with their broken equipment and I would fix it. If they had girlfriend problems, they would come tell me. If they had school problems, they would come asking for help. If they're hungry, let's go eat. They all sensed that I was different. The majority. Not all. And the majority of the boys in school still respect me even today. They still have the same *aloha*, and that's a credit to them. I have the utmost respect for my schoolmates. Especially the boys. The girls are different because the girls always tend to be a little more accepting.

I remember my classmates from University, the boys from the outer islands . . . All of us used to go and stay at one of our classmate's apartments on campus. One day I told them that I had something important to say, and I wanted all of them to be there. So I called all of them to this grand thing in the apartment. They're all sitting there looking at me. "What's up?" I started to tear, I didn't know what to say. I just said, "You guys know I don't like girls, yeah? Well, I have a boyfriend." And they looked at me like, "So? So what? What do you want us to do?" I said, "I would understand if you guys didn't want to be my friends anymore. If you didn't want me coming around here anymore." But they said, "Eh, no act stupid! We *expect* you to be here. You're one of us." So they all shook my hand and said, "Hey cuz, no matter what, you're still one of the *braddahs*, you're still one of us." I said, "*Oh really?*" And now when they look at me, the *aloha* they have for me, the respect for me, are still the same. That's the main thing. Even if they still shake my hand or whatever

— hey, they could be throwing rocks at me, they could be beating me over the head if we were in other places, other parts of the world. So the way I see it is, it's all good. They said, "Hey, just tell your boyfriend he better make sure he treats you good. Otherwise we're gonna go kick his ass." I was like, "Oh! *Lovely*..." [laughs] That makes you feel fish, makes a girl feel like a real woman. What's nice is that I can still come to the table at one of our school functions or graduate functions, and I can *still* sit down with them. They're not going to push me away.

***

Mahu, in our communities now, are known to be a lot of things. One of the good things is that they are the caregivers. They will either care for the young, the babies and kids around the house, or they will care for the elderly, which is something I did. Or they are the teachers. They teach *hula*, crafts, *lei*-making, chanting, singing. They sew clothes, they clean the house. They have immaculate houses — but don't come to mine! *Do not come* to my house, because I do not portray a good *mahu* in that way. [laughs]

Mahu are, in many ways, the keepers of the Hawaiian culture because they know the chants. *Mahu* are the ones who teach *hula*, the stories, the *mo'olelo*, of all the different places. They remember all the aunties and uncles, they know the genealogies. And they're the talented ones in the family. Or at least the more recognized ones.

The American Indians have a really nice way of putting it. They say "two spirited." So I like to borrow that and apply it to *mahu*, and have it mean "two spirited." Not "hermaphrodite" or "homosexual," like you find in the Hawaiian dictionary. Because *mahu* could mean a guy who likes a guy, but is somewhat soft, and likes to have relations with the same sex. Or it could be like us. And many, many others. So, if you're anywhere within that two-spirited realm, the word *mahu* could apply to you. People like this have an aura... They give off both man and woman. But *mahu* is not something that somebody would necessarily *choose* to be called. There's a confusion that *mahu* is the only thing that we're supposed to call you. No. We'll call each individual what they would like to be called. Either by their name or by queen or by woman or by whatever. They're all names. But traditionally, the correct term is *mahu*.

From all of the history books that we have today, you don't see a whole lot about *mahu*. Except for the idea of homosexuality or homosexual relations. And that is where the chiefs had to maintain their bloodlines. Being human, they had desires, needs, wants . . . they needed relief. So they selected someone to share their bed area. And that was accepted. *Moe aikane*. That was someone who was close to the chief, maybe because of his particular skill in dancing *hula*, or fishing or hunting, and they usually were always seen in each other's company. Or, the *aikane* would have a favorite spot in the court. He would be afforded a certain kind of status and be treated very well. I say "he" because you don't really see too many references of women being with women. Unless, of course, you look in the Pele and Hi'iaka stories. Because Pele's youngest sister Hi'iaka is known to have her *aikane*, and they are *wahine*. But you don't really have a lot of documentation about certain aspects of Hawaiian life because people took them for granted. They weren't necessarily looked upon as being abhorrent. Or they weren't looked upon as being derogatory or negative.

Traditionally . . . But what can I really tell you about "traditionally"? I'm twenty-seven years old! But from what I've studied and from experiences in the South Pacific with other Polynesians who tend to be closer to my own traditional culture, I bridge what I read with what I experience, and my knowledge of language, to span the miles. So I look at that and in my head, I'm making the association, "Oh, *this* is what it must have been like in Hawaiian history and Hawaiian culture." When you look at our Polynesian cousins, and although the term is just slightly different, it is very similar and the concept is the same. Because in other areas of the South Pacific there is the word "*mahu*" — in Tahiti or Society Islands, the Marqueses Islands, and all of those areas. You can find it in Rarotonga, as *ma'u*. You also find *fa'afafine* in Samoa and *fakafefine* in Tonga. The latter means "to be in the way of a woman." There's always a term for these kind of people.

Mahu are mentioned in certain islands in chants . . . There's a place called Ka Pae Mahu in Waikiki. It was said that four wizards arrived there . . . In English they have such peculiar terms, calling these four individuals "wizards." But then again, it says, "*mahu*" in Hawaiian. Why would you call somebody "*mahu*" if they weren't really *mahu*? Up until this day people know what *mahu* are, and that carries on from generation to generation. So if you take it all the way back, why are they going to call somebody something that they're not? So in the story of Ka Pae Mahu, they were healers from Tahiti. They came and brought healing and medicine and those arts. Not necessarily that our ancestors didn't come with it before, but they introduced more healing to the islands. They were known for possessing that *mana*.

***

I tell people that nowadays there's all this talk and action for keeping the Hawaiian language and culture alive. Well, that includes all the aspects of culture, including the ones that tend to be sensitive. Working for Ke Ola Mamo gives me opportunity to work with the Hawaiian community. So in conjunction with teaching the Hawaiian language, I taught two classes to elders, or *kupuna*. I asked them what would they do if somebody in their family was *mahu*. They just looked at me and repeated, "What would you *do*?! You don't *do* anything! You love them. You don't kick them out — that's your family. You cannot help it, that's how they were born." Some people say God made them that way. Some people say *that's just how they are*. And they have roles. They're known to take care of the family and clean; they're the ones who keep the family together. They're known to be the go-getters, the ones who get out there.

When your culture is dictated by your environment. . . . We think of our native peoples, who have a great respect and symbiotic relationship with the land and their environment, including the spiritual aspect. Through Western conquest and in America they called it "manifest destiny." Manifest destiny meant that it was inevitable for America to conquer, to rule, to dominate — and that involved not only the political spread but the religious spread as well. And no matter how you look at it, it was this same concept of manifest destiny that we can apply to other European countries. What were the great powers? Great Britain, France, Germany, The United States of America, Spain . . . When you have the

Western people coming in and assuming the dominant role over other native peoples across the world and subjecting some to slavery to the point where they are annihilated or something like the Holocaust, where people were slaughtered in the millions, then that really shows us a culture that is *not* symbiotic, but rather is one-sided in many ways. Religion has a lot to do with it. When we look at the origin of Christianity, people fought. There was bloodshed to spread Christianity. *Bloodshed.* The Crusades. So the Christian world which we live in today is based greatly upon those great events in history. I have accepted Christian prayer as an essential part of daily life, yet I never forget the traditional deities. I have a great respect for the old religion because I am a *mo'opuna* of my *kupuna* and all of those who went before them. The old ways bear too much responsibility. Most people can't nowadays can't handle that, so I don't teach them too much about stirring up the old ways. I can, but it's not for everyone.

We see that we are very Western-influenced, so now the symbiotic relationship — where everybody is in harmony, where everybody has a role — has become displaced. In precontact Hawai'i the more generous estimates are of a population of a million plus. With the coming of Cook our people died by the thousands. Population decimation was rapid, and within ten years our population was reduced to a mere hundred thousand. With that much population decimation . . . You know what it's like when you go to one funeral, so imagine to have family and friends drop around you like nothing . . .

***

If we can be the movers and the shakers, and be examples . . . Not to say that there haven't been other transgendered girls who came before us, because we're young. A lot of the old-timers who are now fifty, sixty, or even in their late forties, they look at us as being so young, we're pups. They went through the really hard times, the times when they had to wear a pin that said, "I'm a boy." The girls have it easy now; the social climate is so accepting compared to what it was. But I think that's why my mother never wanted me to go like that, because her only memories of that kind of stuff were that they had to wear pins which said they were boys, you were discriminated against, you fought all the time, you engaged in only prostitution, drugs, all of that kind of stuff. Now there is the threat of disease as well. But if we can change some of the Western norms that have been imposed upon us, that would be a benefit. Because then the girls wouldn't be so reclusive, they wouldn't be so ashamed, and they wouldn't resort to risky behavior. Why do the girls have risky behaviors? Because this is their only chance to be with somebody who wants to pay attention to them, even if it's only for a sexual favor. If you tie that back into culture, you've got to use our native culture which tells us that we had a *place*. And which tells us that we were all right. We were the spiritual people, the spiritual keepers, officiating over the spiritual matters of the land.

For example, in order to truly understand the meaning of *hula*, you have to be in both worlds. In order to interpret the poetry. In order to understand, or even to receive some of these things. Our people were very selective over who was to receive what knowledge and information. A lot of the *mahu* were entrusted with certain knowledge because they were particular about detail. They were particular about different aspects of the culture. They paid attention. They were meticulous. They were thorough. They were articulate. They care. They have the sensitivity for caring and the soft side that is more associated with *wahine*. Yet they have enough aggressiveness and enough strength — the backbone side. Not to say that Hawai'ian women were not strong. Hawai'ian women were very, very strong. But the *mahu* had both qualities of both man and woman in them. So naturally you would want to give knowledge and information to someone who is going to work wonders with it. You could teach a roomful of men and women, but who is going to retain all of that knowledge, and who is going to make it a point to retain it, perpetuate it, and appreciate it? The *mahu*. Now, I'm not saying that anybody else wouldn't. But nowadays, it just tends to be that way. I can't explain it. But *mahu* are very respected in that way. Although when somebody hears "*mahu*" in the local community, you might get the people who — and they tend to be very, very Christian-oriented, unfortunately — say, "Ugh." They want to pray for you, as if it were some sort of illness. This is an aspect of Christianity that bothers me because it tends to be condemning of different creeds and beliefs. But in our native culture, to be *mahu* was OK because you had your role. And that was one of the roles — to be the caregiver, the spiritual leader, the cultural leader.

Myself and a dear *tita* of mine, Kauaʻi Iki Olores — she is not only a sister to me, but also a mentor — we are known for doing many, many public cultural presentations and spiritual offerings. We go around town, and sometimes when all of the Hawaiian events are happening, we'll get a call, "We need people to chant. Can you please come chant for us?" Sometimes they say, "We have money, we can pay you." Sometimes they say, "This is for *kokua*, for *aloha*." We always try to help those people because they are there for us when we need it. And our role is not to necessarily take sides in, let's say, the struggle for sovereignty. Rather, our role is to provide spiritual guidance and leadership. We're like a spiritual door, a spiritual voice.

Wouldn't it be much better to have a religious leader who had the *mana* of both *wahine* and *kane* in them? That way they are themselves a stronger individual. Because both man or woman can either stand or fall on their own. But when you have both together . . . with the right attitude, nothing can push them down.

I was born in Minnesota in 1942, right after the Second War started. I grew up in a lot of places. I lived in Minnesota, South Dakota, Texas — I really grew up in Texas . . . I also moved to Indiana, California. I've been around.

My mother passed on when I was around three. My father sent me to live with an aunt and uncle in South Dakota . . . Actually, my grandmother took care of me, and we lived in my aunt and uncle's home; they were very loving people. Then my father remarried and decided to bring me back to his home. That was a troubling time for me. Apparently his new wife wasn't too happy with me, so I was sent to my mother's parents' home in Texas, and I stayed down there for a number of years until I was a freshman in high school. I moved back to Indiana, stayed up there one year; moved to California, San Diego, stayed there one year, and then said, "I've had enough." I was back with my stepmother and my father, and I just didn't want to stay around any longer, so I decided to join the military as a way out. That's how I started my military career.

As I remember it — and I've thought back on this a number of times — the earliest recollection I have of anything along the transgender line was when I was in South Dakota. That had to be when I was between three and six or seven. I was living in a town that had about forty people, an old prairie town that had dwindled to a few houses and people. Through the years, all the prairie towns experienced some type of catastrophe . . . In this particular one, some of the homes had been burned by prairie fires and some had been physically moved away to be set in other farm locations, so there weren't very many people or houses left. My aunt and uncle had owned a general store there, run the post office, this and that . . .

229

As for the kids in town, there weren't very many of us, probably six or seven who were around the same age. I remember when we would play in this farmhouse — all of us kids would be over there, and I always wanted to wear the dress. I don't know how I even got away with it. Maybe because there were more boys than girls . . . But I just liked that; I thought that was great. And that's my earliest recollection. I think I was too young to understand, but I do remember that I liked to wear the dress. We would go up into the attic and find these old clothes, and I don't remember what the circumstances were, other than maybe we were playing house. But during that time, it wasn't a major thing in my life. I think that when I was that age, I was more interested in playing. You were forced into certain roles. As a boy, you had to do boy things.

I do remember the feelings I had later in those younger years. Wishing and hoping. I think probably a lot of us went through that stage where we'd go to bed at night wishing that we'd wake up and that thing would be gone. That there would be something else there — or nothing there. [laughs] But I don't remember acting on anything at that time; I was just thinking about those things, wishing and hoping. You know, you're put into a role when you're that age that you don't really have a lot of latitude in, especially if you're not with loving parents, and I just wasn't. And when you're in someone else's home a lot, you just can't do what you want to do. Whether that would have made any difference at that age or not, I don't know.

When I was in the fourth grade I was shipped off to my grandparents' on my mother's side, in Texas. And that's where it began, really — the cross-dressing, or the dressing up, or whatever you want to call it — much more strongly. I was probably about ten years old. I very distinctly remember reading in the newspaper when Christine Jorgensen had her sex change. That was such a shock because it meant there was a ray of hope for me. It was just so much . . . I was a young boy at the time, but I remember reading it in the newspaper and of course it was on the radio, and in the magazines . . . I can still see these pictures of her, wearing her little fur cap and fur coat. I remember asking a friend's father, who was a physician . . . I don't remember how it went, but I asked him, "How did Christine Jorgensen change her sex?" He replied, "Oh, do you want to do that too?" I knew he'd read me then. Of course, I didn't know if he'd really read me, but I was very afraid. I don't remember what I said next, but obviously he was smart enough to know that there must be something there. I mean, what ten year old boy asks about a sex change? During this time I asked my grandmother if I could wear her old clothes. I wanted to dress up like a girl. And she was very open to it. I don't think she realized what I was, or why I wanted to do that. She didn't have any problems with it because we lived in the country. That is, if I were around the house, then that would take up the spare time in which I could be doing something improper outside, like throwing rocks. So she said OK. I remember her saying, "Wear whatever you want." So of course I would go and put on all her clothes . . .

A lot of times my grandparents would have friends over — they used to play canasta — and they would have me come out and show everybody, and they would all ogle. I was pretty cute when I was young, and I could just about pass as a girl. Many people used to tell me, "You should've been a girl." It was because I had a lot of Swedish blood in me, and I had the pink cheeks and puffy face — just a typical female look when I was young. So I got that reaction all the time.

I always had clothes — my grandmother would just leave the clothes in the room after a while; she didn't care. But sometimes she would get angry with me. I remember one time I was wearing her new girdle. [laughs] She caught me wearing it out somewhere. I guess my shirt had come up and she saw that I had on her new girdle under my boy's clothes. I couldn't have been more than ten or twelve. She got excited because she had just bought it and hadn't even worn it yet.

Of course, that was also a time when I was experimenting with sexual urges. Let's face it, that was part of it. That was part of being a cross-dresser, there's no question about it. Your hormones are raging at that age, or beginning to rage. And I remember I had terrible feelings after I had my sexual orgasm — I don't know what it was, but I just had to take off all my clothes immediately and then wouldn't think about it for a while. So even though I really wanted to be a girl, whenever I had an orgasm, I felt I was doing something completely wrong, and that I'd I

better get out of those clothes right away and should never do that again
— shame on you , shame on you, shame on you . . .

I've never given it a lot of thought, but I imagine everyone who is
transgendered has those same feelings. But my grandmother was very,
very good about that. She would never say anything, and I could do
whatever I wanted, anytime I wanted. I don't really know if she realized
what I was doing. So I always had clothes, and I could always dress up. I
tried to dress up anytime I could. Always.

As a young boy I would go downtown, and walk up and down Main
Street. I would go past all the dress shops, and I'd dream and I'd dream
and I'd dream about this dress or that dress. I'd also dream that I would
sneak in and get locked in the ladies' department store. I'd just go through
it all night long and try on all these dresses. Maybe that's a typical dream
we all go through; I don't know.

I spent a lot of time downtown looking at those stores. I really did.
I'd go down to the movie on Saturdays, it was nine cents back then, and
I'd see the double feature cowboy movies, with a couple of cartoons and
an episode of some serial feature. Then after the movie I'd spend another hour or two hours going up and down the street, looking at all the
girls' and women's dress shops. You know, they had a lot more dress
shops back then. Such pretty clothes, too. So feminine. Now they're kind
of wishy-washy. It was an exciting time in my life.

That went on until I was a freshman in high school. Then I was
shipped — I'm saying shipped [laughs] — I was sent back to my father to
live with him again, and with my stepmother. This was because I was
really getting into too much trouble with the friends I used to go to
school with. I was still with the "boys," because you pretty much had to
be, because of the peer pressure . . .

So I was sent back to my father. Obviously that was a shock. I had to
leave all my grandmother's clothes, go back to Indiana, and continue in
high school. But I also continued my love of dressing up. Every opportunity I could get, when nobody was around the house, I went up and got
into the old clothes in the storage room or attic and put them on. Naturally, the opportunities were far and few between. But I got into a routine
where I would window shop all the time. And I read newspaper after

newspaper after newspaper trying to find . . . at that time, then, as a high school freshman, I was trying to figure out, Who was I? Where was I going? Where did I come from? What made up all these ideas in my mind? *Why was I like this?*

I took every avenue of investigation I could in our high school library. I went through every periodical. I mean, I went through *every-thing*. I got all the research books, all the books you had to ask for. I always looked under transvestism. I tried to find anything. But there wasn't a lot written back then. This was in the fifties, so there weren't a lot of periodicals or reference materials available. What little there was, you'd quickly find.

I also used to go to the bookstore, the magazine shops, at least once a week, and go through every periodical that had come in that week. I can remember looking for *anything* on sex-change, transvestism. . . . These were the two key words, I suppose. I read newspapers and Time magazine, Newsweek, Life and Look — I scoured everything I could. I suppose, if there was any plus to being transgendered, it was that I im-proved my reading skills tremendously, having to go to the book store and magazine shops and go through this stuff week after week after week. [laughs] So I became quite an expert in that; I found out where to look and where to go in the magazines. Actually, most of the time, if there was anything on tranvestites or sex-change, it was on the cover of the magazine, so you really didn't have to look. They didn't bury that kind of stuff back then because it was very sensational.

I stayed in Indiana until my father was transferred to California. He was in sales and worked for a big company. We were transferred to San Diego, so I moved out there. I stayed another year, and I really didn't have the opportunity to dress up too often. When I finished my sopho-more year — I had just turned seventeen — I decided to ask my father if he would sign for me and let me go into the military because I just wasn't getting along with my stepmother. Plus this burden that I had . . . I thought that maybe if I went into the military I could get rid of this problem. I think a lot of us felt that way, and probably still do, trying to achieve something that would let us overcome all these feelings. But obviously you know where that went — it didn't go anywhere.

So I went into the military in 1959. I joined the Air Force. I continued my magazine and newspaper and periodical thing. I still had not yet met another person such as myself. That was 1959, and I was stationed in San Antonio. *Transvestia* magazine came out around that time; I got my first *Transvestia* somewhere in San Antonio. The feeling I had when I first found this magazine — it's impossible to describe. Actually, I don't remember if it was actually *Transvestia*, but it was some sort of correspondence magazine related to cross-dressing. And, well, my heart would jump and I'd be very excited — not sexually excited, but just excited like, "My God, here's something that I had been looking for all my life," so it was like I found gold. I just couldn't get enough of it; I wanted to read everything. Of course those magazines probably cost three or four dollars apiece, a lot of money at that time. They were really overpriced. . .

After about six or seven months in San Antonio I got reassigned to Mississippi. When I got to Keesler, down in Biloxi, I got put in the barracks, and there was a gay cook there. We went together to New Orleans. And New Orleans was, and still is, the place where everybody went to have fun. So being eighty miles down the road from New Orleans, on payday we'd get some money in our pockets, and off we'd go. As I remember it, we went down to the French Quarter, to Bourbon Street, and we drank our beer . . .

Somehow, I got into a bar that had some queens. But at that time, you couldn't cross-dress in public; it was against the law in New Orleans. They would put you in jail right away. So you just couldn't cross-dress in New Orleans at the time. There were only two times a year you could cross-dress, and that was Halloween and Mardi Gras. But somehow I found out there was a club that featured female impersonators in Jefferson Parish, just on the other side of the Mississippi River. Of course, I knew about this kind of thing from reading my magazines. I don't remember now how I got out there; I think I took a taxi, and went into the club, and somehow I met up with one of the girls.

I forget how we first met. I think they used to come out after the show and cruise around and get people to buy them drinks. I met this Italian boy — I think her name was Jackie. Very pretty. Of course, they all wore these fancy gowns in the show, and that was very exciting to me.

I was very, very taken aback with the show; it was another heart-stopping thing for me. I was excited just to be around these people; there were so many of them, maybe six or ten in the production. Very nice people. So I met up with this one, and I don't remember exactly what happened, but we got back to New Orleans after the show, which was in the middle of the night, probably three or four in the morning. Somehow I told him I wanted to dress up . . . And, well, how can I describe this . . . I was taken home; I got taken home. Of course, he was a queen, but he was gay. He wanted to please me, but he also wanted other favors from me, and in that regard . . . he was very gentle, I've got to say that. And I was . . . stupid, I guess you could say. I wanted to wear his dresses, I suppose, when it gets right down to it. Because they were so beautiful. Now remember, I was eighteen at the time, and I had never really gotten all dressed up, with makeup, wig, the whole bit. I had never done it. So over a period of a year or so, I was able to transform myself . . .

I would go down and stay there with him on the weekends and wear anything I wanted. I went to Mardi Gras, and friends fixed me all up. I was out on the streets with all these queens, and of course queens are loved by everybody as they are in a lot of places. So we went to a lot of parties, big time, in the big hotels, just had the time of our life. I was in heaven dressing up, because I had saved money and bought a wig of my own, and he made my dress, out of a very nice brocade material. I bought shoes and lingerie. I was very happy. That was my first Mardi Gras.

I continued see this fellow, this queen, for a couple of years, until I was promoted and transferred to Florida. By this time I had become more adapted to procuring my own stuff, doing my own thing, although I didn't keep clothing in the barracks. After I was reassigned, I went back to New Orleans for a couple of Mardi Gras, and I bought a bunch of stuff. I would dress up as much as I could. I spent a lot of time in New Orleans . . .

Then I got reassigned to go overseas, to Taiwan. So I packed up all my clothes, took them down to my grandmother's and said, "Look at all these clothes I've got." She thought they were so pretty and nice. I asked her to keep them. Naturally, I didn't want to take them overseas because, being in the military, you can imagine what they might think if my suitcase were to be opened — why was I carrying all these women's clothes?

Anyway, I went overseas and I met up with a woman whom I had told about myself, who I was, what I liked. She had never met anybody like me before, but said "OK. I guess it'll be OK." So I wrote to my grandmother and she sent a bunch of stuff over. I bought some more stuff through catalogues like JC Penny and Sears and Roebuck, and had it all shipped in. I also had a lot of clothes made, girls' stuff.

I lived in Taiwan for . . . I can't remember, three or four years. I was the night manager of the officers' club, so I made a lot of extra money. I had plenty of money. And you can have stuff made for next to nothing. At the time, I was living downtown in Taipei. There weren't enough military quarters for us, so another fellow who was also a night manager at the officers' club and myself went and rented a new apartment together, and we each had our own bedroom. I was driving a brand new '65 Mustang at the time, the first one on the island. That was back when everybody was bicycling around, and here was this young punk American driving around this maroon Mustang.

So, I was going with this girl who later became my wife. I bought a lot of clothing. I dressed at every opportunity I could. But it was very difficult to go out in Taipei. I went out only three or four times because, first of all, I wasn't Chinese; there were very few Americans. I was super tall, and I was read — I didn't know what I was doing. I had nice clothes, very beautiful clothing, stylish and chic, but I was read every time. So I didn't go out very often. I didn't want to get caught. You always have that hatchet hanging over your head in the military. One wrong move and you're gone.

After I got married I left Taiwan and returned to the mainland. I had decided to get out, to leave the military. I had nine years in, and that was enough. I'd had enough of it. I wanted to go and have a sex change. So when we got back to the US mainland, we moved to Texas where I had grown up. I got a job down there, but it paid meager wages. We had some savings, but they were soon on their way to depletion. It was during the Vietnam War, and we talked it over, and I said, "I think I made a mistake." Here I already had nine years in the military, and I could have spent another eleven years and then retired. I said, "That's just not very long." So we decided that we'd try to return to the military.

Now let me predate all this. Before we decided this, my wife became pregnant. So that stopped my sex change in mid-stream. Because I felt an obligation. I'm a person that feels you have to take care of those things you might do incorrectly. And that was one of them — that my wife got pregnant. I didn't want her to have an abortion. So she had our child just after we signed up to go back into the military.

I didn't return to the Air Force, I went into the Army. Actually, the Air Force didn't want me, thank goodness, because I ended up going much further in the Army in only a short amount of time. So I went back in the military, and I continued to cross-dress all the time; it was just part of my life. I went to basic training again out in El Paso, and then came back to Fort Sam Houston for medical training as a medic. I didn't really want to go through that because they had already given me a job in the army when I signed the papers — they had said I could go back into administration.

I talked it over with my wife and told her that I didn't want to be in the medical field. Maybe I should've stayed in it, but I didn't. So I went and told the folks at the personnel office that there had been a mistake, that I should've been in administration. I had already gotten some rank back, too, which they didn't realize. So they said, "We'll just keep you here." So I stayed in San Antonio.

As I remember it, during this time I continued to cross-dress. That was satisfying enough for me. I had an accepting spouse, so it went along fine. We had the child . . .

I had alerts from the military to go to Okinawa and then to Germany, but it seemed like every time I got an order to go somewhere, I'd get promoted again. So I got promoted out of the Okinawa assignment. Then a few months later when I got orders to go to Germany, I got promoted again. Then I got orders to go to Okinawa again. All during this time the Vietnam war was going on. Each time I had orders I told these people, "God, just let me go, because I know the next time it's going to be Vietnam!" Yeah, those two orders came but they wouldn't let me go. They wanted to keep me because I was doing such a good job.

That's hard to believe, but they don't want you to leave. If you do a good job in any business, anywhere, people don't want you to go. They said, "Well, you can't go on that assignment because you got promoted." Then I got my third promotion, but they couldn't hold me back from that because it called for my new promotion grade in Okinawa. So I went to Okinawa and I stayed for . . . four years, I think. This was all during Vietnam, which finally wrapped up when I was in Okinawa. So I never got to Vietnam.

My wife was with me in Okinawa. We had another child there. And then we got reassigned to Italy. I forget how many years we stayed there. And all this time nothing unusual happened, other than my cross-dressing. I continued to buy clothing here and there.

My children began to be an issue, so I had to be very, very quiet about it and cross-dress only in the bedroom, but I could survive on that. I didn't particularly care for it; I wish I could've gone out. Of course, I wished I could have had a sex change — it was still in the back of my mind. But the years went by. The children grew up. We were reassigned to the mainland. I continued to cross-dress and spend money on clothing. I got back into the military's club system, was a club manager, ran a military officers' club.

Previously, my wife had some serious medical problems, and during that time she accepted the Lord Jesus as her savior. Later she became very involved with the church. It was then that my cross-dressing, coupled with the presence of our children, began to cause some tension. When we were in Louisiana, she got into the full gospel businessmen's association meetings on Friday nights, which is a charismatic type of Christianity, and that gave her more courage to condemn my actions. So it began to get a little more heated up around the house when I was dressing. And she, unbeknownst to me, had felt for a number of years that she wasn't comfortable with it anymore. She told me in so many words, but I wasn't smart enough to pick up on it, I guess. So our relationship was growing cold in certain ways . . .

She was studying more and more of the Bible, and apparently getting more frustrated with my actions as each day passed. While we were in Italy, I went to the Baptist Church and accepted Jesus as my savior, and

I began to attend church. But we never talked about cross-dressing; that was something nobody ever talked about. When we moved back to Louisiana later on, she brought up this scripture in the Old Testament that talks about cross-dressing, about men and women wearing each other's clothing. Of course she threw this in my face, and me not being a scholar of the Bible, it became a regular rut in our marriage. There wasn't a whole lot I could do about it, but I still had these feelings, these tremendously strong feelings; it was just part of me. All this time, over these many years, you kind of grow to accept who you are; you don't have a choice in the matter. You've seen all the avenues, you've studied everything you could get your hands on, and you come to a point where you find that you have to either accept yourself or go crazy. And I'm not one to do myself in under any circumstances. The sun's always gonna come up tomorrow, and I want to see the sun come up. There's a better day tomorrow. I've never considered anything other than that — waiting for tomorrow.

Sure enough, I had gotten promoted in Italy, and I was going to get promoted again, but this called for a two year lock-in, and I would shortly reach my twenty years. If I had taken this next promotion, I would have had to stay in for another two years. So I spoke to my spouse, and she wanted to stay in Louisiana because she had found friends there, and because of the church. But I wanted to leave because I found out I was going to be put in a position as first sergeant. I'm not a first sergeant kind of person, as you can imagine. I want to run around in my high heels and dress, and first sergeants are supposed to be big *men*, to lead the *men* of the unit. [laughs] That wasn't me.

After I retired, we decided to come out here to Hawai'i. We came for a few months, but decided that it was pretty expensive, and maybe we wouldn't stay after all. So then we went to Florida. . . . But in October, November 1980 we finally settled out here. We've been here since then.

I lounged around for a couple of months and took it easy because I hadn't had a real vacation in twenty years. Then I applied for a job I found in the newspaper. The first one I applied for I got hired at. I've been there ever since, a moving company. I went to work in December of 1980 as office personnel. The owner was an older guy. He liked to move around. He didn't like staying in any one place too long, so after about a year he decided to sell the company. He had been staying at one of the Hilton Hawaiian Village condos, then moved out to a house in Foster Village, then decided he didn't want to stay there. He said to me, "Why don't you move into this house in Foster Village? Just pay me a little bit of money." I had been living in a two bedroom apartment in Waikiki, and now I was able to move to a three bedroom home in Foster Village, a beautiful place. He sold the company to a younger fellow, in his late twenties, who bought the company in order to move to Hawai'i, just as a business to have. And our company has flourished quite well for the last twenty years. We've been very successful.

After we moved to Foster Village, and for the next two or three years, my marriage was still on those slippery slopes. I forget the year now, but it was in the early 1980s that my wife and I separated from sleeping in the same room. I moved to the *lanai* and she stayed in the bedroom. Within another year or so she said she had to divorce me, even though I wasn't really cross-dressing anymore. I'd given it up for my kids because they would be smart enough to go into Mama's room and find my stuff. So even though it was a tremendous burden for me, I gave it up. I wanted them to grow up without any hindrances from me. I guess you could say I sacrificed myself in certain ways for them. But I did continue to read all the magazines . . .

I also enveloped myself in church. I spent all my free time taking my kids to church, letting them be in the youth groups and do all that stuff. I got involved in the audio and video ministries and helped build the church. We had a brand new church up on Red Hill. I spent all my free time up there during the construction period of a year or two, working every minute I could. It took my mind away from a lot of this kind of stuff. When you give to somebody else, you forget about yourself. So I just gave everything that I had, all the time and effort. I just didn't find time to think about myself. My kids were more important. I knew the life I had gone through with a stepmother, and I wanted my kids to have a decent upbringing.

But we did get a divorce. At the time my wife said that she knew I was still that way, and that she couldn't take it because it was against the

Bible. So we had a mutually agreeable divorce, just signed the papers and that was it. But she continued to stay at our house, and we continued to bring up our kids together. The legal papers said that I had responsibility for the children, and she had none. But we still were a family. We didn't even let anybody know about our divorce for five or six years. That, apparently, gave her some assurance somehow . . . I told her that I didn't mind, if that's what she wanted and it made her happy. She was a great mother, she brought up our kids well. I never had a bit of problem with my children, not a bit. Great kids. Both are college educated. One's teaching now, the other is a housewife. Both graduated from the University of Hawai'i. And my wife contributed most to their upbringing, to their values and their spirituality. Most of it is attributable to her, not me. Well, I did spend a lot of time with them, and I'm sure I had a little bit to do with it, but most of it was her.

After our divorce, I continued to be involved with the church. Then, when our oldest child was ready to graduate from UH, and the other one was at Leeward [Community College] and getting ready to transfer to UH, I said to myself, "My kids have finished. I've brought them up. I've fulfilled all of my fatherly responsibilities with them. It's my turn now. I'm divorced. My spouse is no longer my spouse; she has nothing to do with me. One of my kids is graduated, the other one is almost there. I'm going to look at my life-long wants and needs."

So I began to accumulate a few items again. Because there was just something there — it never leaves. It's always lurking in the background. It wasn't as strong during the period of my kids' older, formative years growing up, but it was still there. I don't know . . . I had always . . . I would still go to the store and end up in the women's section, looking . . .

Not too long after that, I bought a bra and stuck it in my desk drawer for some reason, rather than putting it in the suitcase where I stashed all my stuff. As I remember it, we had some of my daughters' friends over. They were going to get some pictures out of the desk during a conversation, and I was sitting out there at the time, in the same room. My daughter jumps up and says, "Oh, let me get these pictures." She opens the drawer and there's my bra. So she gets the pictures and shuts the drawer. Later on I found out that she got together with her sister and asked, "Where did that bra come from?"

Actually, my spouse had clued in my daughters about my previous cross-dressing experiences, although they never told me about it. So they put two and two together, and when they came to me and asked me what the bra had been doing in there, I told them the whole story about my life.

When I first told my children about myself, they weren't accepting. And that's perfectly understandable to me because they only knew me as their father. Well, obviously I am still their father, and they still call me "daddy." Even today, after I've fully transitioned. But they don't call me "Rebecca." They call me "daddy." And that's fine; I don't have a problem with that — I'm their father.

One of my daughters is more open to me than the other one. The other one dislikes it. She always has something to say about it. The other one is more understanding. They have different personalities. And the other one has two boys; I have two grandsons, and she and her husband don't want me to . . . associate any of my ways with the boys. They feel that the boys will possibly think that it is an acceptable thing to do, which they don't believe is right. They still feel that what I am doing is incorrect, and in their eyes I shouldn't be doing it. But then again, they're not in my shoes. I wish I didn't have to do what I'm doing, but to live with myself, I have to . . . I don't *have to*, obviously; I went through it before. But to be at peace with myself, I need to do this. I need to be who I am. It's not something I flaunt or want to do, but I'm just doing it because it's part of me.

My daughters . . . One is more liberal than the other. But you never know, they might flip-flop their ways down the road. Who can say? They've gotten accustomed to me more. When my grandsons are around I try to wear a big t-shirt and shorts, nothing flaunting. But my oldest grandson, he's asked me before, "How come Pop Pop" — he calls me "Pop Pop" — "How come you like to wear girls' clothes?" I think he must have found it out from his mother grumbling at me so many times. [laughs] I told him, "Well, Pop Pop likes to wear girls' clothes, that's all." And that's enough for him at this point — he's only seven. He'll accept that. As they become older, they'll understand. Especially in Hawai'i. They'll see it all over; there are too many folks around. I think that my grandsons will be open to it, unless their parents beat it into them that it's evil. And even with that, they still might accept me. Who knows? By the time they're old, I'll be real old, too, so maybe I won't even be around at that time, so . . . I'm not worried about it.

***

Anyway, around the time I told my children I found out about Hawai'i Transgendered Outreach. I came to a meeting and met Tracy and Auntie Joan and some of the other girls and, from talking to and seeing the various folks who come through this group, decided that I was going to follow the same road that Tracy had been on: to transition. I felt that I had no more responsibilities to my family, and even though it was a big thing and I could possibly lose my job, I was going to go ahead and do it.

I studied and read and got everything I could on it, and I decided that I wouldn't tell my employer. I didn't want to chance it. I'd been there a number of years already. I had asked him one thing, and he's never questioned me about this, maybe he's forgotten, but I said, "You know, I never let my hair grow. I was always in the military when men were wearing long hair, so I'd like to let my hair grow long to see what it's like." He replied, "Oh, yeah, go ahead. Just keep it kind of neat. But it's all right." So I continued to let my hair grow, and during the next few years slowly but surely I transitioned.

During that first year I didn't do too much. I started electrolysis. I was going about once a week, for a whole year. It took that long just to remove the mustache and some of the beard. I still haven't even gotten more than half of it off. It's turned gray, so it's hard to see now. During that first year I also got in to see a physician, and started on hormones. Previously, I'd been buying them off the street. But a lot of times my supply would run out, and I couldn't get them, so I'd get older ones — I wouldn't know if they were potent anymore, who made them or what they were. Finally I saw a physician and got on a routine prescription. So there were hormones and electrolysis.

And slowly but surely, that was in 1991 or 1992, I began to change pieces of clothing. It was done very, very cautiously and very slowly. Over a three year period I progressed to women's blue jeans, shoes, unisex. But I was always very butch about it. Although my hair was long, I didn't tell anybody anything. Then one morning I was sitting up in my office, and my boss comes in and shuts the door and calls downstairs, "Don't call me up here, I'm upstairs. I don't want you to bother me; don't send any calls up here." Then he turns to me and asks, "What's going on with you, wearing these women's clothes all the time?" I was shocked. I knew it was going to come one day, but it had come when I wasn't prepared for it. I hadn't thought about it for a long time. It was a major shock to me.

I immediately broke down and started to cry. Big time. Of course, the hormones are part of that. They really change your personality and your body; it changes everything about you. So my emotions were just shot. I bawled and bawled and bawled . . . I couldn't stop bawling. I must have cried for twenty minutes. He didn't know what to do. He was nervous. He was embarrassed. I knew the world had come to an end. I was surely going to be fired immediately. But finally when I got to my senses and got my tears dabbed over, we talked for three hours, at least. I told him my whole life story. At the end, he said, "I don't really understand why you're doing it. But I understand that you are doing it." He immediately thought that I was . . . Well, he asked me if I was going to have a sex change. And I said, "Well, I don't know. It's kind of expensive, and I don't have the money." He replied, "I'll tell you what. You go ahead and continue, as long as it doesn't affect the company. If it does, I'll let you know." I assured him I would never do anything to bring discredit to the company. Then he said, "But you can't wear a dress." "Oh, OK, fine." Because I would have agreed to anything at that time. [laughs] It was like being released from jail a second time. I was out of jail! I was free! I didn't have any encumbrances now. I could transition on the job. I worked for only one fellow. And the person who owned the company told me to go ahead and do it. But I was very conservative. Of course, I'm a conservative person. I'm not flamboyant in any way. So I just continued on, but I did buy more feminine things: slacks and tops and pantsuits, things like that. But no dresses. Christmas was about the only time I'd slip into one at work. So I finished my transition, as far as the office went, on that day. Shortly thereafter I became more bold . . .

But I was still going to this mainline charismatic church on top of Red Hill. And through a series of circumstances, I misinterpreted someone's statement to me concerning who I was. I had been invited several times to the house of an officer of the church, someone I knew very well. It was Christmas that I was invited again over to dinner, along with a couple of single people I used to hang around with in the church. I had somehow misunderstood somebody saying something about me, and I had assumed that somehow this fellow and his wife had found out about what I was doing. So I thought I should just try to explain everything to them. I don't remember now what I said, but while we were having dinner, I came out and made some remark . . . I don't remember what I said, but it was something along the lines of, "Why would I want to do what I'm doing at this time in my life?" I just started to talk about it, trying to explain myself because I thought they knew about my transition. Well, they were shocked. "What are you talking about?!" And then I knew it — Oh my God! I've made a big mistake.

So that let the cat out of the bag through the back door. Because I had tattle-taled on myself to my friends in the church, and that was my demise in the church. I was cold-shouldered, and given the friendly "*Adios.*" I was forced out of the church. That's certainly not the way Christians should treat each other, or anybody for that matter. But they didn't want me around anymore. I'm not the type of person to fight or argue, so I packed my bag and left. That was probably the worst thing that ever happened to me. Because I had found a home there. I'd spent many years there and I had a lot of close friends there. I still do have friends there, but some of them are no longer my friends; they won't even talk to me. They shun me. I haven't seen anybody for a while now. When I would see people, they would turn around and walk the other way rather than confront me, which was unfortunate. But I always made a point to talk to everybody I saw, if nothing more than to make them jumpy. People who knew you before get embarrassed when they have to talk to you. That's probably not the correct thing to do, but I did it anyway.

So my transition in Hawai'i took about three years to start, and then I got the approval from my employer, which was the main thing in my life. Because I didn't have any other responsibilities. Certainly my children couldn't tell me what to do. I had already given them the best years of my life . . .

***

I'm on a hormone regimen now. I take injections every two weeks. But my feeling on the sex change at this time — I'm fifty-eight now — is that I don't use what I have now and I probably wouldn't use what I'd get after the sex change. So why waste my money? They don't check under my dress when I walk out the door or walk in a store. Who cares? I'm perfectly happy the way I am. Sex doesn't mean anything to me anymore. It doesn't drive me, it doesn't push me. As I remember my younger years, testosterone drove me, in most cases. But now that the testosterone has been overwhelmed with estrogen, I don't have those "must have" demands on my body and my mind anymore; they're just not there. And it's a wonderful feeling not to be bothered with it. It really is.

Although sex is wonderful. But now that it's over with, I really don't miss it. Probably a younger person could not comprehend what I've said, but as you get older — "Been there, done that," — missing it is no big deal anymore. In fact, it's refreshing not to be bothered with it. And you can remember when you were young, it seemed like every time you turned around you were bothered with it. It's part of your thinking; you spend half your life thinking about sex. Now I can just shove all that out; it doesn't even appear anymore. I can put more energy into other things. Because you lose a lot of that testosterone energy when you get the estrogen in your body. So I really don't care about the physical changes — I don't have to have them.

I know there are some girls out there who just have to have the operation. They think they do. And if they think they do, I guess they do. It's never been a demand on myself. Even though I was determined to have the operation, as I think back over that determination, at the time, when I was in my late twenties and thirties and into my early forties, what was driving that? Was it testosterone that demanded I do that? I don't know. I suspect it had something to do with it. But now that it's not there anymore, it's not a big problem. Plus, the operation is a lot of money; I'm not a rich person. But even if I were, why even take the chance, medically?

But then you get into relationships. If I have a relationship, whether it is with another women or with a guy — which I don't have at the present time — I would have to be swept off my feet, tumbling down the stairs, before I'd even consider it. It would have to be somebody special, something you read about it in the storybooks, love at first sight where you just melt in somebody's arms. It would have to be something like that before I'd even consider the operation. And I would assume it would be somebody my age, and sex maybe wouldn't mean that much to them, either. But who can say? Maybe a relationship would change these feelings I have.

But at the present time I'm happy just the way I am, living as a transgendered woman as best I can. I mean, I pass — unless I open my mouth. People read me, but I'm not concerned with that. It depends on how you conduct yourself, how you appear to people. I always walk around as a woman. I act as a woman, I dress as a woman . . . I'm not flamboyant; I try to be stylish, I try to dress my age as best I can.

And I enjoy being a girl. I enjoy going to get my hair done, my nails done, taking care of myself, pampering myself. Bubble baths and those things that are so important to the stereotype of a woman. But I enjoy them, and I take pride in myself. I try to look my best and spend time on my clothes, if I can. I'm very busy working now. It seems like as I get older, I'm working more than I did when I was younger.

I hate to wear pants. I wore pants all my life, so I want to wear a skirt as much as possible. I want to wear a dress. But that's kind of difficult, because most women want to wear slacks and shorts. [laughs] Oh, I do, too, but every opportunity I have I wear a dress, I want to dress up! Because I don't have that many years left to do that. I've had all my blue jeans days and combat boot days. And those days are gone. [laughs]

JENNIFER AND PHOEBE

My name is Jennifer Kamaunu; my birth name is MacRay Kamaunu. My ethnic background is Hawaiian-Irish-Chinese. I'm eighteen and come from Farrington High School.

Hi. My name is Phoebe Narvaez but my birth name was Joseph. I'm nineteen years old and also a graduate from Farrington High. I am Hawaiian, Chinese, Puerto Rican and Indian.

Jennifer: In preschool I never hung around with the boys, only with the girls. But I didn't think anything of it — just that I liked hanging around with girls. I didn't know I was transgendered or anything like that. When I moved to Kalihi I started to see different things. Because when I was living in Waimanalo, there wasn't too much I could see because my family was isolated. When I moved to Kalihi I made new friends, one of whom was Phoebe. She was very flamboyant. Seeing her made me feel more comfortable and helped me be who I am today. When I was in elementary school I did have a girlfriend. But that was just to experiment and see what I really wanted. But I really didn't want that. As far as I can remember I was always with the girls; I just felt like one of the girls.

Phoebe: The first thing I can remember about being transgender was in preschool — I can recall playing with my sister's Barbies, running upstairs to my mom's room, grabbing her make-up and *mu'umu'u* dresses and dressing up and prancing around the house. I always knew I was what they call "*mahu*." I just had that feeling. I was never attracted to girls, but I always had a sense of feeling for boys. It's just that I never really liked girls, I always thought of them as being friends . . . I just wanted to be one of the girls.

Jennifer: I think being this way in intermediate school, we were more favored by the teachers. Because the teachers saw that we needed more attention than normal students. We had good relationships with all our teachers in intermediate school; I loved all of them. They were all cool to me. I thought I would have a problem interacting with male teachers. Because to me, guys are kind of scary. Just interacting with them is frightening because you don't know if they're going to like you or not, knowing what you are. The teachers in intermediate and high school were really cool about it. They didn't treat us any different from the others. One thing that was different was that we could joke around with the teachers. All the teachers would understand where we were coming from. I guess it's because a lot of teachers in Farrington have been there a long time, and they've seen a lot of queens come in and out of that school. So a lot of them already had experience with the "t." Even some of the younger teachers were really cool with it. One of my favorite teachers was twenty-four when I first met her, and I enjoyed her class. Everyone hated her, but not me. I liked her because she was so funny. She would always make me laugh. What surprised me was the P.E. teacher. It was this guy, Mr. —. He was really, really nice. Extra nice to me. I'm not sure why, but ever since I met him he had this extra treatment for me because of the way I was; I was the only queen in the class at the time. You know, in P.E. classes you get boys who are always going to harass you. But he would tell me, "Never mind what they say, they're all stupid." I looked up to him because he supported me.

The only time when I dressed up to go to school was to perform [for special events]. But then when I became a senior I started to dress up to go to school every once in a while, whenever I felt like it. Everyone would ask me, "What's the special occasion today?" And I'd say, "Oh, I don't know, I just felt like dressing up." It was kind of funny because all the boys would say, "Whoa! Who's that? Who's that?" And I'd turn around and they'd be, "Oh my gosh — It's you!" But usually I'd dress up and perform because that was the only way I could dress up with telling my mom. If I told my mom I was performing, then she would let me dress up. And one thing that was really important to me was being honest with my mom because I didn't want to lie to her. Every time I lied to her I felt so guilty.

Phoebe: For me, school would be hard sometimes, but it was mostly easy. Some of the students tended to shy away from me because of how I acted — I was always flamboyant and didn't care how anyone saw me. If you didn't like me — Oh well, you'd better stay away from me. I would let anyone know how I felt by just telling them. A lot of the teachers took me under their wing because of the way I was. I had a reading disorder, dyslexia, so I had to take special classes to learn how to cope with it. After that the teachers learned to be nicer. They were nice already, but it's just that they became more generous by giving me more food. They always used to give me treats . . . [laughs] So I always thought of myself as being special. But some teachers used to slip and would call me "stupid" or "dumb."

A lot of the students accepted us. We didn't really have any problems in school. Like for me, I didn't really have any problems with anybody. If you had a problem with me — Oh well, that was your fault. Some people would shy away from me, but as soon as they got to know me, that's when they became closer. If I didn't know anybody in the class I would keep to myself, but one or two weeks after that class was in progress, everybody would become friends with me. Everybody loved to sit by me because they could have a lot of fun. And they always used to tell me, "I want to go there with you, I want to do this with you." [laughs] But school was really fun. I enjoyed it and wish I was still there, "but life goes on." You take whatever life throws at you and do the best that you can.

Jennifer: Yeah, the students think it's so fun to be around you. It was the same thing with me. If I was in a class and didn't know anybody, I'd be really quiet. But after a couple of weeks passed by I'd get more comfortable and start getting louder and louder. And everybody would be friendly.

There weren't any assholes who really harassed us. It wasn't that bad. And I think it was easier for me and Phoebe because we played sports, too — volleyball.

Phoebe: People would see me playing and ask, "Wow! How come you're so good? How do you do that? Can you teach me how to do that?"

Jennifer: A lot of the boys would come and support us at our volleyball games. It was really accepted. Although there were other queens at school who had it harder than we did.

Phoebe: I think it was because they weren't comfortable with themselves. A lot of them were hesitant to come to school because they were so afraid of the harassment from other students. To us, we didn't care.

Jennifer: I didn't give a shit.

Phoebe: Yeah.

Jennifer: If you're going to harass me, try!

Phoebe: Yeah. You can *try* harassing me, but . . .

Jennifer: Some of the other girls had it harder because they weren't from the same neighborhood as us — we were from a rough neighborhood. Everyone at school knew where we were from and it surprised them to see that we lived in a ghetto place. It was easier on us than on other queens at the school. Because I know other queens got harassed a lot. But the one problem with them was that they didn't know how to open their mouths. Sometimes I would open my mouth for them.

Phoebe: Yeah. A lot of them didn't know how to open their mouths and stand up for themselves.

Jennifer: If a guy is ripping in the hall, I don't care. I'll turn around and bitch the hell out of him.

Phoebe: Yeah. I would yell at him. I wouldn't care.

Jennifer: I don't care if I'm being loud and standing up for my rights.

Phoebe: Yeah, you've just got to make sure you know how to back up yourself. [laughs]

***

Phoebe: For us, the Chrysalis support group didn't start until the middle of our junior year.

Jennifer: I had first heard about it from another queen from Wai'anae, Vanessa. She played on the Wai'anae volleyball team and was telling me that they had this group in Wai'anae, called Chrysalis, for transgendered teens. She said that they were going to start one in Farrington, but I said that I hadn't heard anything about it. And then when the group did start, some of the teachers from the Teen Center called us in.

Phoebe: They did everything discreetly. They didn't want anyone knowing about the group because they were afraid of gay-bashing.

Jennifer: So they would call us in and ask us questions, like who else we knew who was transgendered. We'd give them names. But sometimes we'd act stupid and give them the name of somebody who wasn't transgendered. [laughs] Just to have fun.

Phoebe: Chrysalis was a support group for transgendered teenagers only. Because there were a lot of support groups already out there for gays, they tried keeping it for transgendered people only. So the organizers told us to think carefully about the people we were choosing to join our group. The Chrysalis group really helped us because April, our mentor, is the one who really opened our eyes to the different communities that are out there and the different things that people do. "Don't be afraid to be transgender," she said. "There are a lot of girls out there who have good jobs, who go out there and *do it*."

Jennifer: It was cool because she brought in guest speakers like lawyers . . .

Phoebe: And retail managers . . . They told us, "If you stick it out and live your life the way it is, things are just going to get better."

Jennifer: It was kind of trippy, because at the time I thought transgendered people, queens, all turn out to be prostitutes . . . Or they have their change, get married and stay home and become a housewife.

Phoebe: Yeah, they're very low class.

Jennifer: But it took Chrysalis to make me realize that queens have futures.

Phoebe: Yeah. It opened our eyes *big time*.

Jennifer: You could be anything you want to be.

Phoebe: Yeah, you can do whatever you want to do, regardless of your gender. It really opened my eyes. It was trippy talking to those people. We even got someone from prison who had just been released. She had been going to school and became a lawyer. She actually got her degree in prison. When she came out she went to work at a law firm. And I was just shocked. She said it was so hard inside there, but she stuck it out. I was like, "Wow. That's trippy." I was amazed by it.

Jennifer: One of the speakers who came to us was Crystal, who is from Farrington. She said she was the first queen to walk with the girls in the graduation ceremony. Because we have the choice whether to walk with the girls or boys during graduation. Even for proms . . . Farrington has a history of having a lot of queens. When I went to the prom in drag, it was no problem. The principal was just in awe; she came up to me and said, "Oh my gosh — how do you walk in those shoes?!" "Very carefully."

Phoebe: Yeah, Chrysalis opened our doors. What April is doing right now with it is really great!

Jennifer: She is making the younger queens open their eyes, so they can see that you don't have to be ashamed to be transgendered. Because it's not like we choose to be this way. It's just that this is the way we are.

Phoebe: It's just the way we feel.

Jennifer: But we do choose to get surgeries like breast implants and sex changes . . .

Phoebe: To make ourselves look more womanly and ladylike.

Jennifer: It's how we feel. In our hearts we feel we are women, so we're going to take steps to make ourselves look like women.

Phoebe: It's just that April was the one who had the guts to go out there and make that group. And so far it's working fine.

***

Phoebe: For me, my family life was kind of on the rocks because my dad was an alcoholic. He loved to gamble a lot, so he was really abusive. I always got the end of everybody's shit. I was the one that always got beaten up and yelled at. I didn't get anything special from my family. The only one I got special treatment from was my mom. She was the one that did everything for me. Whatever I wanted she gave to me. There are five altogether in my family, two boys and three girls, and I'm the youngest one. My brother didn't really accept me at all. Any time he saw me acting like that, he would hit me. Just the fact that he would hit me made me *more* determined to be a woman.

I had it easier later on because of my dad passing. So that was an obstacle I didn't have to worry about anymore. I didn't have to worry about getting beaten up every day by my dad just because of the way I was.

After my mom died . . . that was the biggest problem I would have to overcome because she had supported me in the way I was. So I learned to take one step at a time and just do what I had to do. As for my sisters, one of them didn't like it at all because of her religion. She is Mormon. She tried to make me be a Mormon, but I told her, "No, I don't want to get baptized to be a Mormon. I feel the way I feel and you feel the way you feel. If you want to call me your brother, your sister, whatever, you may do so. But just remember — I am related to you by blood and I don't care if you disown me or anything because I will always be your brother or your sister or whatever you want me to be." My other two sisters really accepted it. And my brother is learning to accept it, slowly learning. Right now he's in rehab. He's a druggie, that's why. That my family is slowly learning to accept the "t" makes it better for me. I would rather go through all the hardship *now* than later because it's going to hurt later on. Especially if any of my siblings pass away and I never got to hear them say, "I love you for the person you are." That's what I really want to hear from them. Because that's what you wait for. To hear them say, "I don't care who you are, I love you for the person that you are." That's the thing that I'm waiting for — unconditional love.

Jennifer: It was easier for me to come out because my older brother was a queen. He's not a queen anymore; he's just gay. But it was easier for me because he started dressing up first. But my mom and dad always knew that I was like this. I think that if any parent is a good parent, they're going to know. How can you not know? If you communicate well with your children, you're going to know. Now my dad accepts it, but before it was really hard for him. One of the reasons was that he had two queen sisters, and he just hated queens with a passion. Older queens told me that my dad would beat them up every day when they were younger. But I think my mom helped to change him. Because my mom is a very intelligent woman. She worked for years trying to change him and I think it's worked, because now he's a totally different person. He's not violent anymore. At first, when I started to dress up, he would be against it. But a couple of months ago I went home and I was all dressed up, face and all, and he told me I looked pretty. I was so surprised and thought, "Oh my gosh!"

I have a brother who is like my dad used to be. But he has to accept me being a queen. Because I'm eighteen, I've graduated, I pay my own bills . . . So his opinion doesn't matter. If he paid my bills, then his opinion would matter. But he doesn't. The rest of my family — there are nine of us all together — accepts it, even my little brother. And my sisters — they love it. They love it because I get to do their makeup and hair. [laughs] They love going out and looking really pretty, with everybody asking, "Oh my gosh, who did your hair? Wow, your make-up is nice!" They love it.

***

Jennifer: We go out a lot and meet people from all different places. Some people aren't surprised by us because there are a lot of transgendered people where they're from. But a lot of those who've already been exposed to transgendered people respect the fact that the queens in Hawai'i look like women. Because where they're from, people who are transgendered don't look like women. So they're surprised that the queens in Hawai'i can pass as women. A lot of them don't even know what transgendered is. We say, "We're transsexual." And they're like, "What is a transsexual?" So we tell them, "We're dudes." A lot of them trip out, but are eager to learn about it; they're very curious. I met a lot of guys from Australia — when I tell them I'm a transsexual they're really curious. "Oh, you are? What do *you* like to do? What gives *you* pleasure?" They're really interested — "When did you know you were like this? How does your family feel?"

Most people I meet are really interested to learn about it. Sometimes when they find out — and they're with their friends — they're like, "Ugghh!" And they dis it. But then they come back by themselves and want to know more about it or they want to get with us. So when people are in a group it's a whole different attitude from when they are by themselves.

Phoebe: Being transgendered and in public . . . sometimes it can be good, sometimes it can be bad. There were a few times when we got into physical altercations with other people because they couldn't handle it. They were so narrow-minded. I've been with a few guys I like to label as "roughnecks." "*Haole* roughnecks." They're from places like Alabama. They say they don't like it, but in actuality they do. They're curious about it and are willing to learn more about how we live and what we do. I have no problem in answering all the questions they ask. For me, being in public is a lot better because you can express yourself to people who are not exposed to the transgender community and really let them know that we're out there and that we're living a life, that we're making something of ourselves. If you want to learn, we're there to help you. But if you want to be narrow-minded, then you go ahead and do your own thing. But don't come over here and dis us. Because we're not doing that to you. Respect us for the people who we are and we'll respect you for who you are. You live your life, I'll live my life.

Jennifer: That's what I cannot understand. Sometimes we'll go out and people will trash talk to us and every time they do that I just feel so confused. I go up to them and ask, "What did we do to you? What did we do to you to make you feel that way?" Every time we go to Jack In The Box it's always like that. We're just standing in line or standing outside and someone will *always* say something.

Phoebe: Always, always.

Jennifer: Sometimes guys will be trash talking and I'll go up to them and say, "What is your problem? I didn't do anything to you. I don't even know you. You don't know me. You don't know what I'm about." They say, "Oh, well, you're dudes and you dress in girls' clothes." And I'm like, "So what? You're a dude and you dress in baggy clothes. What's the point? There are girls who dress in guys' clothes. What's the point? It's just clothes!"

Phoebe: A lot of them just have really narrow minds or want to look good in front of their friends.

Jennifer: But Lord knows, when they're by themselves it's a different story . . .

Phoebe: Girls can be really, really bad about it. Especially when they're in a bunch. Girls can be really jealous.

Jennifer: Especially when they're with their boyfriends. Because guys will always look — that's just the way guys are. When they see something, they'll always look. Anything with tits and ass — they're going to look. [laughs] And girls get really jealous when they see their boyfriends looking at us. So that's when they start talking shit about us. They're just lucky because we're males; legally, on paper, we're males. If I were a female I'd go straight up to her and slap her face!

Phoebe: Yeah, if I had a choice and somebody was talking shit like that, I wouldn't hesitate to crack them. [laughs] It's really bad.

Jennifer: Yeah, they are so ignorant.

Phoebe: I would think girls would be a lot more open-minded about it. But some of them are really narrow-minded. "Ooh — you're boys! Don't dress like that! You're supposed to dress like boys!" I look at them and think that women should have more open minds because of all the stuff that they have to go through, but actually they are really narrow-minded.

Jennifer: But there are also a lot who are open-minded.

Phoebe: Yeah, some tell us, "Oh, you're pretty."

Jennifer: They look at our beauty and say, "Oh my gosh — why can't I do that? You're a guy and you can look like that; I'm a girl and I can't even look like that." A lot of them like exotic beauty and are just obsessed with that look.

Phoebe: Some of them are really nice . . . You just always have your bad apples.

Phoebe: We know we're going to get harassed, especially when we go to Jack In The Box. But we're just like, "You know what — Fuck it. We're going to go over there and eat in front of all of them." [laughs]

Jennifer: And everybody is just staring at us.

Phoebe: Even though we don't see them staring, we can feel it. All that bad tension.

Jennifer: We can just feel the vibes . . .

Jennifer: When I go out and people harass me, I try to ignore them because I just think they're stupid. If they're not paying my bills, if they're not helping me out in any way, then they mean nothing to me. So I don't really care *what* they say.

Phoebe: We're used to it already, that's why. We just walk away.

Jennifer: The only time I get mad at someone is when they start getting physical. That's when the high heels are coming off!

Phoebe: Yeah. It's when they start throwing stuff that we get really mad. If you're going to say something, say it. Don't do something stupid.

Jennifer: We've had stuff thrown at us. A lot of queens would try to ignore it, but us, we do something about it. Whether it means chasing the person down or calling the cops, we're going to do something about it.

Phoebe: Yeah, you just better hope you can back yourself up if you do something. We're not going to just stand there and let you get away with it. It only happened once or twice where I ignored a person and they got mad. And they started coming after me. I was thinking, "Oh my God — what am I going to do?!" [laughs] It's funny, because you're ignoring them — they're calling you "faggot," "*mahu*," and you're like, "Really? Oh yeah? Really?" And they'd be like, "What?! What did you say?!" Then they'd get really mad.

Jennifer: You know what's so funny? Every time we go out, I'm usually the one . . . If someone's saying something, I don't say anything. I'm like, "Oh well, let it go." While everyone else is saying something. But when it comes down to it, they come up to me — and I'm the shortest one out of all of them. I'm like, "What is your problem, *braddah*?!"

Phoebe: Because we're all tall, that's why. They always tend to pick on the smaller ones. It's kind of funny. But as long as we have each other to back each other up, we feel a lot safer than being by ourselves.

Jennifer: It's really good that we can rely on each other.

***

Phoebe: Ever since I was young I wanted to play professional volley-ball; that's all I wanted to do. For me, I was on the way to reaching that goal with receiving awards and that sort of thing, but after a while I wasn't getting the attention I thought I deserved. Because I wanted to go to college, and received only one scholarship to a school. I thought that maybe I deserved more. I was thinking, "If they find out the way that I am, they're going to be discreet about it and brush me off." So I said to myself, "If I'm not going to be able to make it as a guy, then I'm going to do it as a lady." Because regardless of what anybody thinks, that's really my ultimate goal right now — to get my sex-change and to play professional volleyball as a lady. I want to make it out there in the sports world, even though people might look at me weird — because I don't really care if they know whether I'm a sex-change or not, as long as I get to do what I want to do. I just want to get my change and play professional women's volleyball. That's what I want to do. I want to represent my country in the Olympics. [laughs] Actually, all my life Tee Williams has been a role model to me in volleyball. Because she's been so good. Plus, she's African-American, so I can imagine some of the barriers which she had to break. So that's one of my goals.

My other one is to get a good job and make it out there. Even though it doesn't mean with a spouse . . . I just want to do what *I* want to do. I don't want to have to look over my shoulder all the time, worrying about what other people are thinking about me. That's one thing that I don't want to do. I just want to go out there and be myself and show the world that I *can* do it. It doesn't matter what you are or where you come from, your background or anything. Just do what you want to do and feel comfortable doing it.

Jennifer: My goal is to be a fashion designer. I really love fashion; I'm very artistic. I like to express myself in art. So I'm going to go back to school, but after my transition. At least when I feel that I'm passable. Because if I don't feel I'm passable, then I'm not going to want to do anything. Another goal of mine is to get married — and have a big wedding. I want to make my wedding dress . . . I just want to have a fabulous wedding . . . that would be so cool. I know only of one other queen who had a nice wedding — Michele from Farrington — she's a real popular queen. I want to have a really nice wedding like hers. Get married to a nice guy.

Phoebe: Yeah.

✳✳✳

Jennifer: Some of the prettier queens act really shady to the queens who are not so pretty or to those who are just starting out. With me, I'm really polite to everyone I meet. If I see a new queen I'll go over and introduce myself to her and get to know her. I don't care how you look. To me, everything is in the way you carry yourself. If you carry yourself in a proper way, a presentable way, you should be fine. You may not be the prettiest person in the world, but it's all in the way you carry yourself. That's one thing my mom taught me — There's a time and place for everything. And you have to carry yourself with the time and place. When queens do act shady, like if they don't want another queen to come with them because, "Oh, you're going to clock my t," I think that's so sad. If they're so scared of getting their t clocked, then they're not being honest with themselves. For me, I could care less if somebody clocks my t. I think if someone knows my t, then that's better because then they know what I'm about and who I am.

Phoebe: I think that the queens who neglect other queens have an image problem with themselves. Maybe they act that way because they don't want to be recognized as ugly or anything like that. To me, every queen starts off ugly, because when you get in that transition period and you're getting rid of everything and you're getting your surgeries and whatnot — you're going to go through an ugly stage. Every queen goes through it. And for those queens who neglect the other ones, I feel they have something wrong with themselves which they can't really confront. If you can't confront your fears, it's not going to make you a better person. If a person has a bad attitude you should kill them with kindness. [laughs] You're going to make them realize what they're really doing is wrong, that the way they present themselves is wrong. There are too many bitches out there, so you should be nice to everybody. And in return you're going to get it back. That's how I feel — just be nice.

***

Jennifer: In the *mahu* community we have queen mothers, but it doesn't matter who's older or younger — it depends who came out first. I know a couple of queens whose mothers are younger than they are. It's because the mothers came out before their daughters did.

Phoebe: The so-called queen mother I have is called Jade. A queen mother is someone who is there for you in your time of need. But this person has never been there for me! [laughs]

Jennifer: I really can't consider her a queen mother because we grew up with her. When we came to Farrington she was a senior, yet she still denied she was a queen. She had a mustache and everything. It was only when we came to Farrington and we didn't care what anybody thought — that's when she came out.

Phoebe: I think it's because she didn't have the same support group that we did.

Jennifer: She didn't have other queens in the school who supported her. I was her daughter before, but I couldn't respect her in that way because I didn't feel like she was a mother. She was more like a peer. One day I got into a fight with her and I said, "You're not my mother anymore." I have a new queen mother, Fou, although I haven't seen her in a long time. I respect her because she is older and has been through a lot. I remember when I first met her, she wanted me to start on hormones, but I didn't want to because I was still playing volleyball. She was always telling me, "Girl, you are going to be so pretty."

Phoebe: For me, I would rather look at you as a sister than as a mother. You're always going to have someone there to help you, but why would you think of them as a mother? From my perspective, you only have one mother, and that's your biological mother. Everybody else that you meet are your sisters or your brothers or cousins. So for me, Jade is not really a queen mother, she's just a close friend. So I would rather think of you as a sister because I get closer to you that way more than a mother would. But I've never had anybody who was there for me when I was down because I've never had a bad situation that I had to be pulled out of. I've never had those kinds of experiences. But if I do have those experiences, I would want someone to be there for me, someone I could count on, depend on, to help me through my tough times. With both of my parents dying when I was young, I really had to depend on myself and pull myself forward. I had to think of life as a daily step by step thing. I had to do it myself. So I can't really say I had a real queen mother.

***

Jennifer: When I was a sophomore I started cruising around town — the streets — and meeting a lot of the queens. But I wouldn't work on the streets. I'd just come out and cruise and watch how they work. My junior year is when I started to work. I was really, really scared at first. But after a while I got used to it. At the time I could make a lot of money. It was really good at the time to work there because it was very busy. But it's different now — it's much slower. Before it would be really good business and you could make a lot of money in one night. Before, no matter what time you came out, you would have made something.

I felt scared when I first started to work out there because I was working on the backstreets. That's where a lot of the drug addicted queens work. I was scared that I would go with some guy and he'd shoot me and leave me somewhere. I was also scared that I would get picked up by a cop. So I started to work and hang around with some of the queens. They pointed out the dates they knew and the ones they didn't know. They told me who the good dates were. I wasn't so scared after that. But after I got busted — that's when I was really scared. Even now, I'm really paranoid to date someone. I'll only date someone I've dated before, or who somebody else has dated. Or if I always see him around picking up girls. But I will not date someone I don't know or have never seen before. Because I'm so scared of getting caught again. I'm so scared to date people I don't know. I'll have to tell the guy, "I don't know you, so I don't want to date you. Maybe if you can tell me who you dated before and I'll talk to them and see if they dated you, then I'll date you." This one guy said, "I can't remember her name." So I said, "Oh well, honey, you're out of luck."

But the streets are not like before, when you could make a lot of money. Now you can make your money, but it's harder because a lot of queens are coming out and they're starting to charge less. That's how they bring all of us down. Because as soon as the dates find out they're charging less, they're only going to go to them; they're not going to think about coming to us. Why spend a hundred dollars when you can spend twenty bucks? If I were a date, I would just want to spend twenty bucks. I wouldn't want to be spending a hundred dollars.

I've never come across a transgendered girl who had a pimp. Everyone works independently. I think the women prostitutes get pimps for security . . . Everyone has their areas. Merchant [Street] is all queens. Back streets — half are queens, half are girls, but most of them are drug addicts. In Waikiki there are certain places for us to work. We only stand at a certain area. Or like around the gay clubs. We don't go to the other corners to work. But I've heard of some pimps coming up to some of the girls and telling them to get off the street, that they don't belong there and to go back to wherever they came from. It's because we're taking their business. A lot of guys have come up to us and told us that we look better than a lot of the real girls who are standing on the other corners. I guess it's because a lot of them are so skinny and fragile-looking — they don't have any meat on their bodies. We're so heavy-set over here. [laughs] But some of the pimps are cool; they'll come around and date us. I've never dated a pimp . . . at least I don't think I've dated a pimp . . . if he was I didn't know . . . but a lot of my friends have dated pimps.

A lot of the pimps will come up to us with their girls to watch us work. They'll say to their girls, "Look at them. You don't see them sitting down." I think the pimps don't bother us because they know how it is in prison. The queens rule the prison. Because, you know guys — they have sexual urges. If they want it, they're going to find something that looks closest to a girl as possible. And there are queens inside who just rule. Some of them are really rough. That's why the pimps respect us. Because the queens can get really rough.

Phoebe: The first time I really worked the street, I was introduced by her [Jennifer]. It was just to go out at first. After a while I got curious and thought to myself, "Oh, I wonder if I can ever make money doing this?" So I tried it, and after a while it got better and better and better. I started dating more and more. I guess there is a certain thing the dates look for, and I guess I got it. So far it's been good. I've never been caught yet, and

I dread the day I do get caught because I'm an adult now. So the penalty would be stiffer.

Working the street and prostituting . . . the way I think about it is, even though it's illegal, you do it, but you do it smart. You make your money, do what you have to do, and then you go home. You don't go over there hanging around and showing everybody that you're a prostitute. One of the strategies I use is that I ask my dates for their ID. And if they're a date, they'll give you their ID. So that's been working for me. But I think you can basically tell who the cops are. Because the undercovers will push you right into it. They'll get down to the nitty-gritty right away. Some dates just want to talk and negotiate. For the cops it's more like, "I have a hundred dollars, get in, let's go." That's how you know it's them — they want to get it done already and get you arrested and go pop another girl. So you have to be careful. And if you do go with a date, try to get his number so you can work out of your house. [laughs] Because then you can work when it's convenient for you.

Jennifer: Yeah, us — we're vampires.

Phoebe: Sleep all day, stay up all night.

Jennifer: Usually we sleep all day and get up in the late afternoon. Then we stay up until six the next morning. That's our daily routine, everyday.

(Together): Sleep, get up, go to work. [laugh]

Phoebe: Yeah. And we hardly ever have fun. Last Sunday was the last time we had fun in a *real* long time. We went to Bayfest and then to a club afterwards . . . In this profession, you're hardly ever going to have fun. Especially now, because you don't know if you're going to go out on the street and be able to make money.

Jennifer: So we try to work as much as possible.

Phoebe: Yeah. So we can get it done now and then won't have to worry about it later. Because some nights it can be really bad. We go and stand out there for nothing. We've only got the palm trees talking to us. [laughs]

***

Jennifer: At first I enjoyed working because being like this [i.e. a queen], you don't get too much attention from boys. But when you go somewhere like the street where guys look for queens and they're horny, that's when you start to get a lot of attention from boys. So when I first came out I started to get a lot of attention from boys. And I really liked it. But after a while it dies out and you don't feel the same way anymore. So now . . . I don't enjoy doing it anymore. I don't enjoy it at all. But I do it because I have to do it — I have to pay the bills.

Phoebe: The attention is good. But after a while you just get sick of it. It just becomes a daily routine. "Give me your money." "What do you want?" "Let's get it on." All that kind of stuff. Some of the guys know that it's just a routine for us. But some guys get mad because we don't put any effort into it.

Jennifer: Yeah, they say, "You're only in it for the money!" And I'm thinking, "Why else would I be doing this?! You've known us for only five seconds and you want us to fall in love with you." [laughs]

Phoebe: That's how some guys are. They tend to fall in love and then want you to be their girlfriend.

Jennifer: Yeah, so sometimes you've just got to play that role.

Phoebe: It's like a circus act. [laughs] If you have the right attitude you can make a lot of money. But if you're a real bitch it's going to be hard. So as long as you treat your dates nicely, you'll know that they'll be back. And with some of them, you can even get connections. I mean, some of them have really good jobs, so if you ever need a car or a loan, you know where they work and you can go to them. And if they don't want to help you . . .

Jennifer: "I'll tell your wife!" [laughs]

***

Phoebe: I see myself as a regular person. I actually don't see myself as a lady yet, because of the person I see in the mirror. Until I can see myself in the mirror as a full woman, I won't think of myself as a lady. Right now I just think of myself as a transsexual. I know myself as a transsexual and I will not deny this to anybody who asks me about it. I think of myself this way now because I don't have the tools, as I put it, to be a lady. Right now I'm developing, and there are certain terms that are OK for me.

Jennifer: Like she-male. [laughs]

Phoebe: Yeah. I think "she-male" is an OK term. Or transsexual. But if you were ever to call me a faggot, that's when I would say something. Because "faggot" is a real bad term. So right now transsexual for me is fine because I know I'm a transsexual. Not a lady. I would like to think of myself as a lady, but the person I see in the mirror doesn't look as lady-like as I would like her to look. Inside I've always felt like a lady. That's why I want to make my appearance look more ladylike. It's going to take time. But as soon as I get there, everything I'm doing now will stop. Being flamboyant . . . It's all going to turn around. Because I'm going to want my life to revolve around being a woman, a lady.

Jennifer: I just consider myself as myself. When people ask me, "Are you gay?" I say, "No, I'm not gay." I have always looked at myself as a normal person who just likes guys. A regular relationship between a guy and a girl. But it's just like Phoebe said. Until I can be passable, looking in the mirror and feeling that I look like a female, then that is when I'm going to consider myself a *woman*. But until then, I'm fine with the terms "transsexual," "drag queen," whatever.

My goal — I want to be a *woman*. Maybe not now, but as I progress in my life I want to become a woman. Being a woman to me means going out in public and people don't look at you like a freak. They're looking at you as a woman. Even if they know what you're all about, they still consider you as a woman because you look like a woman, you have features like a woman, you present yourself as a woman, you act like a woman, you're very ladylike. That's what I consider a woman. I don't really feel passable right now. But I still feel like a woman inside . . .

And as for the word "*mahu*" — *I do not like that word at all.*

Phoebe: Actually, for me, I think "*mahu*" is the politically correct term in the Hawaiian language for people like us. I have no problem with it. I can have Hawaiian people say it, but it's a different story if a *haole* person says it. Because I know they are degrading me. For Hawaiian people, I know they aren't degrading me because that's the only word they know. But those *haole* who use it, they know what *mahu* is, and they use it in a bad way. It's all in the way you use the word.

Jennifer: Yeah. If we call each other "fag" or "*mahu*," it's all right. Because we're like this. But if somebody else said it, that would be totally wrong.

***

Jennifer: It's kind of cool to be the new generation of queens. But it also makes me scared because you see all these *old* queens and they're like, "Oh girl, I used to be just like you when I was young." [laughs] That gets me scared because I think, "'Oh my gosh — one day we're going to be that old." But it's kind of cool because the older queens say, "You guys are the new generation, you guys are going to take over now, you guys are going to be the ones to carry it on." Just like on the streets — the older queens made the streets, but we're the ones who are keeping it alive. Unfortunately some other queens are trying to bring it down, charging less!

It's cool to be the new generation, because in this time and place it seems to be more accepted than before. There are a lot more things we can do to find out who we are and learn more about ourselves. There are a lot of programs to help people like us. So it's kind of cool being transgendered at this time, right now. It's accepted.

Phoebe: I think the new generation of transsexuals is learning the ways of the older ones and then trying to apply that to their daily lives. A lot of the older queens tell us not to do this, not to do that . . . Of course we might be stupid and not listen — that's natural. But we all need to learn from our different experiences. And the older ones look forward to the new generation to come up and do what they did or even do better, to try to break even more barriers. Because with every barrier you break, people will look at you and think of you as a hero or role model. And it's always good to look forward to doing those kinds of things. Like if an older queen didn't get to do it, then why not go and do it. Do what you feel like doing, have fun, and live your life — just make sure that you do it in a good way. If you do fall, at least pick yourself back up and try again.

Jennifer: A lot of the older queens tell me that things are so much easier for our generation because we're coming out so much younger.

Phoebe: Yeah, a lot of us came out a lot younger than they did. I came out around ten. It was before my mom passed away. She had already suspected what I was, but didn't really know until I was about ten. That was when I came out and told her that I liked what I was doing. She said she didn't care what I did as long as I graduated from high school.

Right now, for the new generation so far . . . some of us are doing good, and some of us are doing really, really bad. For those girls who are dropping out of high school, we're trying to help them out, trying to get them back to school. If not . . . If you don't want to go to school and get an education, you'd better get your ass out there and work and make a living.

Jennifer: A queen once told me, "It's 'p' to be a queen, but it's even more 'p' to be an educated queen."

Phoebe: Yeah. Because if you're educated, you can have a high paying job and don't have to depend on the streets for your money. Queens will look up to you big time if you get that education.

***

Phoebe: My final thought would be to those who are narrow-minded and don't even want to look at transgendered people or talk to them . . . Well, you know what? *You have issues.* And you need to solve those issues before you can do anything else. Before you ever call anybody else "faggot," "*mahu*," or anything, you'd better take a real good look at yourself because when you have children, your son might come out *mahu*. And if that happens you'd better make sure you accept him for who he is. So you should always take into consideration what you say to other people, whether they be transgendered, gay or lesbian.

Jennifer: I'd like to say my final thought to all the younger transgendered teens out there: do what you've got to do. Don't take other people's opinions too hard. Because in the end, it's only your opinion that matters. And to the other people out there: I hope this book helps you to understand our point of view. We don't choose to be like this. It's just the way we are.

EPILOGUE

EPILOGUE

The first time I met Ashliana she told me about the Wizard Stones of Waikiki: four huge boulders planted over five hundred years ago in what is now called Kuhio Beach. This was done in order to honor four powerful healers from Tahiti. For Ashliana, along with several other participants in this book, these stones are significant because, according to legend, the healers were *mahu*. This element of the story marks the stones both as a source of pride as well as a valuable connection to the past for present-day Hawaiian and Tahitian *mahu* (interestingly, both languages use this same word to refer to transgendered individuals). The more I learned about the Wizard Stones, the more I felt that they were connected to the present in another way — through this book. And so I would like to end *'O Au No Keia* by examining how the story of the stones may act as an allegory for transgendersim in contemporary Hawai'i. In addition, I will revisit and summarize what I believe to be some of the more dominant themes found within the book's narratives.

The site of the Wizard Stones is difficult to miss while walking down Kalakaua Avenue in Waikiki. As you pass by the Sheraton Moana Surfrider hotel and the new police station on Kuhio Beach, you quickly come upon four boulders set into a dirt platform which is ringed by a stone wall. Encircling these stones are green bushes which are further surrounded by an imposing wrought-iron fence. At the head of the memorial stand two large plaques, one with Hawaiian text, the other with English. The latter reads:

The Stones of Life
Na Pohaku Ola Kapaemahu A Kapuni

275

ATZ

Legend says these stones are the living legacy of four powerful Tahitian healers who once resided near this site at a place called Ulukou. From the court of the Tahitian chief, the names of the four were Kapaemahu, Kapuni, Kinohi, Kahaloa. They came from Moa'ulanuiakea on the island of Raiatea long before the reign of Kakuhihewa, beloved O'ahu chief during the 1500s.

The fame of the healers spread as they traveled throughout the islands administering their miraculous cures. When it was time to return to Raiatea they asked that two stones be placed at their Ulukou residence and two at their favorite bathing place in the sea. Four huge stones were quarried from Kaimuki and on the night of "Kane" thousands transported the stones to Ulukou. Incantations, fasting and prayer lasted a full cycle of the moon. The healers then gave their names and *mana* (spiritual power) to the stones before departing for their homeland.

PiPi Holo Ka'ao

(Sprinkled, the tale runs)

In 1997 the stones were raised onto a *paepae* (stone platform), and an *ahu* (altar) and fence were built to honor and protect them. The largest stone was estimated to weigh 7.5 tons. As part of the project's ceremonies, Tahitians from Raiatea presented a stone from the healers' homeland which they named *Ta'ahu Ea* (The life).

These ancient stones are part of the spiritual history of Waikiki and native Hawaiian people. They remind us of the need to preserve and honor Hawai'i's unique heritage for generations to come.

Department of Parks and Recreation

City and County of Honolulu 1997

Interestingly, there is nothing on this plaque to indicate the stones' connection with either *mahu* or transgenderism except for the name Kapaemahu (one possible meaning is, "The arrival of the *mahu*"). Intrigued after first learning about the Wizard Stones, I began searching for more information by looking through tourist guidebooks to Hawai'i. All mentioned the stones but individual accounts conformed to either one of two versions. Some followed closely the story of the plaque. However, other descriptions related that the "wizards" were in fact "hermaphrodites." My curiousity piqued by this discrepency, I decided to visit the Bishop Museum library to see how far back I could trace descriptions of the stones. With the help of a librarian I located two sources in English for the legend of the stones (one, by James Boyd, is from 1906; the other, by June Gutmanis, is not dated, but appears to have been written in the mid 1980s). Although both writers utilized different source material (including oral history; the examination of state archives and newspaper articles; and personal correspondence with knowledgeable sources), their stories are similar. What follows is a summary of their accounts.

Long before the sixteenth-century reign of the Hawaiian Chief Kakuihewa, four soothsayers/healers from the court of the Tahitian king made their way to Hawai'i. Their names were Kapaemahu, Kahaloa, Kapuni and Kinohi. Gutmanis states that people have used the terms "unsexed" as well as "*mahu*" to refer to the healers. However, she also relates that in more recent stories, Kapaemahu and Kapuni are said to have been males, and Kahaloa and Kinohi females. In his account Boyd writes, "[The four] were received as became their station, and their tall stature, courteous ways and kindly manners made them loved by the Hawaiian people. The attractiveness of their fine physique and kindly demeanor was overshadowed by their low, soft speech which endeared them to all with whom they came in contact. They were unsexed by nature, and their habits coincided with their feminine appearance, although manly in stature and general bearing" (p.140).

After spending a long time traveling throughout the different Hawaiian islands, the four finally settled at Ulukou (or Kou), in Waikiki. Due to their wondrous powers of healing, the fame of the Tahitians spread far and wide, and great numbers of Hawaiians came to visit them. After a period of time, the healers decided that they would leave Hawai'i. In Boyd's retelling, it was because the healers wanted to be remembered in a tangible way for their accomplishments that they asked the people to erect four large stones: two to be placed on the spot where they were living, and two at the spot in the ocean where they were fond of bathing. The healers requested that the stones be collected from the area of the famous "bell rock," at Kaimuki. According to Gutmanis, the healers asked the people to erect a monument commemorating their stay in Hawai'i. It was the people themselves who then decided that four large stones would be an appropriate memorial, and removed them from the "bell rock" quarry.

Both writers agree that the time for the transportation of the basalt stones was set for the night of "Kane, the twenty-seventh night of the moon-month." Thousands worked to move the stones, weighing several tons each, to their designated locations in Waikiki.

After the stones were set in place, the chief healer, Kapaemahu, conducted ceremonies to transfer his spiritual power to one of the stones (which was named after him). A sacrifice of a young chieftess was also made, and her body was placed underneath the stone. In addition, both Boyd and Gutmanis relate that "idols indicating the hermaphrodite sex of the wizards were also placed under each stone." The ceremonies and prayers by which the other three healers transferred their powers to each of the stones lasted for one full moon. When the rituals were finally complete, the Tahitians vanished and were never heard from again.

Regarding the later history of the stones, Gutmanis reports that in the mid-nineteenth century Princess Likelike, the wife of Governor A. S. Cleghorn and mother of Princess Kaiulani, always offered a *lei* to each of the stones and said a prayer every time she entered the ocean. However, by the turn of the twentieth century it appears that all of the stones had been covered by sand. It wasn't until around 1907 that Governor Cleghorn unearthed them. After Cleghorn's death, the stones were offered to the Bishop Museum, which declined to take them. In 1941 the Cleghorn property was leased for the construction of a bowling alley, at which time the stones were apparently buried under the new building's foundations. In 1958, the City and County of Honolulu took over that same area and decided to make it into a park. After the demolition of the bowling alley the four stones were rediscovered.

Because of the stones' history, the Parks Board decided to leave them in that area, and in 1963 they were deeply embedded into the beach sand. Gutmanis writes that due to beach improvements in early 1980, the stones were again moved, this time some fifty feet away. After being placed in their new home under a banyan tree along Kalakaua Avenue, Hawaiian and Christian priests recited blessings over the stones. This is where Gutmanis' account ends. The stones were moved one more time in 1997, at which time they were raised onto a special platform and sanctified with a special ceremony involving representatives from Tahiti, who brought a small stone from their homeland to be placed beside the memorial plaque. Finally, after years of neglect — during which beachgoers often dried their towels on and leaned their surfboards against the boulders — the "Wizard Stones" had regained their glory and become a noted monument on the beach of Waikiki.

Contrary to the accounts of Boyd and Gutmanis, nowhere on the Wizard Stones' memorial plaque does it mention that the "wizards" were, or might have been, *mahu*. This is ironic considering that the last two sentences of the plaque state, "These ancient stones are part of the spiritual history of Waikiki and native Hawaiian people. They remind us of the need to preserve and honor Hawaii's unique heritage for generations to come." It is unfortunate that the Honolulu Department of Parks and Recreation did not see fit to include *mahu* in Hawai'i's "spiritual history" and "unique heritage," even though their existence in precontact Hawai'i is orally well-documented by *kupuna*. Regardless of its worthy intentions, the Department of Parks and Recreation succeeded in obscuring the significant role transgenderism plays in the stones' history by leaving out key information from their legend. Indeed, the plaque's revised version of the Wizard Stones story illustrates how the cultural history and value of transgenderism can so easily be lost. It is for this very reason that the Wizard Stones themselves may be seen as an allegory for the struggles of transgendered people in contemporary Hawai'i.

Although the Wizard Stones are on full-view on Waikiki beach, the hundreds of tourists who pass by them each day are largely unaware of the details of their story. The memorial is located in a conspicuous location, yet the transgendered aspect at its core remains deeply buried, like a piece of history deemed unfit for consumption. Similarly, many people living on O'ahu, whether of Hawaiian background or not, have little or no understanding of the valuable roles *mahu* once played in Hawaiian culture. Present-day transgendered people have drifted from their heritage as well. Rather than claiming their places in society as healers, caregivers, or teachers, many present-day queens on Oʻahu must work the streets in order to survive. Indeed, the word "*mahu*" has lost its cultural salience to such an extent that it has become an insult to throw at gay or transgendered people. Perhaps the author of the Wizard Stones' plaque felt obligated by either fear or shame to ignore the transgenderism of the four healers; in the same way, many families in Hawaiʻi today fail to recognize the specialness of their transgendered children and instead view them as worthy only of condemnation. It is unfortunate that although so many aspects of Hawaiian culture have been reclaimed and reinvigorated due to the Hawaiian renaissance, transgenderism is still largely ignored.

To this day, the Wizard Stones remain silent about their *mahu* heritage. However, it is interesting to note that the stones are reportedly composed of a certain type of basalt known to produce a ringing sound when struck. While the stones themselves are silent, resonant tones nevertheless float on the island trade winds. This sound is echoed in the efforts of a small number of queens of Hawaiian background who have begun to reclaim the term "*mahu*." Exploring the roles their spiritual ancestors played in precontact Hawaiian society, the members of this group want to ensure that this knowledge will never be lost again. The slowly increasing number of queens who are beginning to feel comfortable identifying themselves as "*mahu*" indicates that this group's message is gradually taking hold. *ʻO Au No Keia* is meant to play a small part in this educational process by making transgendered lives visible to the general public. And so, what have we learned about these people's experiences? What do the narratives in this book tell us about being transgendered on Oʻahu today?

One dominant theme in this collection is that the cultural basis of transgenderism in Hawaiian culture has resulted in it being more visible here than on the mainland. One effect of this widespread visibility is that youngsters see and interact with queens from an early age. This is quite different from the situation on the mainland. I have been told by a number of older transgendered people originally from the mainland that while growing up they believed that they were the only transgendered people in the world; they could not imagine there was anyone else like them. Naturally, they felt lonely, frustrated and confused. Today, however, things are different because of the spread of internet sites and magazines dealing with transgenderism. In particular, transgendered people can connect with others like themselves due to the large number of chat rooms that are now available on-line. Nonetheless, there is still the chance that transgendered people on the mainland may grow up without coming into contact with others like themselves. Because they lack role models, social support and a cultural heritage of transgenderism, mainland queens or transsexuals may suppress their feelings of gender dysphoria and instead conform to male gender expectations by marrying and starting a family. Frequently, it is not until mid-life or beyond that transgendered people finally embrace the side of themselves which they had hidden for so many years.

On the other hand, people on the Hawaiian islands with transgendered feelings tend to begin their transition to womanhood much earlier. Although a youngster might be alienated and unaccepted at home, it is much easier to find a support system on Oʻahu than on the mainland because of the opportunites for interaction with queens at school, among relatives, or on the streets. This factor highlights the difference of the ages of transition between local and mainland-raised contributors to this book. For example, Paige told me that when she was a teenager she looked forward to her family gatherings because her aunties, who were queens, always entertained at them. "So that's how I got exposed. I could say to myself, 'You know what, I can be this way, too. I can be *mahu* and an entertainer.'" Tracy, originally from the mainland, also commented on the differences between growing up on the east coast as opposed to Oʻahu. "Where I grew up in Connecticut, the idea of being transgendered in school — in high school — is just . . . like a fantasy for anybody who's like me. But you come out here, and there are lots of transgendered people in the schools, even in the junior high schools, who are braiding their hair, wearing makeup, and being very open about it. Of course, they get some grief, being in a teenage situation — teenagers are like that. But it's a much different mindset. There's the idea that *it can be done*, existing within the person who wants to do it. And that makes a big difference."

The size of O'ahu also plays a part in building a sense of community among those who are transgendered here. Bubbles told me, "In Hawai'i we're afforded the luxury of living on an island that is forty-five miles by thirty miles. To get to a person, it will only take you an hour. People on the mainland might have to travel a day to get to the nearest transgendered person. So they do not have the close-knit family that we have. And when I talk about family, we treat each other as family. Yes, we're all friends, but we're all in this together and all the transgendered people, whether they're pre-op, post-op, transvestite, whatever, in Hawai'i we're all in this together, and we're close — a close-knit family." This Hawaiian concept of *ohana*, or the importance of the family, was emphasized by many of the transgendered people with whom I spoke. Whether or not it is actualized in daily life, there is a general feeling that all of the queens on O'ahu are bound together as a large family, and as such owe one another understanding and support.

Of course, acceptance from blood relatives is also important for queens. As the contributors have shown, levels of familial approval are far from uniform. Parents may either reject their children outright or fully accept them; begrudgingly tolerate their behavior or welcome their new "daughters" into their homes once they fully transition into passable womanhood. Some participants explained it wasn't that their parents disapproved of their transgenderism per se; rather, mothers and fathers were scared for their children. Looking towards the future of their transgendered child, some adults saw only difficulty and pain. One major concern is career options, which are limited for openly transgendered individuals. There is also the likelihood that a person passing as a woman will be fired if her birth sex is discovered by an employer. This situation results from prejudice, as well as the difficulty queens often have attaining higher levels of education.

Although it is at school that some queens make the connections with like-minded friends which support them through their transition, the teenage years are challenging as well. Indeed, both students as well as school officials can be extremely prejudiced, and I have heard many stories about transgendered students who suffered various forms of verbal, physical and/or sexual abuse at the hands of both. Adolescence is hard enough for gender-normative young men and women; it is even more difficult for transgendered youth. Those who are transgendered must spend a great deal of energy dealing with issues of identity, and — in some cases — harassment at home and at school. These tribulations interfere with the progress of queens in their classes and hamper their academic development. As Kaui told me, "I've always believed that education is important, and that's my biggest failure since I was smart in school — I had Bs and Cs and several As. But because of my gender identity crisis I was going through I couldn't focus. I was more focused on why everybody was calling me a fag, why everybody was being mean to me, why I was being rejected by my family."

This is not to suggest that families who fully accept their transgendered children do not exist, for they do. However, if the situation at school deteriorates, a transgendered student may decide to drop out. The burden of paying for hormones, surgery and clothing is quite heavy without a highschool degree. If one has been kicked out of the house, the added expenses of rent and food often leave queens with few job options. Working the streets becomes a necessity to survive. Almost all of the locally-raised participants in this book worked in sex-work at one time or another, and to this day prostitution remains a dominant way of life within local transgender communities. For queens living in a hostile society, sex-work, with all of its frightening hazards and lucrative benefits, is oftentimes the only available path to take.

All prostitutes potentially face a number of dangers, including deadly sexually transmitted diseases, drug addiciton, and possibly fatal violence. For transgendered sex workers, however, the stakes are even higher. Sometimes the transphobia or misguided homophobia of a customer can result in violence directed at sex-workers who are openly transgendered. And for those queens who seek to fully pass as women to their customers, there is always the possibility of refusal of payment or violence if a customer should discover that the sex worker is transgendered. Prostitutes must also contend with police undercover agents, as well as large-scale crackdowns, both of which can lead to arrests, hefty fines and/or jail time. Parents of queens read about arrests and murders in the newspaper, resulting in fear and negative reactions to their children's transgenderism.

Yet the importance of the streets in providing a sense of community for queens cannot be minimized. Although many queens I spoke with stressed that they disliked the daily risks they had to take as prostitutes, these same people appreciated the camaraderie they found among other queens in that working environment. Ashliana told me, "Out on the streets the other girls were really nice people. It was like one huge support group for transgenders. Regardless of what we were doing, everyone knew each other and respected one another. If not, you were taught fast!"

Also, not to be ignored are the large amounts of money which prostitutes can make in relatively short periods of time. Kaui tells of a golden age in the late eighties and early nineties, in which hundreds of dollars could be charged for each client. However, as Phoebe and Jennifer relate, more competitive younger queens are currently under-cutting prices and driving down rates to ridiculously low levels. This factor, combined with increased police interference, suggests that prostitution is becoming less and less of a worthwhile income strategy for queens. Perhaps this is one of the reasons why their interest in education has recently gained strength.

In addition to sex work, "traditional" career choices for queens have been in the beauty and entertainment industries. Customers who might otherwise be prejudiced against queens or gay men often prefer them to cut their hair or do their makeup. The folk wisdom which attributes natural talent for hairstyling and cosmetology to queens makes these fields attractive ones. And while entertainment might have been a viable career for a lucky few in the days of the wildly popular Glade nightclub, nothing on that level of cabaret exists in Oʻahu today. For those members of the revues at Fusion or Venus nightclubs, female impersonation is a sideline rather than a full-time profession.

However, because of the visibility of queens in the sex work and beauty industries, young impressionable queens have looked to people in these professions as role models. Nevertheless, there are queens who have found success in a wide range of careers. April Weiss has been instrumental in bringing together older queens and teenage queens through an organization named Chrysalis. This support group for transgendered teens has been formed at several high schools in Wai'anae and Honolulu. By inviting successful older transgender women to the group to explain how they navigated their way to well-paying, stable jobs, April has provided a necessary forum in which transgender youth can be encouraged and inspired to seek careers other than those which have traditionally been open to them.

Influential queen mothers also emphasize education and encourage their daughters to complete high school and attend college. Like several others, Kaui believes that bettering oneself through education is the only way to break the vicious cycle of sex work and downward mobility. She says that queens need education in today's world because, "back then, the streets were OK, but now everything is education; you need that hook to get a job. You use that as a weapon to get a job in today's society." Jennifer's comments also reflect the prestige that education symbolizes among the young transgendered population, "A queen once told me, "It's 'p' to be a queen, but it's even more 'p' to be an educated queen."

A number of contributors also mentioned the need for safe houses and community centers for queens. Genie, a queen from Moloka'i whose interview was unable to be included in this project, told me, "I'd like to build a house where queens, if they needed to go away, could stay — like a retreat. I want to have education for the young queens, and someone for them to turn to. Having gone through it myself, I know how hard it can be with your family if you don't have their acceptance. So you have to run somewhere. Of course, my family would be welcome to my house, but I would gear it towards transgendered people. It would be something I never had that would have helped me and made it easier for me. That's really my goal."

Auntie Cheryl has the same idea. Currently in the planning stages, "Jill's House" is to be a halfway house specifically for queens who are struggling with drug and alcohol addictions. Besides offering training in various occupational skills, one of Cheryl's goals is to have transgendered counselors available for occupants. At present, queens are typically counseled by psychologists or social workers who do not have the intimate experience dealing with transgender issues necessary

285

for effective treatment. However, several queens are now pursuing degrees in counseling; once they graduate, they will be valuable resources and inspirational leaders for their community.

I would like to conclude with an appreciation of the courage which transgendered people possess. For queens seeking to actualize their true selves, going out in public carries with it the chance of verbal or even physical harassment. Paige told me, "The most difficult thing about transitioning was dealing with society. *Torment.* That was my problem. 'How can I deal with this?' So whenever somebody called me names my feelings got hurt really fast . I was so weak. My heart is so . . . so loving, that I'm *weak.* So I get really depressed sometimes when society just really puts me down and tells me that I'm not supposed to be this way. That *you're a man.* And my mentality was driving me crazy. That's why I turned to drugs — to take away the problems."

I think many people fail to realize that publicly transitioning into womanhood while living in a society which condemns transgenderism requires a great deal of bravery and inner strength. Unfortunately, outsiders rarely have the opportunity to learn exactly why such qualities are so necessary. I believe that by talking openly about the struggles queens have gone through in order to simply be themselves can provide an understanding of their lives which goes beyond one-dimensional images. Accounts such as Paige's can create empathy among those who never before knew what it is like to be *mahu* or transgendered.

More than anything else, I feel that the contributors to *'O Au No Keia* appreciated the opportunity to represent themselves in their own terms on a more in-depth level than usually allowed in newspapers, magazines and TV talk shows. Because people fear what they do not understand, I hope this book will act as a corrective to the misunderstandings and misguided perceptions people have about those who are transgendered. For with understanding comes acceptance. As Bubbles explained to me, "We're all in this together, in this human race, in this world race. We have to think about other people. But the love has to come from within, first. That's why I want to do this book. Because it will give other people the opportunity to see, 'Hey, transsexuals are just like everybody else.' When somebody pricks us, we bleed. When it comes down to it, we are all in this together."

SOURCES

Boyd, James H. (1907) "Tradition of the Wizard Stones Ka-Pae-Mahu," p.139-141, Hawaiian Annual; Honolulu, Hawai'i.

Gutmanis, Jane (n.d.) *Pohaku: Hawaiian Stones*, p. 33-36, The Institute for Polynesian Studies, Brigham Young University: Hawai'i.

This list includes Hawaiian and Pidgin words used in the text, as well as colloquial and specialized terms used by the participants. Language appears in brackets following the word. "Pidgin" refers to the Hawaiian creole language originally developed among the Japanese, Chinese, Portuguese, Korean, Filipino and caucasian immigrants who worked on sugar and pineapple plantations in the late nineteenth and early twentieth centuries.

aikane [Hawaiian] Friend.

aloha [Hawaiian] Love, affection, compassion; hello, goodbye.

aumakua [Hawaiian] Spirit guide

auntie [Pidgin] One's aunt; a term of address used to show respect and/ or closeness to a woman who is older than oneself.

The Big Island Nickname for the island of Hawai'i.

bj Blow job.

braddah / bra [Pidgin] A familiar term of address used between males, similar to "pal" or "brother."

butch A gay man who is masculine or macho in dress and behavior.

butch queen An effeminate gay man; a gender-normative gay man.

to clock one's t When an outsider recognizes that a person is trying to pass as the opposite sex; to cause an outsider to recognize that someone else is trying to pass as the opposite sex.

da kine [Pidgin] Used to refer to something without actually naming it.

a date The sexual (or otherwise) transaction between sex-worker and client; the customer of a sex-worker.

to dis To show disrespect to a person or thing.

drag daughter A queen who is provided with guidance and assistance by a queen mother.

drag queen A gay man who dresses as a woman in public or for performances, rather than full-time.

electrolysis The removal of facial or body hair by means of electric or laser charge.

to be fish To be, or to be impressively similar to, a genetic woman.

to flip To move from one gender identity or sexual behavior to another. For example, a queen flips by giving up cross-dressing in order to marry a woman and live as a gender-normative male.

gender Refers to the social classification of a person as either a man or a woman based on factors such as appearance and behavior.

gender dysphoria The dissonance between a person's assigned sex at birth (as either male or female) and subsequent gender identity (i.e., the feeling one has of being either a man or a woman).

ha [Hawaiian] Breath, life.

haku [Hawaiian] A traditional Hawaiian head *lei*.

hanai [Hawaiian] Adopted; to raise.

hana'ino [Hawaiian] To mistreat.

haole [Hawaiian] Caucasian, foreigner.

haumia [Hawaiian] Unclean.

ho'ailona [Hawaiian] A sign, omen.

hula [Hawaiian] Native Hawaiian dance.

husband Boyfriend.

the Imperial Court An national organization located within the gay/lesbian community which raises funds for various charities through drag shows and other functions.

inoa [Hawaiian] Name.
ipuheke [Hawaiian] Double gourd drum.

john The customer of a sex worker.

kahuna [Hawaiian] Priest; expert in any profession.
kane [Hawaiian] Man.
koho'ia [Hawaiian] To be chosen.
kokua [Hawaiian] To help, support.
kuleana [Hawaiian] Responsibility, authority.
kumu [Hawaiian] Teacher.
kumu hula [Hawaiian] *Hula* teacher.
kupua [Hawaiian] A sorcerer, wizard.
kupuna [Hawaiian] Elders.

lanai [Hawaiian] A porch.
laulima [Hawaiian] Cooperation.
lei [Hawaiian] Garland or necklace made from materials such as flowers, feathers, leaves or shells.
to lick To beat
lomilomi [Hawaiian] Traditional Hawaiian massage.

msm A clinical acronym for men who have sex with men.
mahu [Hawaiian] Hermaphrodite; in pre-contact Hawai'i, a male or female who engaged in both male and female social roles.
mahu [Pidgin] Cross-dresser; gay man.
maile [Hawaiian] A vine-like shrub with dark green fragrant leaves.
mana [Hawaiian] Divine power.
mary Queens often refer to one another by this term during conversation.
moe aikane [Hawaiian] Sleeping partner of the same sex.
mokihana [Hawaiian] An anise-scented native slender tree.
mo'o [Hawaiian] Reptile, lizard.
mo'olelo [Hawaiian] History, tradition.
mo'opuna [Hawaiian] Grandchild.

mother queen A queen who provides guidance and assistance to other queens (who are usually, but not always, younger than she is).

muffy Effeminate.

mu'umu'u [Hawaiian] Woman's long dress, whose style is influenced by Victorian nightdresses.

na'au [Hawaiian] Gut, intestines. Seat of emotions, consciousness.

nails Horrible.

nana ao [Hawaiian] Cloud interpreter, seer.

'ohana [Hawaiian] family

opihi [Hawaiian] A shell fish.

p Good; positive; beautiful.

to pass To appear convincingly as a member of the opposite sex.

piko [Hawaiian] Navel.

poi [Hawaiian] A purple paste made from taro root. It is a staple of the Hawaiian diet.

pono [Hawaiian] Goodness, balance, correctness.

pre/post op Refers to whether a transsexual is either planning to have or has already undergone sex reassignment surgery, respectively.

puna hele [Hawaiian] A favorite.

punani [Pidgin] Vagina.

queen A biological male who lives full-time as a woman, often with the aid of female hormones and/or surgery. Many queens prefer that non-queens use this term to refer to them.

queen mother See **mother queen**.

to read someone To recognize that a person is attempting to pass as a member of the opposite sex.

to rip To harshly criticize.

sex Social categorization of a person as male or female based on physical/biological attributes.

silicone Some queens inject industrial silicone into their bodies in order to fill out body parts and gain feminine curves.

(the) street To work or be on "the street(s)" means to engage in prostitution.

(the) surgery Refers to sex reassignment surgery, specifically for the genitals.

t Shorthand for "transgendered person" or "transgenderism."

tapa Cloth made from the inner bark of certain trees.

tita / ti [Pidgin] A tough girl; sister; used among women to refer to a close friend.

town Honolulu.

transgender I use this word as a general term to refer to people who cross socially appropriate boundaries of gender and/or physical sex. As such, in this book it refers to a wide range of identities, including transsexual, drag queen and *mahu*.

transition N. The process through which a person changes their appearance from male to female (or vice versa for females who are transgendered). V. To go through that process.

transsexual A person whose gender identity is that of the opposite sex. Sometimes, but not always, a transsexual will undergo hormone treatments and/or surgery in order to bring their physical body into alignment with their sense of being either a man or a woman.

transvestite A person (typically a heterosexual male) who enjoys wearing the clothing of the opposite sex.

trick N. The customer of a sex worker. V. To engage in prostitution.

to turn back butch To dress and live as a male after having been a queen.

'ukulele [Hawaiian] Literally "Leaping flea," this small guitar-like instrument was brought to Hawai'i by the Portuguese in the late 1800s.

uniki [Hawaiian] Graduation ceremony.

wahine [Hawaiian] Woman.